In this innovative book, Gary Miller bridges the gap between traditional organizational theory, based in psychology, sociology, and political science, and organizational economics. The former stresses the importance of managerial leadership and cooperation among employees, while the latter focuses on the engineering of incentive systems that will induce efficiency, and profitability, by rewarding worker self-interest.

Miller demonstrates that it is impossible to design an incentive system based on self-interest that will effectively discipline all subordinates and superiors and overcome the role of political conflict or replace the role of leadership in an organization. Applying game theory to the analysis of cooperation and leadership in organizational hierarchies, he concludes that organizations whose managers can inspire cooperation and the transcendence of short-term interest among employees enjoy a significant competitive advantage.

MANAGERIAL DILEMMAS

THE POLITICAL ECONOMY OF INSTITUTIONS AND DECISIONS

Editors
James E. Alt, Harvard University
Douglass C. North, Washington University in St. Louis

Other books in the series
James E. Alt and Kenneth Shepsle, eds., *Perspectives on Positive Political Economy*
Yoram Barzel, *Economic Analysis of Property Rights*
Robert Bates, *Beyond the Miracle of the Market: The Political Economy of Agrarian Development in Kenya*
Gary W. Cox, *The Efficient Secret: The Cabinet and the Development of Political Parties in Victorian England*
Leif Lewin, *Ideology and Strategy: A Century of Swedish Politics* (English Edition)
Gary Libecap, *Contracting for Property Rights*
Matthew D. McCubbins and Terry Sullivan, eds., *Congress: Structure and Policy*
Douglass C. North, *Institutions, Institutional Change, and Economic Performance*
Elinor Ostrom, *Governing the Commons: The Evolution of Institutions for Collective Action*
Charles Stewart III, *Budget Reform Politics: The Design of the Appropriations Process in the House of Representatives, 1865–1921*

MANAGERIAL DILEMMAS
The political economy of hierarchy

GARY J. MILLER

Washington University

CAMBRIDGE
UNIVERSITY PRESS

Published by the Press Syndicate of the University of Cambridge
The Pitt Building, Trumpington Street, Cambridge CB2 1RP
40 West 20th Street, New York, NY 10011-4211, USA
10 Stamford Road, Oakleigh, Melbourne 3166, Australia

First published 1992
First paperback edition 1993

Printed in the United States of America

Library of Congress Cataloging-in-Publication Data
Miller, Gary J.
Managerial dilemmas: the political economy of hierarchy/
Gary J. Miller.
p.   cm. – (The political economy of institutions and
decisions)
ISBN 0-521-37281-X   ISBN 0-521-45769-6 (pbk.)
1. Industrial management.   2. Organizational behavior.
3. Psychology, industrial.   4. Employee motivation.   5. Incentives
in industry.   I. Title.   II. Series.
HD31.M442   1991
658.4'02 – dc20   91-19211
CIP

A catalogue record for this book is available from the British Library.

ISBN 0-521-37281-X hardback
ISBN 0-521-45769-6 paperback

To Neil, who became
a scuba diver, juggler, and logician
all while I was working
on this one book

Contents

Contents

Tables and figures

Tables and figures

Series editors' preface

This Cambridge series – The Political Economy of Institutions and Decisions – is built around attempts to answer two central questions: How do institutions evolve in response to individual incentives, strategies, and choices; and how do institutions affect the performance of political and economic systems? The scope of the series is comparative and historical rather than international or specifically North American, and the focus is positive rather than normative.

In this innovative study, Gary Miller tackles head-on a fundamental dilemma in the organizational economics literature. While the economic rationale for the existence of hierarchy is based on its capacity to correct market failure, this correction unavoidably creates consequences that are incentive incompatible between self-interested superiors and subordinates. How can managers inspire members of an organization to transcend the sort of self-interested behavior that results in shirking? Miller argues that those organizations whose managers can inspire members to transcend short-term self-interest will always have a competitive advantage. He employs modern game theory to provide a rigorous analysis of cooperation and political leadership in hierarchies.

This study bridges the literature on organizational economics and that on organizational behavior to provide new insights into the structure of hierarchies. In the context of the analysis of repeated games, the traditional concepts of cooperation, culture, trust, commitment, and leadership take on a richer meaning.

Acknowledgments

My greatest debt is to two Michigan State University political scientists, Thomas Hammond and Jack Knott. Many of the ideas in this book emerged from a decade-long dialogue with them on the politics of hierarchy. In particular, Chapter 7 is based on one of several versions of a paper written in collaboration with Tom Hammond, "Incentive Compatible Mechanisms Are Not Credible," presented at the American Political Science Association convention in San Francisco in September 1990. Similarly, Chapter 5 is a direct result of a collaboration with Jack Knott on a series of laboratory experiments and a paper entitled "Dilemmas in Teams and Firms." I acknowledge, with thanks, Tom and Jack as coauthors of these chapters.

The book got a helpful start with research supported by a grant from the National Science Foundation entitled "The Politics of Collective Consumption and Bureaucratic Supply" (SES-8218571). The John M. Olin School of Business and an anonymous foundation provided additional financial support. They helped provide valuable research assistance by Francine Reicher (who read and edited the manuscript), Beth Cassani (who provided many details about some of the firms discussed in the book), and Mark Farmer (who provided the figures).

Douglass North and Elisabeth Case are an extraordinary pair of editors — no one could wish for better. Doug offered many important ideas about transaction cost economics that found their way into the book, although they are not stated as deftly as he could have stated them. Both he and Elisabeth were adept at finding my weak spots, and both encouraged me to keep at it. The book is much clearer as a result of Mary Racine's excellent copyediting.

In May 1989 I had the valuable opportunity to present the manuscript at a week-long seminar to James Alt and his colleagues at the Harvard University Department of Government. They contributed to the manuscript collectively and individually. James made me think seriously about the concept of second-order norms, resulting in a serious revision of Chapter 10. Morris Fiorina suggested that I think about Condorcet jury theorems, which greatly strengthened Chapter 3. Kenneth Shepsle's emphasis on credible commitments helped me throughout the book, but especially in Chapter 11.

I am very much indebted to Barry Weingast and his colleagues at Stanford University and the Hoover Institution. I had a very enjoyable chance to present part of the book to them in November 1989 and received a great deal of valuable feedback. Barry's comments were both encouraging and constructive; he challenged me to rewrite much of Chapter 8. I am especially obliged to him for the idea of organizing the book into three parts.

Several friends in the field of political economy provided key insights at crucial points. Randy Calvert presented an extraordinary paper at Washington University, coauthored with Jeffrey Banks, called "Communication and Efficiency in Coordination Games with Incomplete Information." It made me think more seriously about the connection between coordination and cooperation, and it had an impact on the entire book. Collaboration with Terry Moe on several early papers was a valuable learning experience. Cheryl Eavey identified a mistake in my discussion of principal–agency theory. Both Krish Ladha and Doug Nelson read the entire book, and engaged me in long, thoughtful conversations about the fundamental problems discussed herein. Andy Rutten correctly insisted on several rewrites of the Introduction and helped me keep my focus on the big picture. He also supplied me with numerous bibliographical references.

Finally, I acknowledge a special debt to my colleagues in organizational behavior at the Washington University School of Business. In particular, Nick Baloff has been a source of wise counsel and insight for the past four years. The course I team-taught with Nick and Walter Nord was a true educational experience. Both Bill Bottom and Todd Zenger read my work and provided helpful comments. They all helped me with one of the primary goals of this book, which was to make it clear that the theoretical problems treated in the literature on political economy are not divorced from reality but are the stuff of everyday management headaches and conundrums facing ordinary people in any hierarchy.

PUBLICATION CREDITS

The material on Du Pont's incentive plan is reprinted by permission of the *Wall Street Journal*, copyright © 1988 by Dow Jones & Company, Inc. All rights reserved worldwide. Much of the material about the difficulties associated with piece rates came from William Foote Whyte, *Money and Motivation*, copyright © 1955 by Harper & Row. Reprinted by permission of Harper & Row, Publishers, Inc. Excerpts regarding management style in

Acknowledgments

several U.S. companies were obtained from Tom J. Peters and Robert H. Waterman, Jr., *In Search of Excellence: Lessons From America's Best Run Companies*, copyright © 1982 by Tom J. Peters and Robert H. Waterman, Jr. Reprinted by permission of Harper & Row, Publishers, Inc. Much of the material about Sears came from Donald R. Katz, *The Big Store*, copyright © 1987 by Donald R. Katz. Reprinted by permission of Viking Penguin, a division of Penguin Books USA Inc. Information regarding the Ford family is reprinted by permission from Peter Collier and David Horowitz, *The Fords: An American Epic*, copyright © 1987 by Peter Collier and David Horowitz. Reprinted by permission of Summit Books, a division of Simon and Schuster Inc. Much of the information about Ford management practices came from David Halberstam, *The Reckoning*, copyright © 1986 by David Halberstam. Reprinted by permission of William Morrow & Co., Inc. Publishers.

Introduction

In the early days of 1914, Henry Ford made a major decision about the allocation of resources at Ford Company. At a board meeting, he proposed raising the daily wage for his employees significantly above the going market rate of approximately $2.20. Members of the board, amazed at the proposal, responded ironically that if he was going to raise the daily wage to $3, he might as well raise it to $4 or even $5. Ford accepted the challenge and made a place for himself in history by announcing the $5 day. Approximately half of the company's anticipated profits, a sum equal to $10 million, were set aside for the new plan, which went into effect on January 12 of that year (Meyer 1981).

What do the social sciences have to say about Ford's decision to impose a $5 day? In what terms is this historical fact to be analyzed? Was it a simple, profit-maximizing act on Ford's part? Or was it fundamentally a political act?

TWO LITERATURES ON HIERARCHY

Since the inception of organization theory, there have been two rather distinct literatures on the topic of organizational control. One views organizational control as a mechanistic problem of designing incentive systems and sanctions so that self-interested and intrinsically unmotivated employees will find it in their own interest to work toward the organization's goals. In other words, management is seen as shaping subordinate behavior through the correct system of rewards and punishments. This literature is associated with, for example, Frederick Taylor, the father of scientific management, who was a devout advocate of incentive wage systems as a way of motivating subordinates.

1

More recently, economics has contributed to this literature the "principal–agency theory," which falls almost entirely within this mechanistic approach. According to this theory, agents are perceived as having distinct tastes (such as the desire to limit risk taking or costly effort), which they pursue as rational maximizing individuals. The principal's job is to anticipate the rational responses of agents and to design a set of incentives such that the agents find it in their own interests (given the incentive system) to take the best possible set of actions (from the principal's perspective).

"Leadership" has a negligible role in this approach, since the manager's goal is essentially the engineering of the organizational "machine." If a manager has engineered the correct system of incentives, then she does not have to "lead" or "inspire" subordinates to do the right thing; they will find right actions to be in their own interest. Competitive forces in the market for managerial talent and for capital automatically tend to discipline the self-interested behavior of the actors involved, with the benign result that "agency costs" are kept to an efficient minimum (Jensen and Meckling 1976; Fama 1980).

This entire literature contrasts sharply with the second, more organic view of organizations, which is centered primarily in political science and organizational psychology. From this perspective, resource allocation results from the decisions of individual leaders. The literature regards the manager's primary job to be one of leadership – that is, inspiring a willingness to cooperate, to take risks, to innovate, to go beyond the level of effort that a narrow, self-interested analysis of the incentives would summon.

An early example of this approach is Chester Barnard's *Functions of the Executive* (1938). Barnard regards organizations as fundamentally cooperative groups of individuals, and the executive's chief job is not so much to shape the self-interested behavior of subordinates as to inspire them to transcend self-interest. Other executive abilities, he claims,

> will not be put forth, will not even be developed, without that sense of responsibility which makes the sacrifices involved a matter of course, and which elicits the initial faith in cooperation. . . . Organizations endure, however, in proportion to the breadth of the morality by which they are governed. This is only to say that foresight, long purposes, high ideals, are the basis for the persistence of cooperation. (282)

Effective leadership is by no means automatic from this perspective. While competitive market forces may tend to reward the more efficient leaders, other leaders may be able to insulate themselves from the disciplining force of the market by political stratagems that result in governmentally enforced entry barriers or restrictions in the capital market. The result may well be persistent inefficiencies within the hierarchy (Perrow 1987).

The contrast is clear. Economists assume that subordinates respond to incentive systems in a self-interested maximizing way. Barnard urges managers to inspire subordinate "sacrifice" by the "breadth of the morality" that they exemplify. Economists regard Barnard's urgings as futile; political scientists and behaviorists feel that organizational economics is based on a chokingly narrow view of the possibilities of leadership and is politically naive.

The primary purpose of this book is to explore the literature of political economy as the theoretical bridge between the two literatures on hierarchical organizations. The first two-thirds of the book argues that a narrow, neoclassical version of organizational economics self-destructs. While the economic rationale for the existence of hierarchy is based on its capacity to correct market failure, the internal logic of self-interested behavior by both subordinates and superiors cannot be shown to sustain a vision of hierarchy as a smoothly running, efficient machine. On the contrary, results described in the literature of social choice theory, principal–agency theory, and incentive compatibility reveal built-in logical inconsistencies that make it impossible to design an incentive/control system that simultaneously disciplines the self-interested behavior of both superiors and subordinates. For every incentive system that has other desirable characteristics, there will always be an incentive for some individuals to "shirk" – to pursue a narrower definition of interest that results in equilibrium outcomes that everyone in the organization can recognize as deficient.

This being the case, I submit that those organizations whose managers can inspire members to transcend short-term self-interest will always have a competitive advantage. The final third of this book argues that modern game theory provides a theoretical structure for a more rigorous analysis of cooperation and political leadership in hierarchies. As such, it has a clear methodological link to organizational economics; however, the game-theoretic analysis legitimizes many of the substantive concerns of the more organic literature of organizational psychology and politics. In the context of the analysis of repeated games, the traditional organic concepts of cooperation, culture, trust, commitment, and leadership take on new and vivid meanings.

COASE ON HIERARCHY

While this book attempts to bridge organizational economics and organizational behavior, the starting point for the analysis lies squarely in organizational economics. This discipline began, slowly and hesitantly, with the work of economist Ronald Coase in 1937. Coase assumed "that the distinguishing mark of the firm is the supersession of the price mechanism" (389). Within the firm, coordination is achieved not directly by price, but by the work of the entrepreneur "without the intervention of the price mechanism" (388):

The main reason why it is profitable to establish a firm would seem to be that there is a cost of using the price mechanism. The most obvious cost of "organising"

3

production through the price mechanism is that of discovering what the relevant prices may be. (388)

Discovering prices, and "negotiating and concluding a separate contract for each exchange transaction which takes place," can be prohibitively expensive. It is the size of the transaction costs that makes it worthwhile for an entrepreneur to direct activities within a broad grant of discretionary authority:

For this series of contracts is substituted one. . . . The contract is one whereby the factor, for a certain remuneration (which may be fixed or fluctuating), agrees to obey the directions of an entreprenuer *within certain limits*. The essence of the contract is that it should only state the limits to the powers of the entrepreneur. Within these limits, he can therefore direct the other factors of production. (391; emphasis in the original)

According to Coase the "master–servant" relationship could be defined by the ability of the employer to "direct" the actions of the employee within certain broad bounds. Coase claimed that the existence of the firm depended on the advantages of replacing voluntaristic market transactions with hierarchical direction. From this perspective, Henry Ford's decision to impose a $5 daily wage was a significant step away from coordination by the price mechanism and toward the creation of hierarchical authority. It was an example not of profit-maximizing behavior within the market, but of a successful attempt to "supersede" the price mechanism by direct hierarchical coordination.

INSTITUTIONS MATTER: COASE AND THE SUBSEQUENT DEVELOPMENT OF ORGANIZATIONAL ECONOMICS

Coase has been a central figure in the subsequent development of the economics of the firm, stating as he did the clear premise that institutions influence the nature of transactions. Transaction costs have emerged as a concept that is fundamental to our understanding of industrial organization.

Many of the lessons of Coase's analysis, however, have been resisted by organizational economists. Many have assumed that virtually all of the lessons learned from market economics can be easily transferred to transactions in the hierarchy. In particular, some organizational economists have continued to insist on the market-like nature of internal firm contracts and on the efficacy of the price mechanism, often as a justification for continued use of the heroic assumptions of the neoclassical model.

For instance, unlike Coase, Alchian and Demsetz (1972) insist that hierarchical firms like Ford Motor Company do not partake of political authority:

It is common to see the firm characterized by the power to settle issues by fiat, by authority, or by disciplinary action superior to that available in the conventional market. This is delusion. The firm does not own all its inputs. It has no power of

4

fiat, no authority, no disciplinary action any different in the slightest degree from ordinary market contracting between any two people. I can "punish" you only by withholding future business or by seeking redress in the courts for any failure to honor our exchange agreement. That is exactly all that any employer can do. (777)

Alchian and Demsetz clearly differ with Coase about the distinct nature of the master–servant contract, which Coase regards as the distinguishing characteristic of the firm. Unlike Coase, they see a fundamental continuity between contracts in the market and those in the firm.

Jensen and Meckling (1976) agree with Alchian and Demsetz that the relations between the firm and the employee are contractual and thus exorcised of politics:

Contractual relations are the essence of the firm, not only with employees but with suppliers, customers, creditors, etc. . . . The private corporation or firm is simply one form of legal fiction which serves as a nexus for contracting relationships and which is also characterized by the existence of divisible residual claims on the assets and cash flows of the organization which can generally be sold without permission of the other contracting individuals. (310–11)

The focus on firms as a nexus of voluntary contracts allows the power of market economics to be applied to these contracts. Competitive market forces in a nearly perfect capital market and other markets drive those relationships involving the firm to efficient contractual forms. As Fama (1980) claims, "The firm is disciplined by competition from other firms, which forces the evolution of devices for efficiently monitoring the performance of the entire team and of its individual members" (288–9). For these economists, unlike Coase, the fundamental coordination mechanism within the firm, as well as among firms, is the price mechanism, not hierarchical direction. Furthermore, they assume that the price mechanism is capable of disciplining efficient outcomes inside the hierarchical firm.

Williamson and Ouchi (1981) have explicitly recognized the inevitability of efficient contracts as a fundamental principle of what they call the "efficiency hypothesis":

Except when there are perversities associated with the funding process, or when strategically situated members of an organization are unable to participate in the prospective gains, unrealized efficiency opportunities always offer an incentive to organize. (355)

Thus, if there is a different, more efficient way of organizing a production process, there is always a reason to find a contract that will result in that more efficient process. In much of organizational economics, the persistent theme is the hierarchy as a nexus of voluntary contracts, permeable to competitive market pressures and responding swiftly and smoothly with efficient organizational forms and procedures to changes in those market pressures.

Introduction

The elegance of organizational economics, the fact that it is based on the same parsimonious set of initial assumptions that have served so well in the microeconomic analysis of markets, and the force of the logical arguments based on those assumptions have combined to give the nascent field an impact far beyond that implied by the number of those who have been working in it. Even behaviorists have recognized that organizational economics has been the source of new theoretical insights in an area that was sorely in need of them.

THE ANOMALIES OF ORGANIZATIONAL ECONOMICS

The precision and rigor of organizational economics have led to a number of rather specific predictions. As might be expected with such a young science, these predictions unfortunately turn out to be false. The existence of these anomalies prompts a reorientation of organizational economics around the notion of political authority, which is attempted in this book.

For instance, in a recent article in the *Journal of Finance*, Baker, Jensen, and Murphy (1988) present economics with a puzzle. As they point out, economic theory assumes that there are competitive market pressures driving firms to their most efficient contractual forms. Yet the incentive systems being used in firms are not those that economic theory would regard as most efficient. Many firms have followed Henry Ford's example by paying more than the market wage, by paying a flat daily wage not directly linked to individual performance, and by not discriminating among employee types. Typical incentive systems are less likely to link pay with performance, and more likely to be egalitarian, than current economic theory would predict.

Baker, Jensen, and Murphy (1988) explore the possibility that typical firms use inefficient incentive systems as a result of managerial shirking—"managers have few incentives to structure and enforce value-maximizing contracts with subordinates" (614). According to this possibility, Henry Ford was simply making his own job easier when he raised the daily wage to $5, a caprice that has since been followed by countless other undisciplined managers. The problem with this hypothesis is that it does not "explain why competitive forces in the product, labor, and control markets are not sufficient to induce economically efficient compensation policies" (615).

If, however, competitive market forces do require economically efficient compensation policies, then economic theory is deficient in being unable to explain why those incentive systems consistently chosen by firms are efficient. "Ultimately, it may be that psychologists, behaviorists, human resource consultants, and personnel executives understand something about human behavior and motivation that is not yet captured in our economic models" (615).

Either way, current economic theory of the firm is deficient. Either competitive market pressures are less likely to discipline hierarchies than economists have imagined, or else there are reasons outside of current economic theory that egalitarian incentive systems are more efficient than those typically prescribed by economists.

Stiglitz (1987) describes inconsistencies between typical labor contracts and those predicted by the economic theory of efficiency. Because employees are risk averse, it is agreed that efficient contracts would insure employees against the risk that is associated with an uncontrollable economic cycle; training costs should be borne by the firm; flat wages would allow firms to retain workers of a given quality at a lower wage. "None of these predictions conform to what is actually observed" (50).

The same puzzle has been noted by other economists (Akerlof and Yellen 1986; Liebenstein 1987). Market forces should promote efficiency, yet we observe incentive systems in hierarchies that economists tell us should not be efficient. Can it be that hierarchies persist in the use of inefficient incentive systems? Yet the very rationale for the existence of hierarchy in a market economy is efficiency: When markets cannot be perfectly efficient due to information asymmetries or other problems, competitive pressure must reward those firms that organize themselves as hierarchies.

An even greater anomaly underlies the entire U.S. labor market. Virtually every market in the United States clears. If there is a line of extra buyers or sellers, the price is forced up or down until demand and supply equilibrate. The exception is the labor market. There are and have been a large number of providers of labor who are involuntarily unemployed – in effect they are queued up to give their labor. Yet the wage is not decreased in order to increase demand and decrease supply, as normal neoclassical economics would predict. There is an extensive literature devoted to this one anomaly. As is shown in Chapter 3, whatever the causes of the anomaly, its implications for hierarchical authority in the firm are enormous.

"Stickiness" in labor markets is obvious, and there are numerous possible sources; but capital markets are generally assumed to be among the most fluid and frictionless in the country. Yet even here, there are anomalies that directly concern the firm and its hierarchy. Competition in the capital markets should force managers to act as if they had the same preferences as stockholders. But in fact, empirical investigation of standstill agreements, greenmail, and poison pills suggests that the capital market is not allowed to be as perfect a disciplining device as economic theory would predict. As a result, managers may have more room for discretion, and discretionary authority, than would otherwise be the case.

It could be that these empirical anomalies in organizational economics are the result of flawed data gathering, data analysis, or interpretation. Yet the most precise, controlled laboratory experiments, conducted in settings designed to test rigorously the logical implications of some aspect of organizational economics, have themselves demonstrated anomalies. Bull, Schotter, and Weigelt tested one implication of principal–agency theory, which is that in the presence of uncertainty, a rank-order tournament incentive system should work better than a piece-rate system. The results were striking. In a piece-rate system, subjects converged to equilibrium effort levels rather quickly. In tournament experiments, in contrast, the economic model performed relatively poorly. There was little convergence over a long period of time. Furthermore, in tournaments in which subjects were either disadvantaged or advantaged, disadvantaged subjects exerted a great deal more effort than economic theories predicted. Participants in these situations seem to engage strategically with one another in ways that are not completely understandable; "as a practical matter, it appears that a cost to choosing a tournament system over a piece rate system is that the principal must bear uncertainty as to how the agents will react to the tournament" (Bull, Schotter, and Weigelt 1987: 29).

Another group of laboratory experiments was performed to test a basic premise of organizational economics, which is that individuals facing the task of producing shared public goods by means of collective action will be totally stymied by the free-rider problem. The experiments revealed much higher levels of contribution in small-group collective action experiments than should be observed (Marwell and Ames 1979).

All of these empirical results are anomalies from a perspective which assumes that, regardless of institutional context, maximizing behavior and efficient outcomes follow immediately and automatically in the firm. In experiments as well as in the field, however, the strategic behavior of individuals in situations involving extreme interdependence is beyond the ability of current neoclassical economic theories to explain. It is in these situations that institutions matter most, because institutions provide cues to individuals about how others are likely to behave in these complex settings; thus, it is imperative to try to understand how institutions shape and condition the behavior of interdependent individual choice (North 1988).

INSTITUTIONS MATTER: MARKETS VERSUS HIERARCHIES

Like Coase's 1937 article, and unlike much of the subsequent work in organizational economics, this book assumes that coordination within the firm takes place by hierarchical direction rather than by the use of the price mechanism. And as argued by the foremost developers of Coase's theories, the institutional switch from market to hierarchy makes an enormous difference in the behavior of individuals; institutions matter (Williamson 1975; North 1990b).

Introduction

Institutions and information

As students of institutions have emphasized (North 1990b), institutions simultaneously determine the rules of the game and condition the choices of individuals under the rules. For instance, different institutions can shape the flow of information among individuals. A competitive market, it appears, is an outstanding mechanism for conveying information and disciplining individual behavior. Consequently, individuals in the market institution very quickly learn to act "as if" they were the perfectly informed maximizing agents of neoclassical economic theory (Plott 1986: 301–28).

However, in other institutions – such as hierarchies – information is a scarce commodity, requirements for cognitive skills may be great, and individual behavior may deviate markedly from that assumed by the neoclassical model (Hogarth and Reder 1986; Simon 1986; Tversky and Kahneman 1986). Individuals may even be rewarded for strategic misrepresentation of private information (Halperin 1974). In such a setting of information scarcity, shared beliefs about how the world works – ideology – may play an especially important role (North 1990b). Henry Ford's decision to impose a $5 daily wage was in large part a result of his own ideologically driven conceptions about how employees would respond to a wage that was more than twice the market wage and to the queuing for Ford jobs that would result from this wage.

Institutions and motivation

Even the kinds of incentives designed to motivate individuals may differ across institutions. In competitive markets, individuals are assumed to be relatively anonymous price takers, and there is little opportunity for sidepayments based on multidimensional networks of social relationships; the automobile buyer has little to offer for a particular auto besides an amount of cash that is very close to the market price for that brand and year. In the hierarchically coordinated transactions within the firm, employer and employee may spend years in close personalized exchange; the sidepayments available (to both parties!) in their attempts to influence other members of the hierarchy may include social acceptance, personal services, or other motivating factors besides cash.

As North (1988) notes, "Human motivation is simply more complicated than simple wealth maximization. Human beings do trade off wealth or income for other values, and because the price one pays for one's convictions are frequently lowered by institutions, institutions are important to choices" (2). Hierarchies, unlike markets, institutionalize long-term mutual commitments that make it easy to trade off social acceptance and esteem against wealth. As I argue in Part III of this book, this may well make

9

possible a level of cooperative effort that is the most convincing advantage that hierarchy has over the market.

Institutions and property rights

As Coase argued in 1960, in the presence of transaction costs, resource allocations are altered by property rights structures. The hierarchical firm clearly develops rules (formal and informal) for defining property rights that determine resource allocations within the firm. Slaveowners sometimes found it advantageous to grant slaves a partial property right to their labor so that they would be motivated to work to earn their freedom (Barzel 1989); similarly, the owner of a firm may choose to "share" ownership in the firm for motivational purposes. The "constitution," or institutional rules and norms by which property rights are defined within a hierarchical firm, becomes a central political issue within the firm, providing one more distinction between the market and hierarchy. As I will discuss in Chapter 2, Ford's decision to enact a $5 day can be seen as a political act redefining property rights within the firm.

Institutions and efficiency

Given that institutions condition the availability of information, shape incentives, and define property rights, are efficient outcomes inevitable? As Coase pointed out, directors of hierarchical firms attempt to coordinate internal resource allocation without the benefit of the price mechanism. This initiates a process of political decision making that may enhance the goals of the emergent political figures in the firm, but there is no guarantee that the results will necessarily be efficient. North (1988) argues:

While political institutions facilitate exchange amongst bargaining parties, there is no implication of economic efficiency as an outcome. Efficient political exchange can, given the interests of the parties, create or alter economic institutions that may raise or lower the costs of economic exchange. (14)

North has pointed out an important reason that political institutions may produce allocations of property rights that do not result in economic efficiency. A ruler may prefer a system of property rights that guarantees him more net tax revenue over one that encourages economic growth for society as a whole. This claim is isomorphic to a result described in Chapter 8 regarding conflict between profit maximization and efficiency in the firm.

For the firm, unlike the medieval state, external market forces may be a means by which internal political inefficiencies are disciplined. At the same time, firms develop and use their external political power to insulate themselves from market discipline – witness the business lobbying for successful antitakeover legislation in Delaware and Pennsylvania. Overall, the best approach may be to take the degree of efficiency resulting from economic and political forces within and around the hierarchy as an open question, subject to empirical investigation.

THE POLITICAL ECONOMY OF HIERARCHY

For all of these reasons, there is no simple way of extrapolating from the behavior of rational individuals in voluntaristic markets to the behavior of rational individuals in authoritative hierarchies. It will be argued in Chapter 2 that one of the primary purposes of Ford's decision to impose a $5 day was to make sure that the labor market in his industry would be transformed from one that was competitive, fluid, and voluntaristic to one in which a decision to work for Ford Motor Company meant a long-term commitment to a system of political authority. With the creation of political authority at Ford Motor Company came a series of other, essentially political problems: the aggregation of disparate preferences into authoritative social choices, the centralized design of incentives, the inevitability of group conflict, the creation of social norms, the potentials for political leadership, the necessity of resolving constitutional issues of power, and the credible commitment of power.

Why hierarchy? The creation of political authority

Part I of this book confronts the issue of political authority in a firm. I agree with organizational economists who state that the reason for the creation of a hierarchical firm is the failure of market efficiency. The reasons for market failure involve the different transaction costs of negotiating and enforcing contracts (Coase 1937). They include team production externalities (Alchian and Demsetz 1972), market power (Klein, Crawford, and Alchian 1978), and information asymmetry (Williamson 1975).

However, the efficient organizational form in the presence of these problems is not simply a nexus of ordinary market contracts. As Chapter 2 demonstrates, the same factors that cause markets to fail can limit the process of bargaining to an efficient contract. The new literature on mechanism design points to the desirability of a coercive authority if two mutually dependent sides bargain in the context of information asymmetries.

Furthermore, as Chapter 3 reveals, the literature on social choice theory argues for a rather extreme centralization of this coercive authority if the firm is to meet certain minimal conditions of rational group decision making. But how is such an authority to be established? Part I ends with a discussion of the means by which a firm can use long-term contracts to provide a barrier against the voluntarism of competitive markets.

Managerial dilemmas: the use of political authority

Part II asks how well the hierarchical firm can correct for the incentive problems generated by information asymmetry, monopoly, and team production externalities. Clearly, hierarchy can at times improve on market inefficiency or the failure of voluntary cooperative action. But the primary theme of Part II is that the same factors that promote inefficiency in the absence of hierarchy confound the managers of hierarchical organizations. A close analysis of hierarchy, using impossibility results well known in social choice theory and mechanism design, suggests that the natural outcome of self-interested behavior in a hierarchy should be persistent inefficiency. Hierarchy does not permit a perfect realignment of individual with group interests.

The theme of persistent inefficiencies is a traditional one in organizational behavior, but not in organizational economics. While this book recognizes that the presence of competitive market forces drives hierarchies to realize potential efficiency gains, Part II explores the logical limitations on the ability of hierarchies to realize those efficiency gains through manipulations of formal contractual and incentive systems. While a great many contractual forms and incentive systems have been proposed, the best economic analysis argues that in every such system there must remain incentives for at least one individual to persist in behavior that leads to organizational inefficiency. I conclude that a determined effort to follow economic analysis to its consistent conclusions leads to a confirmation, rather than a denial, of the theme of persistent organizational inefficiency.

Cooperation and leadership: the deployment of political authority

And yet the pressures of the marketplace reward those hierarchies than can (and do!) achieve the efficiency gains that self-interested behavior under any incentive system leaves unrealized. If narrow self-interested behavior under formal contractual systems cannot realize all potential efficiency gains, there must be a competitive advantage for hierarchies that can induce non-self-interested intrafirm cooperation.

Indeed, the evidence is mounting that, at least for some industries, there is a competitive edge for intrafirm cooperation. Firms with apparently identical formal contracts, organizational structures, and incentive schemes may perform quite differently, depending on the nature of individual expectations and beliefs, social norms, and leadership. Part III therefore proposes an answer to the Baker, Jensen, and Murphy conundrum regarding hierarchical incentives and inefficiency. Any formal incentive system leaves room for self-interested behavior leading to persistent efficiency losses. Consequently, a hierarchy that can induce the right kind of cooperation – defined as voluntary deviations from self-interested behavior – will have an important competitive edge over other firms.

Intrafirm cooperation, like persistent organizational inefficiency, is a traditional theme of the organizational behavior literature. But the behavioral theory of intrafirm cooperation (like the behavioral theory of persistent inefficiencies) is vague, ill-defined, and informal. Can formal economic theory provide any insight into a topic that has historically been considered by economists to be beyond the pale of economic analysis?

Part III argues that the theory of repeated games can make an important contribution to the analysis of cooperative behavior in the hierarchy. It provides a flexible tool for understanding the wide range of behaviors that distinguish firms with identical formal economic incentive systems. At the same time, this analysis suggests that the key differences among firms are of a political rather than strictly economic nature. The firm must be regarded as an arena for political leadership, ideology, and goal setting rather than simply for managerial manipulation of economic incentives and formal structure.

PART I

Why have hierarchy?

Lehman Brothers Kuhn Loeb was until 1984 one of the most prestigious investment banking partnerships on Wall Street. A partnership can be visualized from an economic perspective as a roughly symmetric voluntary contractual relationship among a nonhierarchical team of players – a "nexus of contracts" in every sense of the term. If one partner feels he can do better elsewhere, he can buy his way out of the contract. Because arrangements are roughly symmetric and because all contracts are voluntary, an economic analysis would indicate that there is little rationale for political strategizing, and still less justification for bitter competition for a position of political "authority" in the firm.

Such a perspective, however, fails to capture the relevant aspects of the bitterly political infighting that led to the dissolution of the firm in 1984. In July 1983, securities trader Lew Glucksman, coleader of the partnership, demanded that Peter Peterson resign as chairman of the firm. Peterson, who had been secretary of commerce under Nixon, found all avenues of appeal cleverly anticipated and blocked by the Machiavellian plots laid by Glucksman. The board of directors accepted Glucksman's demands to be appointed chairman and paid Peterson the necessary severance pay. This development dramatized, but did not heal, the rift between the aggressive securities traders led by Glucksman and the more traditional investment bankers in the partnership. Rumors flew, and counterplots were hatched. More and more partners demanded that they be bought out; each departure made the firm more vulnerable to the next. Within ten months, Lehman Brothers was forced to sell out. It became just one of the hierarchical subsidiaries of the Shearson/American Express bureaucracy (Auletta 1986). Those partners who remained found themselves in the new position of being subordinates in a long chain of hierarchy.

Why have hierarchy?

Hierarchy can be defined as the asymmetric and incompletely defined authority of one actor to direct the activities of another within certain bounds. Hierarchy, as defined in this way, is characteristic of contractual relationships in Shearson/American Express, as in many other firms (but not all; see Barzel 1989: 46–8). The rights of employees are often relatively vague, the responsibilities even more so. In exchange for a wage (which may be determined in part by the subjective valuations of a supervisor), the employee recognizes the right of an employer to assign tasks, set performance standards, determine working conditions, and dictate codes of appropriate interpersonal behavior with clients, supervisors, and other employees. Limits on personal autonomy are fixed in the employment contract that would not be regarded as legitimate in other contractual relationships: While a homeowner would not presume to tell a plumber or electrician how to dress while she was repairing his home, an employer can fix codes of appropriate dress that may be arbitrarily changed after the employment contract has been entered into.

Since few people like to have their activities directed by another, the desirability of hierarchy is questionable on the face of it. There are other ways of organizing human activity; the first three chapters of this book focus on competitive markets, negotiated contracts, and democratic voting procedures, respectively. Each of these alternatives has proved to be viable for some set of human interactions; so why do we organize so many of our business firms, our governmental agencies, even our nonprofit hospitals and charities as hierarchies? In the case of Lehman Brothers, why was it efficient for the partners to sell out to a hierarchically organized conglomerate?

A superficial answer to this question is: economies of scale. A large banking firm can share the cost of overhead over a much larger number of transactions and thus operate more cheaply than a smaller partnership (Auletta 1986: 232). But large scale does not imply hierarchical organization. Barzel (1989) points out that economies of scale in the use of capital equipment may be achieved by a contractual arrangement in which the skills of several specialists are obtained without hierarchical obligation.

For example, Galoob Toys operates on a very large scale indeed, but relies almost exclusively on contractual market relationships rather than hierarchy. A small staff (115 employees) contracts with inventors to design the toys, with manufacturers to make the toys, with retailers to distribute the toys, with advertising firms to publicize the toys, even with collection agencies to collect the revenue (*Business Week* 1986:63). Executive Vice-President Robert Galoob says, "Our business is one of relationships" – in particular, market relationships. These market relationships allow Galoob to realize the benefits of large scale without hierarchy. Why is Galoob's avoidance of hierarchy in favor of market contracting the exception rather than the rule?

Why have hierarchy?

This question is especially compelling in the face of the fundamental theorem of welfare economics, which states that, in a broad range of circumstances, competitive markets allocate resources efficiently. That is, the resource allocation that results from competitive markets cannot be changed to make everyone better off; all the mutually beneficial trades will be realized by the market. Hierarchical decision making, in these circumstances, cannot reallocate resources in any way, without hurting at least one person.

While the fundamental theorem of welfare economics applies to a broad set of circumstances, any efficiency advantages for hierarchy must depend on exceptions to the theorem. Such exceptions are known as instances of "market failure" – market equilibria that fail to allocate resources efficiently. The efficiency argument for hierarchy applies to precisely those circumstances in which markets fail.

What are the circumstances that cause markets to allocate resources inefficiently? As Coase (1937) pointed out, the failure of market actors to contract efficiently may be attributed to the relative costliness of negotiating, monitoring, and enforcing contracts with factor inputs. Whenever conditions are present that make such transactions costly, markets may fail to achieve the efficient equilibria they could achieve in the frictionless case.

Chapter 1 discusses three reasons for high transaction costs and market failure. The first of these is information asymmetries:

In the textbook characterization of firms, the inputs purchased in the market are assumed to perform the tasks expected of them automatically and fully. This would hold true if the relationship between inputs and outputs were costlessly observable, because then inputs' owners could be remunerated strictly on the basis of their contributions; such costless observability is one of the features necessary (and indeed sufficient) for costless transacting to exist. (Barzel 1989: 46)

In the presence of an information asymmetry, the consumer and producer of labor may fail to achieve what would otherwise be a mutually advantageous market exchange; hierarchy may be the best way to realize the potential benefits of these transactions.

Externalities constitute a second potential reason for market failure. In particular, in a team production process, each person's level of productivity may be determined by other actors' efforts. This can provide opportunities for individual shirking and can make it especially costly to reach a satisfactory contract for the efforts of any one member or all members of such a team production technology.

A third reason for market failure is the acquisition of market power by a small number of participants on one or both sides of a market. In a "thin" market, actors are not simply price takers as in the competitive market, and one or both parties may be vulnerable to what Williamson aptly calls "opportunism" – self-serving misrepresentation of information

(Williamson 1975; Williamson and Ouchi 1981: 348–53). The result in the marketplace is an inefficient underallocation of resources to monopoly-produced goods.

Whenever any of these factors is present, a competitive market will yield an inefficient allocation of resources. As Coase (1960) demonstrated in his famous theorem, these allocative inefficiencies could be corrected by contracting, assuming clear specification of property rights and costless negotiation and enforcement of contracts. However, these transaction costs may be large, and larger under some institutions than others. As shown in Chapter 2, the best political-economic analysis suggests that information asymmetry, externalities, and market power can limit the efficiency of negotiated solutions to competitive market failure. The same analysis points out that hierarchical authority can be an efficiency-enhancing institutional feature (Farrell 1987b: 120).

While Chapter 2 establishes the desirability of authority, Chapter 3 raises the possibility that democratic voting may be used to reach authoritative group decisions. Here again, however, the problems that generate market failure and negotiation failure can be shown to lead to systematic failures in voting processes. Perhaps the strongest result in political economy, the Arrow theorem, establishes the case not just for hierarchical authority, but for dictatorial social choice.

These results suggest that, at least in some circumstances, groups of individuals are faced with a dilemma. Most people would prefer the voluntaristic or participatory exchange of competitive markets, bargained contracts, or voting democracies. However, these transaction arenas may result in large allocative inefficiencies in the presence of information asymmetry, externalities, or market power. Allocative efficiency and reduction in the transaction costs of negotiating and monitoring contracts may require that some persons in the group receive an asymmetric and incompletely defined grant of authority to direct the activities of other members. Sometimes, as in the case of Lehman Brothers, the result is the dissolution of partnership contracts based on bargaining and voting among partners and the imposition of strict hierarchical authority.

1

Market failures and hierarchical solutions
The tension between individual and social rationality

> Every team member would prefer a team in which no one, not even himself, shirked.
>
> Alchian and Demsetz (1972: 790)

Virtually everyone agrees that working in hierarchies is at times unpleasant. Yet most people in the twentieth century spend most of their time in hierarchical organizations – supervising subordinates or being supervised by their own superiors.

This was not always the case. In the early nineteenth century, most economic activity was carried out in small cottage industries consisting of individual tradesmen and a small number of apprentices. Even our largest federal bureaucracies were only loosely hierarchical, with most postmasters and land agents working as individuals miles from the nearest "supervisor" and showing a marked tendency to set their own policies (Crenson 1975). Most economic activity took place among individual farmers, buyers, wholesalers, importers, and exporters (Chandler 1977).

Today, most of our goods are produced by large corporations instead of individual wheelwrights or weavers, and even our food is produced in large part by agribusiness. Law enforcement is provided by a large hierarchy instead of the night watchman, and education is provided by another bureaucracy instead of the individual in a one-room schoolhouse (Knott and Miller 1987). Yet there is a good deal of unhappiness with hierarchy, centering around doubts concerning both its efficiency and its effect on individual autonomy or liberty. While concerns about government efficiency and intrusions on individual liberty are an ongoing theme in U.S. society, similar doubts have begun to be voiced about corporate bureaucracies.

In 1986 Richard Darman, deputy secretary of the treasury in Reagan's administration, gave a speech at the Harvard Business School in which he expressed concern about the "corpocracy." He saw in business managers a lack of adequate preparation for the future; a weakness in identifying emerging rules of the game; a hesitancy in associating with unfamiliar forces of change; an inability to formulate and execute creative strategies of adaptation; and a general slowness of foot that left them, like Sonny Liston, sitting in a corner on a stool when the bell rang for the crucial rounds. (Darman 1986: 5)

Others have been even more critical. Management consultants Peters and Waterman (1984) remember the sixties, when "American management was touted by many, at home and abroad, as the primary asset that America could export to the world"; today, they regard the well-run companies in U.S. business as a "saving remnant," outnumbered by stodgy and inefficient firms (xvii).

Doubts about both public and private hierarchies raise the issue: Why have hierarchy anyway? Why not simply allow individuals to pursue their own interest in competitive markets? From an ethical standpoint, markets have the advantage of granting individuals autonomy. Each person in a free and open market can buy or sell as it suits his or her own tastes, unconstrained by the authority of king or bureaucrat.

Furthermore, in the marketplace the advantages of individual freedom can frequently be obtained at no efficiency cost. Welfare economists have demonstrated the efficiency of competitive markets: When individuals buy and sell private goods in competitive markets, the resulting allocation of resources cannot be changed without at least one person being hurt. Central to this efficiency result is the assumption that all individuals act for themselves, in pursuit of individual self-interest. Hierarchical constraints imposed on the pursuit of individual self-interest can only be harmful.

This result has often been used to buttress arguments against government regulation: Why have government regulation when regulations can at best be nonconstraining and at worst distort the efficient resource allocation processes of the market? The same question can, of course, be asked of private hierarchy: Why have corporate hierarchy when the rules and dictates of hierarchy can at best be nonconstraining and at worst distort the efficient resource allocation processes of the market?

Government regulation has been defended by pointing out the existence of market failure. Market failure may exist when any of the built-in assumptions of welfare economics – competitive markets, private goods, and costless information – are not met. The explanation for private hierarchy, as well as government regulation, must rest with the same causes of market failure. In the absence of competitive markets, private goods, or costless information, autonomous self-interested individuals can converge on inefficient outcomes. Because of market failure, hierarchical control may serve to improve, rather than impede, efficiency.

Market failures and hierarchical solutions

There would be no need for large, hierarchical social units if individual rationality were always sufficient to yield efficient social outcomes. Game theory has proved to be an effective way of thinking about the interaction between individual self-interest and group efficiency. This section reviews some basic notions in game theory, concepts that will be useful later in the analysis of hierarchy.

Individual rationality in games

Smith and Jones are two prisoners serving time for grand larceny. The district attorney, Ms. Doe, has an unsolved bank robbery and believes that Smith and Jones are the perpetrators of the crime. She is planning to run for governor and would like to get them to confess, since this would add a major conviction to her record. She enlists the aid of the prison warden, who conducts a surprise search of their cells, revealing hidden weapons and drugs. She knows that she can use this information to get a conviction on the minor charge of concealed weapons and drugs. She considers two alternative plans, plan A and plan B, intended to elicit a confession from the two convicts.

Plan A. The goal of plan A is to get both prisoners to confess to the crime, making it easy to convict both of them. Ms. Doe promises the harshest possible punishment for either one if he is the only one to confess, but promises to go easier on them if they both confess.

The district attorney confronts Smith and Jones and makes the following commitment: If just one confesses to the crime, the one who confesses will have the book thrown at him, receiving an additional twenty years in jail for both the bank robbery and the minor charges; the other will get no additional years. If both confess to the crime, each will get an additional five years in jail for the bank robbery. If neither confesses, both will receive two additional years for the hidden weapons and drug charge. Each must make his choice without knowledge of the other prisoner's choice.

The district attorney has created a game for Smith and Jones. A game is a social interaction involving at least two players, in which each player has at least two possible courses of action and the payoffs are associated with the players' action choices. In this game, shown in Table 1.1, Smith has one best choice no matter what Jones chooses to do. If Jones does not confess, Smith gets a lighter sentence by refusing to confess as well. If Jones

Table 1.1. *Individual self-interest as an aid to social efficiency (plan A)*

	Jones confesses	Jones does not confess
Smith confesses	Smith gets 5 additional years Jones gets 5 additional years	Smith gets 20 additional years Jones gets no additional years
Smith does not confess	Smith gets no additional years Jones gets 20 additional years	Smith gets 2 additional years Jones gets 2 additional years

confesses, then Smith can get off free by not confessing. Smith then has a dominant strategy, which is defined as a strategy choice that is best for the choosing player no matter what choice his opponent makes. Similarly, Jones has a dominant strategy, because he is best off not confessing, whether Smith confesses or not.

The outcome reached when both players choose not to confess is a stable one; that is, each player is satisfied that he has made the correct choice, after the other's choice is revealed. Neither player could make himself better off by each changing his mind. In game theory such an outcome is called a Nash equilibrium (Tirole 1988: 206).

The game created by plan A obviously fails to achieve the district attorney's goal. Rational self-interested choice by Smith and Jones leads to a stable outcome in which they both refuse to confess. Is there any way to design the game that changes the calculations of Smith and Jones?

Plan B. With plan B, the goal is to get either prisoner to confess, as long as either one implicates the other. The district attorney then promises to inflict the harshest possible sentence on the one who does not confess.

She confronts Smith and Jones and makes the following commitment: As in plan A, if neither confesses to the bank robbery, she will guarantee each of them an additional two years in jail on the drug and weapons possession charge. If both confess to the crime, both will get an additional five years for the bank robbery, again as in plan A. If just one of them confesses, implicating both of them, the one who confesses will get off free on both the bank robbery and the minor charge. The one who fails to confess will receive an additional twenty years in jail for both the bank robbery and the minor charges. This is summarized in Table 1.2.

Here again Smith has a dominant strategy – but now his dominant strategy is to confess. If Jones fails to confess, Smith can evade both the bank robbery and minor charges by confessing. If Jones confesses, Smith will have to confess as well to avoid having twenty years added to his sentence. The same reasoning applies to Jones. Both will confess, and that outcome is a Nash equilibrium – neither, knowing that the other has chosen to confess, will want to change his mind.

Table 1.2. *Individual self-interest as an obstacle to social efficiency (plan B)*

	Jones confesses	Jones does not confess
Smith confesses	Smith gets 5 additional years Jones gets 5 additional years	Smith gets no additional years Jones gets 20 additional years
Smith does not confess	Smith gets 20 additional years Jones gets no additional years	Smith gets 2 additional years Jones gets 2 additional years

Social efficiency in games

With plan B, the district attorney has structured a situation in which individual self-interested behavior works against Smith and Jones. Each is led to confess, and thus each achieves for himself an outcome that both could agree is inferior to one they could achieve if both refused to confess. An outcome that all players could agree is worse than some other outcome is called "Pareto suboptimal." Any other outcome is Pareto optimal. Regarding just the preferences of Smith and Jones, the Nash equilibrium achieved by plan A is Pareto optimal. The Nash equilibrium reached by plan B is Pareto suboptimal for Smith and Jones.

Pareto optimality is the weakest possible requirement for group efficiency; if an outcome is not Pareto optimal, a change could be made that would benefit at least one person without hurting anyone else. There would seem to be no objection to making such a move; consequently, a failure of a weak condition like Pareto optimality is a clear violation of group efficiency.

With either plan A or plan B, Smith and Jones could have only two years added to their sentences by not confessing; but with plan A, that outcome is easy to achieve, whereas with plan B it seems impossible to achieve. The main point of this analysis is that, with plan B, Smith and Jones would have to behave in a radically different way than with plan A in order to achieve the same outcome and the same payoff.

With plan A, each convict has only to consult his own self-interest and play his dominant strategy. With plan B, the same outcome is achievable only if the two players find some way to coordinate their choices; for only if each individual chooses the individually irrational option can both individuals be better off.

Under plan B, failing to confess is definitely worse for Smith and Jones no matter which choice the other makes. But if both convicts select their individually worst, dominated alternative, both will be better off than if each selects the best choices. Only if Smith and Jones figure out a way to convince one another to make individually irrational choices will they achieve the payoff that they could achieve with plan A simply by acting in their own self-interest. Obviously, this necessity makes plan B unambiguously a harder game for the convicts.

In fact, the incentives constructed in plan B are so compelling that it would be very easy to imagine that Smith and Jones would be forced to confess to the bank robbery *even if they were both innocent.* An innocent Smith could be convicted by Jones's confession, or vice versa, and the incentives in Table 1.2 are the same whether they are innocent or guilty. If the district attorney really wants to increase her chances of being elected governor, all she has to do is find two plausible candidates for each of the unsolved crimes, implement plan B, and use the confessions to obtain convictions.

Nor is this just an academic possibility. The women found guilty of witchcraft during the Salem witch-hunt were in a dilemma similar to that of Smith and Jones: The hope was that the naming of other witches would add sincerity to one's confession and induce the authorities to look favorably on one's cooperativeness. Similar games (with or without physical torture) are used in police states to generate confessions from "subversives," along with the names of "coconspirators."

The authority to create incentives that induce innocents to confess to crimes they did not commit is a terrible power. The possibility that people in hierarchical authority may misuse their ability to create incentives for others is a continuing theme of this book. It underscores the main question of the present chapter: Why should people give up the voluntarism of markets, free contracts, or democratic voting to create hierarchical authority in firms or governments?

The Invisible Hand versus the Prisoners' Dilemma game

Plan A and plan B represent two very different kinds of social interactions depending on whether or not self-interest is sufficient to achieve Pareto-optimal outcomes. A game like plan A in which individual self-interest is sufficient to guarantee a Pareto-optimal outcome is an "Invisible Hand" game. In such a game, the Nash equilibrium is Pareto optimal. The players do not have to communicate ahead of time; they do not have to bribe or coerce one another or contract with one another. No group interaction of any sort is necessary to achieve a Pareto-optimal outcome.

Plan B, in contrast, is known as a "Prisoners' Dilemma" game. Because the Nash equilibrium is Pareto suboptimal, individual self-interest is simply a trap rather than a sufficient mechanism for group efficiency. With plan B, Smith and Jones must use some sort of social interaction other than individual pursuit of self-interest if they are to achieve an efficient group outcome.

This Prisoners' Dilemma game, and all such games, raise the fundamental issue of individual and group interests in conflict. When group well-being can be achieved only if each individual behaves irrationally, what is to be done? What are Smith and Jones to do? How can they achieve the preferred outcome of two years each in jail rather than five years each? There are a variety of possibilities, but none of them are necessary in an Invisible Hand game.

Consider communication. Suppose Smith and Jones were allowed ten minutes alone in an interrogation room before they decided whether to confess. The obvious theme of the conversation would be the mutual gains to be achieved if both were to resist the self-interested temptation to confess. They would probably also make a mutual compact not to confess. Then, as they found themselves alone facing the district attorney, Smith might well think: "If Jones sticks to our compact, I can get off free by confessing! But if he squeals, I will be buying a twenty-year prison term if I don't confess. In fact, he is probably thinking the same thing I'm thinking now, which means he is probably going to confess; so I have to confess, too." It is obvious that simple communication is not sufficient to escape the dilemma.

A hierarchical solution to the Prisoners' Dilemma game

The fundamental aspect of the dilemma is that individual choice, which we tend to regard as a very good thing, is costly for Smith and Jones – and all other individuals who are trapped in Prisoners' Dilemma games. The characteristic common to all these games is that, if someone would just force each player not to take the alternative that seems attractive to each in equilibrium, then both would be better off. The use of "force" in this way can be called the hierarchical solution to group inefficiency. That is, in hierarchies some people are granted coercive authority to induce others to do what they would not otherwise find it in their interest to do. Hierarchy is the price people may choose to pay for efficiency in groups.

One institution has evolved to provide a Pareto-optimal solution to the problem facing Smith and Jones: the Mafia. If Smith and Jones are members of the Mafia, they face a different set of payoffs than those described in Table 1.2. A Mafia member who squeals on another mafioso knows he will be murdered, either in jail or after he has been released. A mafioso in Smith's position may well consider the five or twenty years in jail that go with not confessing better than the death sentence that goes with confessing. Better yet, each knows that the other knows this, so that each can be confident that the other will not confess. The Mafia thus replaces the incentive system designed by the district attorney with a system that creates a different dominant strategy.

Joining the Mafia puts one in the position of having a potential death sentence hanging over one's head. One would not expect this to be an attractive option for most people; yet people do voluntarily give up a degree of liberty – that is, the right to choose individually preferable outcomes

25

without having to worry about sanctions – in order to achieve the gains that are possible through coordinated play. Bank robbers may well do this voluntarily because they know that the alternative is a dilemma like the one Smith and Jones face under plan B. For this "service" – which deprives them of their individual liberty – they are even willing to pay the further price of a share of their take. These are the extremes to which individuals in social dilemmas are driven. The insufficiency of individual rationality leads people to seek group solutions to their problems – even coercive solutions.

The dilemma behind the dilemma

While "Prisoners' Dilemma" refers to a rather specific type of game in which each individual has a dominant strategy not to cooperate, the same dilemma occurs in any game in which the Nash equilibrium is inefficient. I call such games – including games in which individuals do not have dominant strategies – "social dilemmas" or "social traps."

At one level, then, the social dilemma is a dilemma facing the participants in the game. They have to choose, as individuals, whether to pursue their own interest or seek some cooperative solution that may provide potential efficiency gains. At another level, a naturally occurring social dilemma poses the necessity of a trade-off between two core values of individual autonomy and social efficiency. In any of these games, individual self-interested choice will lead to the inefficient Nash equilibrium. Individual liberty must be purchased at the cost of efficiency, or vice versa.

This is an uncomfortable choice at best, and it is very important, therefore, to know how pervasive and unavoidable are social dilemmas. If they are rare, or if there is some formula that allows for their solution without the imposition of hierarchy, social groups can avoid the dilemma of liberty versus efficiency. If, however, they are widespread and intractable, groups must make difficult choices. The widespread and growing phenomenon of hierarchy in the modern world must be intimately connected with the pervasiveness of social dilemmas.

MARKET SUCCESS AND MARKET FAILURE

The originator of the phrase "invisible hand" was Adam Smith, who questioned the value of much governmental intervention in the marketplace:

As every individual, therefore, endeavours as much as he can both to employ his capital in the support of domestic industry, and so to direct that industry that its produce may be of the greatest value; every individual necessarily labours to render the annual revenue of the society as great as he can. He generally, indeed, neither intends to promote the public interest, nor knows how much he is promoting it. . . . he intends only his own gain, and he is in this, as in many other cases, led by an

26

invisible hand to promote an end which was not part of his intention. Nor is it always the worse for the society that it was no part of it. By pursuing his own interest he frequently promotes that of the society more effectually than when he really intends to promote it. (Smith 1776/1952: 194)

Competitive market for private goods: the invisible hand

In their analysis of competitive markets, economists have demonstrated that Adam Smith's insight was absolutely correct: Under certain conditions, individual pursuit of self-interest does serve as an engine for social welfare. This is the fundamental theorem of welfare economics: "A competitive [market] equilibrium is Pareto optimal (that is, a benevolent and fully informed social planner could not replace the competitive allocation of goods with another feasible allocation that would increase all the consumers' welfare)" (Tirole 1988: 6).

As producers seek to maximize profit, they cater to the demands of consumers. The competitive buying behavior of consumers in markets serves as a perfectly adequate signal of their tastes. Producers also utilize inputs of labor, capital, and raw materials in such a way as to keep costs to a minimum. The net result is an efficient allocation of resources to alternative uses. The decentralized market by itself will have already discovered and exploited all mutually beneficial transactions, making hierarchical direction unnecessary.

The fundamental theorem of welfare economics is justifiably used to bolster the hope of neoclassical economists that it is unnecessary to face the choice represented by the prisoners' dilemma – liberty versus efficiency. In the presence of competitive markets for private goods, liberty and efficiency support one another. Hierarchy is an intrusion on individual liberty that can only interfere with efficiency.

However, the smooth and efficient operation of the market economy is dependent on the clear specification of property rights and the ability of market participants to negotiate, monitor, and enforce contracts at a low cost. There are systematic reasons that these conditions may not apply. In this case, efficiency losses may well be restored by means of an asymmetric grant of authority to one party.

Three causes of market failure

Three primary conditions are placed on the fundamental theorem of welfare economics. When any one of them is not met, individual self-interest leads to inefficient Nash equilibria – a social dilemma. Each of these three occasions for market failure can be used to support a different explanation and rationale for the existence of hierarchy.

27

Information asymmetry. One condition of the fundamental theorem of welfare economics is symmetric information – one side must not be deprived of vital information available to another side. As demonstrated by Akerlof (1970), when buyers (for instance) are faced with asymmetric information, inefficiency can result.

Akerlof's example is the market for used cars. Imagine that some proportion of the sellers of used cars have "premium" used cars – cars that are in better mechanical shape than others with identical mileage because the owners have driven them with care and spent a great deal of money on upkeep. There are also some buyers who would be willing to pay more for such used cars. These two groups – the owners of premium used cars and the interested buyers – are natural trading partners. Both could be better off making deals at prices higher than the prices of "lemons."

The problem is that, because the quality of the used cars on the market cannot be verified, these trades will not be made. Every seller has an incentive to claim that his or her car is one of the premium cars, even if it is in fact a lemon. Buyers cannot sort out the true from the false claims, and therefore refuse to offer a premium price. Because they cannot get the premium price, the owners of the good used cars may refuse to sell. Both the owners of the better cars and the interested buyers are worse off than they would be if the quality of the car were knowable.

Of course, a mechanic can give his expert and presumably objective opinion of the value of a used car, and his services are available for a fee. This goes a long way toward solving the problem; but in another sense it further illustrates the problem, since the fee, whether paid by the buyer or the seller or by both, in some combination, is a deadweight loss. The cost of finding a trustworthy mechanic and paying for his services is a cost of transacting that is itself a manifestation of the inefficiency caused by the information asymmetry.

A further example is illustrated by professional services, such as those of a physician. When a physician claims that a patient needs an operation, the patient has no way of knowing whether the operation is in fact required. For example, many news reports have revealed that thousands of unnecessary hysterectomies are performed in the United States every year. A patient, knowing that physicians have a monetary incentive to perform unnecessary surgery, may refuse to visit a physician even for an annual checkup.

Monopoly power. A second condition of the fundamental theorem is market competition. A competitive market is one in which no single buyer or seller can have an impact on the equilibrium market price by withholding her sale or purchase. To the extent that a seller has that kind of impact on the market, the seller has acquired some degree of monopoly power. It is generally recognized that monopoly power (or monopsony power, in the case of a single buyer) creates incentives that lead rational individuals to suboptimal group outcomes. The temptation for the monopolist is to increase prices in order to increase profits. However, doing so causes buyers to decrease the amount of the good consumed. The harm done to buyers from increased price and decreased consumption is greater than the benefit achieved by the monopolist in the form of increased profits, resulting in a market inefficiency.

Externalities. A third condition for efficient markets is that the transactions in the marketplace have no impact on third parties. When a buyer purchases a scarf, the scarf keeps no one but the buyer warm. However, some transactions do have effects, called externality effects, on people who are not involved in the transaction. The purchase of a loud stereo system may cause neighbors pain; the purchase of a tree may provide benefits.

Whether the externality is positive or negative, a normal economic buyer will not consider the externality in purchasing the good. Individually rational buyers tend to purchase more and more of a good as long as the extra benefit from an additional unit exceeds the price. They stop buying when the extra benefit exactly equals the price. In the case of a positive externality, however, all the people in a neighborhood might be better off if, for example, they all chipped in and purchased a tree that no individual could afford. To take another example – everyone in a neighborhood might like to live in a flower-filled environment but the cost (in terms of financial expense, time, and hard work) of filling one's own front yard with flowers would be significant. Consider Ned and Edna. They live across from one another, and each would like to see flowers out of his or her window, whether those flowers were in his or her own yard or across the street. In fact, each would be willing to pay $20 to see one yard full of flowers and $45 to see two yards full of flowers. However, it would take $30 to rent the tools, buy the seeds, and hire someone to tend the garden.

The payoffs for all possible combinations of gardening efforts are listed in Table 1.3. If Ned gardens, Edna is better off not gardening, because she gets $20 worth of benefits for free; this is better than getting $40 worth of benefits at a cost of $30. However, if Ned does not garden, she is still better off not gardening, because obtaining one garden is worth $20 and costs $30. Thus, no matter what Ned does, Edna is better off not gardening. The same is true for Ned. The Nash equilibrium of the game is for neither one to have a garden. However, individual rationality is once again a trap, since both would be better off if both did what neither one has any reason to do.

29

Table 1.3. *Consumption externalities inducing a prisoners' dilemma*

	Ned gardens	Ned does not garden
Edna gardens	Edna gets $45 − 30 = $15	$20 − 30 = −$10
	Ned gets $45 − 30 = $15	$20 − 0 = $20
Edna does not garden	Edna gets $20 − 0 = $20	$0 − 0 = $0
	Ned gets $20 − 30 = −$10	$0 − 0 = $0

Note: The following assumptions are made: (1) Each derives $45 worth of benefit from two gardens, and $20 worth of benefit from one, and (2) each must pay $30 in order to garden.

Externalities are often much broader than those facing gardeners in a neighborhood – large-scale irrigation projects and national defense are some of the broadest. These could conceivably be supplied through a market contract involving a large number of affected parties. However, the costs of organizing the group, negotiating the multiparty contract that would be necessary to purchase the public good, and monitoring the contract enforcement would be large.

The cost of such a market transaction is even greater when problems of information asymmetry are considered. The value of a neighborhood garden or of a large-scale irrigation project is not absolute or intellectually knowable. It is determined by the summation of the private valuations of the citizens who might benefit (or be hurt by) the public good. Each citizen may have compelling reasons to misrepresent his or her private valuation of the good.

These transaction costs being what they are, it becomes prohibitively expensive to negotiate a new contract for every public good. It would be cheaper simply to arrange a contract known as a "state," which would have the authority to tax citizens for the provision of the package of public goods. Because of this, the classic solution to the problem of externalities has involved some degree of hierarchy – a means of changing the incentives facing individuals to encourage investment in underproduced public goods and to discourage investment in overproduced public bads.

SOCIAL TRAPS IN PRODUCTION: SPECIALIZATION IN TEAMS

Firms have discovered that specialization of effort creates the potential for large improvements in efficiency. The problem is that this specialization implies some degree of information asymmetry, market power, and externalities. The very production processes that offer the promise of large efficiency gains simultaneously increase the costs of transacting under normal competitive market institutions.

Team production externalities

A group of individuals may find that a certain technology makes possible a production function that is highly interactive – the more effort one person exerts, the more productive other members of the group may be. This is what Alchian and Demsetz (1972) call a "team production function." Just as "public goods" may not be consumed at all without cooperative group action among consumers, "team goods" may not be produced at all without cooperative action among producers. The production of team goods, like the consumption of public goods, is a social trap. Efficiency in either case requires coordinated – even hierarchical – interaction.

As an example, suppose that Calvin and Cathy can separately produce $40 worth of profits each, and together can produce $80 worth of profits. This simple production function is *not* team production, because each individual's marginal productivity is independent of the other team member's effort. In such a situation, there are no gains to be realized by the two of them working in the same organization. Each person could sell his or her own output, and no group effort could possibly realize greater efficiency. Market competition alone would be sufficient to discipline each worker to produce the optimal amount. Without team technology, the two are in an Invisible Hand game: The Nash equilibrium of their production decisions is Pareto optimal.

Suppose now that Calvin and Cathy can each produce $40 worth of profits working alone but can produce $90 of profits working together, perhaps by specializing. In such a situation, there are real productivity gains to be made from working together, because each person's productivity increases from the other one's working harder. This is the defining characteristic of team production.

Now suppose the two of them are working in a cooperative relationship in which they sell the product of their joint efforts at the market price and then split the revenue. The benefits of each person's effort would be divided equally, but the costs would be experienced individually. In such a case, the production efforts have production "externalities" that result in prisoners' dilemmas just as surely as do consumption externalities.

In Table 1.4, both individuals would be better off working hard than shirking. However, that higher level of effort is not an equilibrium. If the other works hard, each person is better off shirking. If the other one shirks, each is better off shirking. Each person has a dominant strategy to shirk, despite the fact that both are worse off when each chooses his or her dominant strategy.

31

Table 1.4. *Production externalities inducing a prisoners' dilemma*

	Calvin works hard	Calvin shirks
Cathy works hard	Cathy gets $45 − 30 = $15	$20 − 30 = −$10
	Calvin gets $45 − 30 = $15	$20 − 0 = $20
Cathy shirks	Cathy gets $20 − 0 = $20	$0 − 0 = $0
	Calvin gets $20 − 30 = −$10	$0 − 0 = $0

Note: The following assumptions are made: (1) Their profits equal $0 when both shirk, $40 when just one works hard, and $90 when both work together. Profits are split equally. (2) Each must pay $30 in psychic costs when working hard, $0 when shirking.

Team shirking has been documented by social psychologists, who call it "social loafing" (Latane, Williams, and Harkins 1979; Edney 1979). When confronted with a simple group task like pulling a rope, cheering, or clapping to produce noise levels, individual effort declines with the number of co-workers. "We have found that when the individual thinks his or her own contribution to the group cannot be measured, his or her output tends to slacken" (Latane et al. 1979: 104). This was found to be true in both German and U.S. cultures and for a large number of tasks. Nor can faulty coordination of effort explain the decline in group effort. When blindfolded and convinced that others were pulling with them,

people pulled at 90 per cent of their individual rate when they believed one other person was pulling, and at only 85 per cent when they believed two to six others were pulling. It appears that virtually all of the decline in performance could be accounted for in terms of reduced effort or social loafing. (106)

The Nash equilibrium of this game is very stable but totally inefficient: Everyone loafs, yet they all realize they would be better off if no one loafed. All members might agree to work harder; they might even hire a cheerleader to spur themselves to maximal effort. But this would clearly not be a stable outcome, even if it were temporarily achieved.

As another example of shirking, let us consider the franchising problem. People go to McDonald's because they want a clean place to eat a meal quickly. Customers tend to think that a given McDonald's is clean, not necessarily because they have been in that restaurant before, but because they have been in other McDonald's restaurants before. But each McDonald's benefits from the fact that other franchise holders are keeping their restaurant clean. What would happen to one franchise holder's profits if he cut corners on keeping his own franchise clean? His profits might go up, because he could reduce his labor costs and still attract customers by relying on the general McDonald's reputation. It is a prisoners' dilemma.

The franchise problem is simply the team production problem writ large. The franchisers as a group do better by having a national reputation for cleanliness, but without a special disciplining process, each franchiser would have an incentive to "free-ride" on the efforts of other franchisers, leaving all of them worse off.

Team production, information asymmetry, and market power

Just as specialization implies the existence of externalities in production among team members, it also creates the conditions for information asymmetry and market power. Each specialist, by definition, knows things that other specialists do not. This can easily lead to conflict between specialists.

A scenario is easy to imagine: A downstream specialist complains about the poor work of an upstream specialist. The upstream specialist feels that she is doing the best she can given the materials and that the problem would be resolved if the downstream specialist simply modified his technique somewhat. The downstream specialist says that the upstream specialist does not realize the technical difficulties and extra cost involved in the proposed modification, and so on. In a world of perfect information and costless negotiation and monitoring, such problems would easily be solved; but increased specialization in an organization implies an increased inability to see the other person's point of view. Transaction costs escalate as the degree of specialization increases.

Furthermore, specialization in production leads to a decrease in the likelihood that competitive market forces will solve coordination problems by means of the neutral operation of the price mechanism. When the upstream specialist complains that she is getting too little compensation for the amount of skill and effort she is bringing to her tasks, there are not a large number of perfectly substitutable specialists willing to take her place at a readily observable market price. If a large market exists for a given worker's labor, then that laborer is not a specialist. The more specialized a production process becomes, the more it invests its participants with monopoly power. The inevitable effect is an increase in the costs of negotiating separate contracts with each specialist. Thus, specialized team production seems to imply a degree of externalities, information asymmetry, and market power. While specialized team production creates the potential for enormous efficiency gains, it also creates the conditions for market failure.

The proposed solution to market failure: hierarchy

Just as externalities in consumption lead to the emergence of authoritative collective consumption units that alter individual incentives in the name of group efficiency, so externalities in production may lead to the emergence of authoritative collective production units that alter individual incentives in the name of efficient production patterns.

Alchian and Demsetz (1972) provide a fairly complete picture of how and why the firm takes the hierarchical shape it does. The problem of social loafing in teams is solved by the presence of supervisors, or monitoring specialists, whose task is "apportioning rewards, observing the input behavior of inputs as means of detecting or estimating their marginal productivity and giving assignments or instructions in what to do and how to do it" (782). This monitoring allows a change in the incentive system in which individuals are rewarded for greater effort and punished for shirking. In short, the purpose of the hierarchy is to realign incentives so that individuals in a team production situation no longer find it in their interest to shirk.

The monitor's task is obviously a difficult one. (We will see how difficult it is in later chapters.) In order for someone to undertake this task, some incentive will doubtless be required. But more important, Alchian and Demsetz point out, the reward for the monitor must be arranged in such a way that she has an incentive to do the job right – that is, to maximize the difference between the payouts to the production inputs and the revenues earned. This can best be done by giving the monitor property rights to the residual profits generated by the team she monitors. The monitor earns her residual through the reduction in shirking that she brings about by observing and directing the actions or uses of inputs.

Managing or examining the ways in which inputs are used in team production is a method of monitoring the marginal productivity of individual inputs to the team's output. To discipline team members and reduce shirking, the residual claimant must have power to revise the contract terms and incentives of individual members without having to terminate or alter every other input's contract. Hence, team members who seek to increase their productivity will assign to the monitor not only the residual claimant right, but also the right to alter individual membership and performance on the team (Alchian and Demsetz 1972: 782). Thus, the organization of the team takes on a hierarchical character, with one central member who monitors subordinates, has the authority to punish and reward subordinates, and owns the profits generated by the team's efforts.

This analysis is a powerful explanation for the existence of hierarchy. Hierarchy is, in the Alchian and Demsetz perspective, an efficiency-enhancing institutional form that helps to resolve the problem of market failure caused by team production externalities. It works by creating a set of incentives – for subordinates and superiors alike – that realign individual self-interest with group efficiency.

CONCLUSION

It is useful to state at this point what this book attempts to do in light of the Alchian and Demsetz picture of the firm. In the first place, the central problem in this book is exactly the central problem identified by Alchian and Demsetz: the tension between individual self-interest and group efficiency in teams. This "social dilemma" is the heart of the managerial problem. Nor were Alchian and Demsetz the first people to observe the centrality of this dilemma. At least since the work of Chester Barnard in 1938, it has been seen as a central problem in the literature on organizational behavior as well.

Furthermore, this book is concerned with the role of incentives, as were Alchian and Demsetz. A hierarchy clearly alters incentives, and these alterations must be seen as efficiency enhancing. I also follow Alchian and Demsetz in being concerned with the incentives that superiors offer subordinates as well as with the incentives shaping superiors' choices.

However, the hierarchical solution to the problem of team shirking is not necessarily automatic or final. In fact, there has been such a long history of organizational conflict surrounding incentive systems that one might easily infer that there is nothing simple at all about solving dilemmas in teams by means of hierarchical monitoring and incentive setting. There may or may not be an "ideal" incentive system that completely aligns subordinate incentives with the goal of organizational profit maximization. And furthermore, if there is such an ideal incentive system for subordinates, superiors may or may not have an incentive to pick that system.

As hierarchies generate profits in excess of what a nonhierarchical team would be able to generate, the problem of distributing those profits appears. In a perfect world, the monitor would be able to assess the marginal productivity of each subordinate and each input, to pay them accordingly, and to keep the excess. However, the next seven chapters discuss the economic and behavioral constraints that keep monitors from following this mechanical path. In practice, the distribution of excess profits in a hierarchy becomes a major bargaining problem. This problem is the focus of Chapter 2.

2

Bargaining failure
Coordination, bargaining, and contracts

> If people come to bargaining already knowing their [own] private val-
> ues for a good, then no arrangement exists that will lead them to trade
> precisely when they should, given that each can choose to walk away.
> So the king's power to coerce really helps to achieve efficiency.
>
> Farrell (1987b: 120)

A breakdown in the efficiency of competitive market processes may create
a prima facie case for hierarchy. Since a social dilemma exists when individual self-interest leads to inefficient outcomes, efficiency would seem to
require a mechanism capable of coercing individuals to do what they would
otherwise have no incentive to do.

But is hierarchy really necessary to escape social inefficiency? Why can't
the individuals facing a social dilemma agree among themselves on the
course of action necessary and voluntarily commit themselves to a mutually
binding legal contract that would resolve the dilemma? A voluntary contract such as this would simply represent an extension of the voluntaristic
market mechanism. Just as a private exchange contract commits a buyer
and a seller to give up assets in return for considerations defined in the contract, a public goods contract could commit two parties in a public goods
dilemma to contribute to the purchase of a public good in return for the
benefits of other parties' contributions.

Indeed, a relatively nonhierarchical form of contractual coordination
called "inside contracting" prevailed in many large-scale industries at the
turn of the century. Under this system, an entrepreneur provided raw materials and a large work space and negotiated contracts with skilled craftsmen and their crews to provide a specified number of components for the
entrepreneur's product. The system had a number of advantages; why was
it replaced by a more hierarchical arrangement?

Bargaining failure

The premise of Coase's classic work (1960) is that, without obstacles to bargaining, rational individuals will always bargain their way to an efficient solution. Only when the costs of bargaining to an efficient outcome are great will there be a need for some hierarchical institution. In his 1937 article, Coase suggests that one should systematically examine the size of those transaction costs in different settings in order to understand why hierarchical firms exist within a market environment.

What are the obstacles to efficient bargaining that might lead to the creation of a firm? A branch of game theory known as bargaining theory has provided a great deal of insight into the bargaining process and why it might not succeed. One of the primary obstacles to efficiency is the multitude of possible contracts that could resolve any given social dilemma. Each of these contracts might have different distributional implications for the players involved. A group of people who are united on the inefficiency of a particular market failure might well find themselves in conflict about how to divide the surplus generated by a more efficient outcome.

In fact, this chapter argues that the same factors that promote market failure can exacerbate transaction costs and create bargaining failure. Monopoly, team production externalities, and information asymmetry have been shown by modern bargaining theory to create barriers to the efficient resolution of social dilemmas. The result is that individuals may find themselves spending much more time negotiating a solution to a problem of group inefficiency than it is worth. This, too, becomes an argument for hierarchy. An asymmetric grant of authority to direct the behavior of others allows efficient outcomes to be imposed that could never be efficiently negotiated.

BARGAINING, PROPERTY RIGHTS, AND CONTRACTS

That voluntary, nonhierarchical contracts can resolve social dilemmas is clearly an empirical fact as well as a theoretical possibility. Interstate pollution-control compacts bind governments to pollute less than they would otherwise have an incentive to do. International treaties resolve dilemmas involving everything from whales to arms reduction. Firms can engage in mutually beneficial joint ventures, with contracts specifying the necessary actions to be undertaken by each party and the division of the resulting revenues.

In each of these cases, coordinated action is achieved by means of a complex contract rather than by hierarchical authority. In a joint venture, for instance, one firm does not become the hierarchical superior of the other, nor is it necessary for either firm to grant superior discretionary authority to any third party other than the normal court system of contract enforcement.

Why have hierarchy?

That nonhierarchical, contractual resolution of market failure occurs frequently is not in dispute. The question for this chapter is: Are there systematic conditions under which nonhierarchical, contractual resolution of market failure must be abandoned in favor of hierarchy?

The advantages of bargaining over hierarchy

As a way of discussing both the potential advantages of voluntary bargaining over hierarchy and the limits of bargaining, let us consider two individuals in a social dilemma. Suppose Sid is bothered by co-worker Cindy's cigarettes. A hierarchical, coercive solution would be a grant of authority to a hierarchical superior to decide whether or not Cindy has the right to smoke. If Cindy were willing to pay $30 in order to smoke in the office, and Sid were willing to pay $45 to work in a smoke-free environment, a decision from the superior prohibiting smoking would be desirable in the sense that it would help Sid more than it would hurt Cindy. At the same time, all the benefits of the hierarchical fiat would go to Sid, and all of the costs would go to Cindy. Coercion would therefore be necessary in order to make the regulation stick; Cindy would have no reason to comply voluntarily.

Both the hierarchical resolution and the necessity of enforcement would pose a variety of social costs. Cindy, at least, would feel oppressed by the violation of her individual freedom and autonomy; even Sid might feel uneasy because the organization for which they both work now has authority over features of their personal lives that are not directly related to work. Furthermore, as documented by a large literature in social psychology, the needless flaunting of hierarchical authority has negative effects on employee morale and motivation (Gouldner 1954).

Furthermore, a hierarchical fiat on the issue of smoking would not be sensitive to considerations of efficiency. The hierarchical superior who ruled on the smoking issue could hardly look inside the heads of Sid and Cindy to see whether the benefits to one outweighed the costs to the other. The superior's decision might have to be made on the basis of a faulty estimate of what would be most beneficial. It would most likely be imposed as a general rule throughout the organization, and thus be imposed on another pair of co-workers where efficiency considerations would go in just the opposite direction. For instance, another worker might find $100 worth of benefit from smoking, while her co-worker would experience only $5 worth of psychic discomfort.

Even more worrisome is the possibility that the hierarchical superior might have no real incentive to seek an efficient solution to the problem. Once he received the authority to make a decision, he might use that opportunity to seek bribes from the parties involved or to extort sidepayments of various sorts. Early shop foremen, who had absolute authority over hiring and firing, habitually sought and received financial, social, and sexual benefits (Nelson 1975: 35–42; Edwards 1979: 59; Jacoby 1985: 17–18, 23).

For all these reasons, a nonhierarchical solution to the problem between Sid and Cindy might well be sought. Coase pointed out, two individuals could feasibly bargain their way to a mutually agreeable contract that would make both better off. Sid could simply pay Cindy something between $30 and $45 dollars not to smoke. Cindy would be paid enough to make it worth her while not to smoke, and Sid would be better off because he would have a smoke-free environment at a cost that would make it worthwhile to him. Coase's solution is basically voluntaristic, and it is based on the fact that the definition of Pareto suboptimality implies that there ought to be ways of dealing with a problem that make everyone better off.

Even more important, perhaps, such voluntary contracts are more flexible than hierarchy. They need go into effect only when there is market failure. In contrast, the no-smoking regulation could just as easily operate inefficiently as efficiently. Let us suppose a different scenario, in which Cindy still values smoking at $30, but Sid now values clean air at only $5. In this case, the no-smoking regulation would hurt Cindy more than it would help Sid, and it would be inefficient to impose the no-smoking regulation. In a Coasian world of perfect contracting, the matter would take care of itself. In this scenario, there would be no contract that Sid and Cindy could reach that would make both better off. Thus, a contract to stop Cindy from smoking would be reached if and only if it were mutually advantageous.

The advantages of hierarchy over bargaining

What kinds of obstacles are there to a negotiated solution to social dilemmas? Coase is most famous for elaborating one obstacle, which he termed "transaction costs" – defined by North (1990) as the "cost of measuring and enforcing agreements" (14).

Problem 1: transaction costs. Measurement costs for Sid and Cindy may be significant. If Sid arrives at work one morning and smells smoke remaining from Cindy's late-night work activities, does that constitute an infringement of his right to clean air? What is the penalty for violation, and who enforces it? It might take an hour for Sid and Cindy to determine how much each of them values smoking or clean air, to determine solutions to measurement and compliance problems, and to bargain their way to a solution. If each is capable of earning $10 an hour, then a solution would take $20 worth of time, even apart from the costs of implementing the contract. But if Cindy were willing to pay $30 in order to smoke and if Sid were willing to pay $45 to avoid having the smoke in the office they share, the efficiency gain from the contract would be only $15. They would be out $20 in earnings in order to achieve a gain that would be only a fraction of that amount. In such a case, there would be no way that they could voluntarily reach a contract that would give each of them more than the $10 gain that would be necessary to compensate each for the earnings lost in achieving the contract.

Clearly, the time spent on bargaining until a solution were reached would be very unlikely to decrease if there were three, four, or forty employees in the office, each with different values regarding smoking and clean air. In such a situation, the time (and potential earnings) spent on bargaining to an efficient solution might be very great indeed. In a university with a hundred such offices, each filled with employees with slightly different aggregate demand functions for clean air and smoking, the time lost by letting each office separately bargain its way to an "efficient" contract could be huge. The work of many universities has been brought to a standstill over less momentous issues. The provost of such a university could easily decide that it would be more efficient to impose a hierarchical no-smoking regulation on all such offices rather than let each engage in Coasian bargaining.

This conclusion follows even without much understanding of what the costs of achieving a contract might include. However, the following analysis suggests some factors that might be systematically related to transaction costs.

Problem 2: incomplete contracts. The simplest contracts might be hard to achieve, but many contracts must specify the rights and responsibilities of the various parties in a variety of contingencies. For instance, Cindy may be willing to bargain away her right to smoke quite cheaply during the morning hours, but greatly value a smoke late in the afternoon, when Sid is about to leave for home anyhow. Or Cindy might be willing to bargain away her right to smoke cheaply on most days, but really need to smoke when she is under a great deal of pressure – although she might not be able to specify ahead of time when those times might be. The efficient contract might well specify that Cindy has options to "buy back" the right to smoke during certain specified circumstances. Similarly, Sid might not mind cigarette smoke except on days when his hay fever is acting up, when he may be willing to pay a very large amount to avoid smoke.

The cost of negotiating contracts with more and more contingencies is likely to increase. And not all such contingencies may be specifiable ahead of time. Cindy and Sid feel that they have reached a suitable contract, but realize when they both show up for extra work on a holiday that the contract does not specify who has rights to what on that specific day.

There may be a special role for hierarchy due to these unforeseen contingencies. Rather than attempting to specify all possible future contingen-

40

cies and programming the responsibilities of each of thirty or forty employees under all such contingencies, it may be easier and cheaper for a contract to leave some contingencies open. But what is to be done if one of the open contingencies in fact occurs? One possibility would be to give one employee a special position – that of "smoking supervisor." The smoking supervisor would have the responsibility of settling all unforeseen contingencies, deciding, for example, whether the pollen count is high enough to trigger a no-smoking rule in deference to Sid's allergies or whether the tension is great enough to allow Cindy that one special cigarette a month. In such a case, a hierarchical solution – the creation of a "boss" with residual authority to make unilateral regulations – would help solve the problem of unforeseen contingencies under an incomplete contract.

Problem 3: property rights and distributional results. As Coase (1960) stated, "If market transactions were costless, all that matters (questions of equity apart) is that the rights of the various parties should be well-defined and the results of legal actions easy to forecast" (19). An absence of property rights can confound a negotiation for an efficient bargain.

In our example, the question of property rights concerns who has a prior claim to the air being breathed. Negotiating a solution is much harder if it is not clear whether Sid or Cindy has a right to the air. Must Cindy compensate Sid for fouling Sid's air, or must Sid compensate Cindy for depriving her of cigarettes? Coase's point was that, as long as transaction costs are not high, either system of property rights will necessarily result in an efficient decision being made about whether to allow Cindy to smoke. However, the distributional implications are quite different depending on who must compensate whom.

In the original Sid and Cindy example, Sid has to pay Cindy because Cindy is regarded as having a right to decide whether or not to smoke. Sid's payment is a way of inducing her not to exercise that right. But Sid might object that he has a property right to clean air in his environment. In place of the no-smoking regulation, he might simply prefer a legal affirmation of his legal right to clean air. Then all the benefits of the Coasian argument could still apply, but in reverse. In scenario 2, in which Sid values clean air at $5, Cindy could pay Sid $20 (say) for the right to smoke, and both would be better off. In scenario 1, in which Sid values clean air at $45, Cindy could not pay Sid enough for the right to putrefy Sid's air, and no contract would be achieved.

With either definition of property rights, a Coasian contract would guarantee that the efficient outcome would be achieved, but the distribution of benefits would be different. Not having the property right to clean air means that Sid has to pay Cindy at least $30 for clean air; having that property right means that he gets the same efficient outcome for free. Thus, while the outcomes of a zero-transaction-cost contract are always efficient,

Table 2.1. *Outcomes under different property right allocations and alternative benefit–cost parameters*

Property right allocation	Scenario 1 (smoking is inefficient): Sid values clean air at $45; Cindy values smoking at $30	Scenario 2 (smoking is efficient): Sid values clean air at $5; Cindy values smoking at $30
Cindy has a right to smoke	Sid pays Cindy $35 not to smoke	No contract (Cindy smokes)
Sid has a right to clean air	No contract (Cindy does not smoke)	Cindy pays Sid $15 for permission to smoke

the interesting question of who gets the benefit is determined by the completely external question of who has which property rights.

Notice that Sid is uniformly better off having his property right to clean air, whether or not he subsequently sells it, as shown in Table 2.1. In scenario 1, it is not efficient for Cindy to smoke, and she doesn't; but without a property right to clean air, Sid must pay $35 to obtain that efficient result. In scenario 2, it is efficient for Cindy to smoke and she does; but without a property right to clean air, Sid does not get paid $15 for having to endure the smoke. Similarly, Cindy is uniformly better off having the right to smoke, whether or not she ultimately sells that right. Either set of property rights results in the efficient outcome, but they have different distributional implications.

Just because the two property rights allocations result in equally efficient outcomes does not mean that the outcomes are the same from the standpoint of the actors. Quite the contrary; the actors will have every reason to fight over the allocation of property rights whether it is efficient for Cindy to smoke or not to smoke. The distributional consequences are just as severe in either case, and the conflict over the institution (who has what rights) will be as intense as the conflict over the policy (whether or not Cindy smokes) that Coase set out to deal with.

Thus, if the problem facing this group is "Shall Cindy smoke?" then Coase's arguments permit Cindy and Sid to resolve that issue themselves – once a system of property rights has been allocated – and we can be satisfied beforehand that the outcome will be efficient as long as the property rights are clear. But if the problem facing them is how to allocate property rights, then Coase's arguments give us no guidance at all. Quite the contrary – Coase's arguments assure us that no efficiency criterion can guide us here, and therefore the property rights allocation must be a purely redistributional question, to be resolved by equity considerations and politics alone. Indeed, this issue – the distributional implications of the allocation of property rights – is at the very core of politics and is unanswered by the Coase argument. Much of the rest of this chapter is concerned with how to think about bargaining and distribution.

Problem 4: distributional ambiguity. Even for a given distribution of property rights, there is a wide range of feasible distributional outcomes. For instance, let us imagine that it has been determined (through some arbitrary political process) that Sid has a property right to clean air and that he must be compensated for any contamination of that resource by Cindy's smoking. Let us say that Sid would secretly be willing to permit Cindy to smoke for as little as $5, while Cindy would be willing to pay as much as $30 for the right to smoke.

Clearly, in this situation it makes sense (i.e., it would be efficient) for Sid to sell Cindy a permit to smoke. But how much should Cindy have to pay? She could compensate Sid by any amount between $5 and $30, and *both* would be better off. At stake is $25 worth of net benefit that could theoretically all go to Sid (if he succeeded in charging Cindy $30 for smoking) or all to Cindy (if she succeeded in buying the right to smoke for as little as $5). There is no way to determine the "correct" amount to pay by referring to any efficiency criterion. The outcome will be determined by "bargaining" between the two, but does that observation help us understand what the final outcome will be? Bargaining is itself a costly process – and all bargaining costs incurred are a deadweight loss. Indeed, as already suggested, if Sid and Cindy spend too much time and too many resources, they could fritter away the $25 worth of net benefit altogether.

Or, just as bad, if they are too stubborn, they could fail to reach any agreement, despite the fact that both could be made better off by reaching one. If Sid insists on charging Cindy at least $25 and Cindy refuses to pay more than $20, they are at a deadlock. Is there any mechanism that would guarantee that they would achieve an efficient contract when one is available, while wasting a minimum of resources in the bargaining process?

A great deal of effort has gone into answering this question, and the answer in general seems to be no. But before we address the question, it would be helpful to spend some time discussing what game theory has to offer the study of distributional bargaining. The following section presents a fundamental model of distributional bargaining known as the "Battle of the Sexes" game.

THINKING ABOUT BARGAINING AND DISTRIBUTION: THE BATTLE OF THE SEXES

This problem of allocating the benefits of efficiency gains is an important one that can lead to a set of other complex issues. One way to think about it is to imagine a simple game that captures the essential features of the

Table 2.2. *The Battle of the Sexes game*

Dale's choices	Roy's choices	
	Left (skin flick)	Right (documentary)
Up (skin flick)	Dale's best outcome Roy's second-best outcome	Bad for both
Down (documentary)	Bad for both	Dale's second-best outcome Roy's best outcome

problem in the same way that the Prisoners' Dilemma game captures the tension between individual rationality and group efficiency.

The classic simple game that accomplishes this is the Battle of the Sexes (Table 2.2). Dale and Roy are a married pair of busy young executives who want to go to a movie together after work. Dale wishes to go to a skin flick ("up") and doesn't want to go to a documentary about Vietnam at all. Roy wants to see the documentary and doesn't really like the idea of going to a skin flick ("right"). While Dale's most preferred outcome is to go to the skin flick with Roy (upper-left-hand outcome), her next choice is to go to the documentary with Roy. The worst possible situation is for her to go to either movie alone. Roy, too, would rather see the skin flick with Dale than the documentary alone.

This game has no dominant strategy: Each player finds that his or her own best strategy *depends on the other player's choice*. For instance, Dale is best off choosing "up" if Roy chooses "left" but is best off choosing "down" if Roy chooses "right." Similarly, Roy is best off choosing "left" if Dale chooses "up" but best off choosing "right" if Dale chooses "down." This results in two Nash equilibria in the game. At the upper-left-hand outcome, Dale has no reason to switch to "down" on her own. Roy has no reason to switch to "right" on his own. The lower-right-hand outcome is similarly stable.

Both of these Nash equilibria are Pareto optimal. From the upper-left-hand outcome, Roy and Dale cannot agree that they would both be better off any place else, and the same is true for the other Nash equilibrium. In this sense, this game does not involve the same conflict between individual rationality and group efficiency that the Prisoners' Dilemma game in the preceding chapter does. A closer analysis, however, reveals a variety of pitfalls that may be anticipated by anyone who has been married.

The problem is that, in a hurried telephone conversation at lunchtime, Roy and Dale failed to agree on which movie to see. Now each has to decide which movie to go to individually, since there will be no time to contact the other before show time. The danger, then, is clear. If each goes to see the movie he or she really wants to see, hoping the other will show up, both could end up in the upper-right-hand corner, which is Pareto suboptimal. They could be sitting in theaters alone, when both would agree that they would rather be with the other even in the less preferred movie. Even worse, if each decides to honor the other's preference, they could end up separately in the wrong theaters (lower-right-hand outcome).

THE POTENTIAL FOR INEFFICIENCY IN THE BATTLE OF THE SEXES GAME

The indeterminacy of the Battle of the Sexes game creates the potential for inefficiency – despite the fact that *either* of the two Nash equilibria is efficient!

Coordination and commitment

This analysis makes clear the desirability of coordination between the players in a bargaining game like the Battle of the Sexes. Coordination can take place in a number of ways. One way is to ask a neutral third party to make a decision. Or each of the players could agree to buy the evening newspaper and go to the skin flick if the headline has an even number of letters and to the documentary if it has an odd number. Each of these techniques solves the problem of ambiguity that makes the game so difficult.

Another way is for one of the individuals to use some strategy that commits him- or herself to a course of action. For instance, Dale could announce during the lunchtime phone conversation, "I am going to the skin flick whether or not you choose to come along" and then immediately hang up. Hanging up the phone is crucial, because keeping the conversation going is a tacit admission that the commitment is negotiable. Hanging up makes it nonnegotiable – Dale would clearly be foolish to go to the documentary after making such a commitment, simply on the grounds that she assumed that Roy would not give in to her position. As long as negotiations cannot be reopened (Dale does not answer the phone), Roy simply has to choose between going alone to the documentary or meeting Dale at the skin flick. As Luce and Raiffa pointed out as long ago as 1957, a credible commitment by one player harnesses the other player's self-interest in a resolution of the problem:

Thus, we see that it is advantageous in such a situation to disclose one's strategy first and to have a reputation for inflexibility. It is the familiar power strategy: "This is what I'm going to do; make up your mind and do what you want." If the second person acts in his own best interests, it works to the first's person's advantage. (91)

A fascinating example of the use of this commitment strategy in the business world occurred during the filming of *The Cotton Club*, directed by Francis Ford Coppola. At one point early in the planning of the film, the money men who supported the film wanted to renegotiate Coppola's contract, threatening to withdraw their financial backing unless he made important concessions:

In the midst of the wrangling, an employee of the law firm appeared, announcing a call from Coppola. . . . [The message] said that Coppola was at the British Airways VIP lounge at JFK Airport, about to board the Concorde for London. If the money men wanted him to stay in town to direct "Cotton Club," they had ten minutes to call him. Otherwise they could reach him in London, where he would be investigating another film. The money men went bananas. (Peters 1988: 12–13)

Of course, the commitment strategy is useless or worse if both people attempt it. If both shout their nonnegotiable demands simultaneously and hang up, each has to consider whether to back down. If neither does (or if both do!), they are back at an inefficient outcome.

Commitment, misrepresentation, and market power

The credibility of one's commitment to one course of action, irrespective of an agreement with the other player, is dependent in part on whether the one making a commitment can show that the alternative to a contract with the other player is not too painful. In the Dale and Roy game, Dale might like to claim that she would enjoy her skin flick whether or not Roy shows up – even if she privately knows that to be false. If she can make Roy believe that, her threat to go there without an agreement with Roy is more credible.

Similarly, it is important to note that the account of Coppola's commitment strategy with his financial backers included the information that he would be in London "investigating another film." This was, of course, much more effective than a threat to go home and fill out an application for unemployment benefits. If the alternative to agreement with the other negotiator is especially attractive (or can be made to seem so), it improves one's bargaining position.

As two parties in a relationship become more and more dependent on one another, the ability of either one to make a claim credibly naturally decreases. This point is illustrated, once again, by the film industry, where "product differentiation" in the form of recognizable star quality is often used by a star to claim that a producer must "need me more than I need you." In contrast, the producer wants to be able to pay a small salary on the grounds that the star's popularity is dependent on, say, a particular television show.

The strategic value of uniqueness is illustrated by an instance of negotiation between Larry Hagman (playing J.R. on the television show "Dallas") and the producers of "Dallas," Lorimar Productions. Hagman wanted to be paid $100,000 for each episode, on the grounds that the show could not proceed without him. "Lorimar not only refused but told Hagman that J.R. could wake up in the hospital after plastic surgery and [find himself being played by] Robert Culp" (*St. Louis Post Dispatch* 1988). Stranger things than that have happened on "Dallas." By convincing Hagman that they had an alternative, Lorimar improved its bargaining position.

BARGAINING, INCOMPLETE INFORMATION, AND MECHANISM DESIGN

The connection between the Battle of the Sexes game and any bargaining situation becomes clearer. If one bargainer can convince a second bargainer that she will not settle for less than a given amount of the bargaining pie, the second player's best response is to settle for that given amount as long as it is more than the amount he would get with no agreement. But there are usually a large number of other equally viable prices on which the two could agree just as easily, each allocating the surplus generated by the trade in different ways. Any of these outcomes would be stable if agreed upon. But just as in the Battle of the Sexes game, the problem is to settle on just one of the equilibrium outcomes rather than having both sides commit to incompatible demands. The bargaining problem can thus be seen as essentially a coordination problem.

Clearly, one of the costs in a Battle of the Sexes game is the bargaining and negotiation that take place as individuals try to determine the distribution of benefits. The short phone call at lunch could easily stretch out into a long argument, as each person presents his or her position and the reasons it is preferable. The time spent is costly, and of course the psychic costs of the dispute can be immense. These costs may in fact swamp the benefits of the exchange altogether. Many couples, in disagreeing over movies, restaurants, or vacations have decided simply to stay at home. Failure to reach one of the viable equilibrium outcomes is another potential source of inefficiency.

The costs associated with negotiating a solution to a game like this may be incurred by the time spent, the resources used in marshaling arguments, the hiring of an arbitrator to make an impartial decision, or the hiring of a lawyer to represent one's position before the arbitrator. The transaction costs associated with bargaining are essentially limitless.

For instance, if things go badly with Roy and Dale, and they decide to get a divorce, they could discover that transaction costs can eat up any benefits they might otherwise receive. Suppose, for instance, that in negotiating the divorce settlement Roy and Dale each make a proposal: Each wants the house and is willing to give the car to the other. Each has two choices: to insist on his or her own position, or to defer to the other. The longer each insists on his or her own position, the more likely it is that the lawyers will get everything in the eventual settlement.

47

Why have hierarchy?

Are there efficient bargaining processes?

Is there any procedure that bargainers can use to guarantee an efficient solution when one exists, with no unnecessary transaction costs incurred in the bargaining process? It turns out that the answer is yes, but only if each side knows the other's payoffs. Asymmetric information is an obstacle to bargaining efficiency as well as to market efficiency.

Ariel Rubinstein (1982) demonstrated that, with symmetric information, one procedure guarantees that the first side to make an offer will fix an offer that the other side finds just barely acceptable. The second side will therefore accept the first side's first offer. A contract is always made when it is efficient to do so, and no time is lost to the bargaining process itself. As long as each side knows the other's valuation of the bargained-for object, efficiency can be guaranteed.

Unfortunately, these desirable characteristics seem to disappear with asymmetries in information. As soon as each side is uncertain about how much the other side would value a contract, there is no bargaining mechanism that will guarantee that the two will always achieve a contract when it is efficient or that valuable resources will not be lost to the bargaining process (see Samuelson 1985 and Sutton 1986 for a survey).

Eliciting private information

If private information is so harmful to the bargaining process, isn't there some way of getting the actors involved to reveal their private information? After all, it has been conclusively proved that it is the incompleteness of information that creates inefficiencies in the bargaining process. Wouldn't both actors be better off simply by revealing, openly and honestly, their stakes in the bargaining game?

Perversely, the revelation of private information in a bargaining process is itself a social dilemma. Each actor would be best off if the *other* actor revealed how great a stake he or she had in the bargaining process, and each would be worst off by revealing his or her own private information accurately while the other lied. Anyone who has ever bargained with a used-car dealer can verify that it is not a good idea to reveal the highest price you would be willing to pay for a car. It is better by far to endure the ritual of a prolonged bargaining process with the dealer. If, however, a car buyer is lucky enough to meet a novice used-car dealer who reveals the true cost of acquiring the used car, it is much easier for the buyer to get a good price on the car. As a result, equilibrium behavior in a bargaining situation is for both sides to guard their private information carefully, with resulting inefficiencies.

This relationship between private information and efficiency has been confirmed by rigorous experiments on bargaining. Roth and Murnighan

48

(1982) have done experiments demonstrating that, when both parties have access to the payoffs of one another, bargaining proceeds quickly and easily to an efficient agreement, whenever one is to be found. But when that information is not available, bargaining becomes much more prolonged and costly, and on numerous occasions potentially efficient agreements are not reached. As Farrell (1986b) says, "A potential buyer may value a house more than its prospective seller does, but less than the seller believes 'most' buyers do. He would then have trouble persuading the seller to lower the price enough to make the deal" (115).

BARGAINING FAILURE AND LEVIATHAN

This chapter began on the hopeful note that, according to Coase, individuals could bargain their way to efficient contracts *without* the "aid" of a hierarchically imposed solution. To the extent that this is true, hierarchy would not be necessary to solve Prisoners' Dilemma problems. Our study of bargaining, however, suggests that there are definite limits on the ability of individuals to find their way to an efficient contract, even if one exists. The basic problem is that the information necessary to guarantee an efficient outcome is essentially private.

Bargainers who do not know one another's payoffs cannot always be expected to find and to agree on an efficient outcome with a minimum of time and energy spent in the bargaining process. Each side will spend time misrepresenting its own preferences, trying to see behind the other's misrepresentations, and engaging in commitment strategies that may backfire in the form of lost opportunities for efficient trades. The problem of distributing the gains from efficient cooperation will be so daunting that the bargainers might lose a large amount of the potential gains to the strategic battle that ensues. The specter that is raised is one of barganing failure – the loss of those very efficiency gains that motivate actors to go to the bargaining table in the first place. A potential solution to this problem may be an incentive system that encourages individuals to reveal their private information. Such mechanisms, known as incentive compatible, exist, but who is to implement them?

Two individuals may agree to submit to an incentive-compatible mechanism as a part of the contract that they voluntarily enter into. One might suppose that it would be worthwhile for both individuals to submit to such a mechanism as a way of generating the efficiency benefits to be derived from the mutual revelation of information about private values. One would assume that it would be individually rational for each individual to do so, meaning that each individual would be guaranteed an amount at least as great as he or she could get by not participating in the scheme.

Here again, however, the possibilities for decentralized bargaining seem to be constrained. A formal theoretical result of Myerson and Satterthwaite

(1983) shows that individually rational incentive-compatible mechanisms are not efficient. If each individual must do at least as well by submitting to an incentive-compatible mechanism as he or she could do separately, there is no way that the incentive-compatible mechanism will guarantee efficient outcomes.

As Farrell (1987b) says, "If people come to bargaining already knowing their private values for a good, then no arrangement exists that will lead them to trade precisely when they should, given that each can choose to walk away. So the king's power to coerce really helps to achieve efficiency" (120).

This suggests that, before people enter into negotiations, they might do well to submit themselves to an authority that can keep them from walking away from the bargaining table once the bargaining has begun (Banks and Calvert 1988). Or to put it in the context of the theory of the firm, organizations with sufficient coercive authority to make subunits of the organization bargain to efficient outcomes will do better than organizations that lack that coercive authority.

Leviathan: the contractarian tradition

At least since the work of Thomas Hobbes, the literature in political economy has had a tradition of advocating Leviathan – Hobbes's gripping name for centralized, coercive authority. The alleged benefits generated by Leviathan in the face of competing individual interests could easily be applied to our understanding of hierarchy.

The situation Hobbes described as the state of nature, in which there is no authority capable of enforcing contracts, presents a social dilemma in which individual pursuit of self-interest is inconsistent with group well-being. In this state of nature, Hobbes argues, if other people are going to be violent, each individual will find it safest to attack them first. If, however, others abstain from violence in the state of nature, the individual will have the opportunity to attain preeminence. "Hereby it is manifest that during the time men live without a common power to keep them all in awe, they are in that condition which is called war; and such a war as is of every man against every man" (Hobbes 1651/1952: 85). This state of war is one that everyone will find so abhorrent that he or she will gladly give up the liberty that led to that state – hence the Leviathan.

A brief review of the U.S. economy after the Civil War reveals the development of the firm as Leviathan. Market processes were in large part replaced by internal transactions, dictated by the "visible hand" of managers (Chandler 1977). Two examples of this process will illustrate the theoretical argument for hierarchy.

Bargaining failure

The decline of the internal contractor

The replacement of market exchange by hierarchy is often regarded as an inevitable result of large-scale manufacturing, but this is not necessarily the case. Many large-scale plants used a "contract" system, even until World War I, that brought market exchange inside the plant (Nelson 1975: 36). Under the contract system, skilled workmen – called "contractors" – "agreed to manufacture a particular object or component in a given quantity at a designated cost and by a specific date. Otherwise they retained virtually complete control over the production process." The contractor could himself hire employees, who normally received day wages. The firm, for its part, provided the materials, power, and the factory building (Nelson 1975: 36).

The contract system was popular well into the twentieth century for reasons that economists would be quite familiar with – it provided all the advantages attributed to the competitive marketplace, and it did so within the large-scale manufacturing plant. The system kept costs low and quality high, and provided the correct incentives for technological innovation. There were sufficient controls for quality, since the work of the contractors – normally components of a final product – was inspected by noncontract employees (Buttrick 1952: 207).

At the same time, the system was popular with the contractors themselves. It provided them with the autonomy and status of an independent entrepreneur, manager, and skilled craftsman within the confines of a large-scale industrial plant. And demand for their work was sufficiently high and inelastic that their profits were consistently high. "In many firms the contractors' earnings far exceeded any foreman's wage as well as the salaries of many company officers" (Nelson 1975: 38).

In the context of contemporary troubles on the manufacturing scene, the contracting system seems idyllic. It provided just the features of a manufacturing process that are so noticeably absent today – craftsmen taking pride in their work, technological innovation, high morale. Why was the internal contracting system – with all of its market advantages – replaced by a system of foremen dictating to wage-earning employees? Why was the market abandoned in favor of Leviathan?

The answer, it seems, has much to do with team production processes, the necessity of coordination, and difficulties in bargaining over surpluses. First of all, it is apparent that technology required ever-greater cooperation among elements of the production process. The components of a rifle or sewing machine produced by craftsmen had to fit together in the final assembly; they also had to flow in required proportions if there were to be no bottlenecks or wastage in the final assembly and marketing. It did no good to have five contractors producing at top speed if the sixth was not; the

51

production process was more than the sum of its parts. As long as the quantities produced were moderate, coordination by means of the internal contracting system seemed to accommodate the necessities of this team production process, but the contracting system "became less useful as manufacturers increased their output to take advantage of growing markets" (Nelson 1975: 37).

While clearly the central management of the firm and the contractors had every reason to negotiate their way to efficient solutions to these team production problems, the negotiation process necessarily involved the issue of distribution of profits. Just as in a Battle of the Sexes game, there would naturally be a large number of possible contracts that could solve the team production coordination problems efficiently but that would allocate the efficiency gains differently. This was evidently a key reason for the abandonment of internal contracting. At Singer Sewing Machine Company, "contractors worked diligently, improved the product, and made high profits" (Nelson 1975: 37). But the management was evidently "unhappy" with the contractors' profits and became convinced that a system of moderately paid foremen supervising wage-earning employees could duplicate the high-quality work of the contractors at a lower cost to the management.

Despite the fact that the contracting system tended to keep costs low and to encourage innovation, management was frequently tempted to squeeze contractors by negotiating lower contract payments. The internal contractors in turn cut the wages of the employees working for them; these employees "often bore the brunt of the downward 'adjustment' in the contractor's price whenever the manufacturer decided that his [the contractor's] profits were too high" (Nelson 1975: 37). When the contractor's employees protested cuts in their own wages, management often abandoned the contracting system altogether. It was largely nonexistent by World War I.

Thus, despite the fact that the system of internal contractors seemed capable of generating sizable profits for the firm, the system was abandoned because of the problem of negotiating the distribution of those profits. From a Coasian perspective, negotiating distribution had relatively high transaction costs. The creation of hierarchical firms economized on those costs.

Vertical integration: General Motors and Fisher Body

"Vertical integration" is the term for the unification of two separate firms when one firm is the supplier to the other. This phenomenon is another example of market exchange being replaced by hierarchical direction.

The market contract. By 1920, the automobile industry was shifting from the use of open, wooden auto bodies to closed metal bodies stamped from highly specific, expensive stamping machines. General Motors, recognizing the importance of auto bodies, sought to establish a stable, long-term relationship with the foremost supplier of those bodies – Fisher Body – by means of a mutually beneficial contract (Klein, Crawford, and Alchian 1978).

While a cooperative, long-term relationship between Fisher Body and General Motors would likely be a highly profitable one, the question of distribution remained. Which organization would receive the lion's share of the profits to be generated? Fisher Body was initially reluctant to enter into a long-term relationship with General Motors, because it would have to make a heavy investment in expensive stamping machines that would be worthless if General Motors subsequently selected another supplier or started making bodies itself. Furthermore, if Fisher Body made such a commitment, General Motors would subsequently be able to lower the price it paid for bodies and Fisher would have little it could do in retaliation. Fisher's becoming dependent on General Motors raised the possibility that all of the gains from the mutually beneficial production relationship would go to General Motors. After the investment had been made, Fisher would have little choice but to go along with an appropriation of all the surplus by General Motors.

Fisher Body therefore wanted a contract that would require General Motors to buy virtually all of its bodies from Fisher for a prolonged period of time:

This exclusive dealing arrangement significantly reduced the possibility of General Motors acting opportunistically by demanding a lower price for the bodies after Fisher made the specific investment in production capacity. Since exclusive dealing contractual conditions are relatively cheap to effectively specify and enforce, General Motors's postcontractual threat to purchase bodies elsewhere was effectively eliminated. (Klein et al. 1978: 309)

However, the contractual arrangement that reduced Fisher Body's dependency raised the opposite possibility that General Motors would be dependent on Fisher and that Fisher could subsequently raise the price of bodies and appropriate an excessive share of the joint surplus. The contract fixed the price for bodies supplied by Fisher to General Motors by means of a "cost-plus" contract. The price was supposed to be equal to costs – exclusive of interest on invested capital – plus 17.6 percent.

After the contract was reached in 1919, the shift toward closed metal bodies increased dramatically in response to buyer demand. This unforeseen circumstance greatly increased Fisher's bargaining position, since Fisher was the acknowledged leader in this technology. Furthermore, the technological improvements and increases in demand meant that a given capital investment produced a larger number of bodies. Hence, Fisher was in an excellent position with its cost plus 17.6 percent contract. Furthermore, General Motors noticed that the cost-plus form of the contract left Fisher with no incentive to look for ways of cutting costs on anything but capital investments. And by excluding interest on capital in figuring Fisher's costs, they had left Fisher with no incentive for improving its capital investment.

Furthermore, severe information asymmetries plagued the negotiations between the two sides. General Motors claimed that the cost could be lowered and still leave Fisher with a wide opportunity for investment, and Fisher claimed that it was on the verge of bankruptcy. The same was true the other way around.

The same information asymmetry plagued issues of product quality. General Motors claimed that Fisher's products were of increasingly poor quality after the 1919 long-term contract was signed. Fisher claimed that it was doing the best it could, given heavily increased output requirements and the inputs available. Was Fisher shirking or doing the best it could? General Motors had no way of knowing for sure.

General Motors then claimed that Fisher should locate its plant near the General Motors assembly plants, for efficiency reasons. General Motors was undoubtedly right about the efficiency of such a move, but Fisher was afraid that it would further increase its dependency on General Motors and thus deprive it of any viable bargaining position for the distribution of gains. It therefore refused to make the move.

One can easily imagine the negotiations between Fisher and General Motors as a Battle of the Sexes game in which each side was trying to decide whether to insist on various favorable contract provisions that decreased its dependency and increased its share of the profits generated. Any failure to agree on a contract would mean that the mutually beneficial gains were forgone.

Given the uncertainties on both sides in this bargaining game, the possibilities of inefficiency by continued negotiation between the two firms as decentralized supplier and buyer of auto bodies seemed excessive. Large amounts of money were being lost to the negotiation process, and worse yet, opportunities for efficiency gains such as the relocation of the Fisher plant were being lost because of strategic concerns about the distributional consequences. The possibility that these efficiency losses could be overcome by hierarchical integration proved compelling to the General Motors leadership: "By 1924, General Motors had found the Fisher contractual relationship intolerable and began negotiations for the purchase of the remaining stock in Fisher Body, culminating in a final merger agreement in 1926" (Klein et al. 1978: 310). Thus, the search for reduced vulnerability resulted in a dramatic restructuring of General Motors to incorporate Fisher Body as one of its primary structural units. The relationship between the two units persisted, but not in the form of a contractual relationship between the market actors. Rather, the General Motors hierarchy now had formal authority to determine uni-laterally "transfer prices," technology decisions, location issues, and investment decisions.

Bargaining failure

The situation between Fisher Body and General Motors seems at first to be quite distinct from the team production problem, because the primary problem seems to be thinness of markets rather than externalities in production. However, the reason the market is thin between Fisher Body and General Motors is that each side gains from a closer, symbiotic relationship with the other. There were multiple competing car companies in the interwar era, but there was only one car company that could do for Fisher Body what General Motors could. And there was only one body manufacturer who had Fisher's expertise in stamped, closed bodies. The properties that made Fisher Body and General Motors uniquely important to one another also, it could be argued, created a team production process between the two. As this occurred, each discovered that the other had an incentive to take actions that were not in the interest of maximum overall production. General Motors had an incentive to try to lower the price it paid for bodies; Fisher Body had an incentive to locate its plant in a less efficient location and decrease product quality. These forms of shirking threatened overall team production.

Thus, the bilateral bargainers in a thin market end up facing the same problems that the members of a team production process do: the problem of achieving efficiency and the problem of allocating the efficiency dividend. Both of these are costly to overcome, and become especially so in the presence of severe asymmetries in information about the performance of the two sides. For these reasons, firms may well decide to internalize, within a hierarchical institution, the kinds of decisions that are the domain of inefficient bargaining in the presence of information asymmetries.

Evidence from the aerospace industry

While the integration of General Motors and Fisher Body is a graphic case, the aerospace industry offers much more systematic evidence in support of the general argument. Economist Scott Masten (1984) provides a fascinating account of the industry. Masten examines the "make or buy" decision of aerospace contractors. He gathers data on a large number of such decisions, coding each decision with regard to whether or not the required component is highly specialized. If it is not highly specialized, there are likely to be a good many potential suppliers of the item; in other words, it can probably be obtained in a competitive market. If it is a specialized component, however, the contractor is likely to be at the mercy of a single monopolistic supplier.

Masten is also interested in "complexity." A complex component is one that involves a great deal of detail and interdependence with other components in the production process. Thus, a relatively noncomplex component can probably be produced autonomously by a separate contractor with little need for cooperation. Uncoordinated production of a complex item, however, may cause the efforts of other component producers to go awry. Component complexity is thus an indication of a team production externality.

Masten calculated maximum likelihood estimates for these variables as they affect the decision of a contractor to use either markets or internal hierarchy as the source of a component. He discovered that an item that is neither complex nor specific is very unlikely (with a probability of less than .01) to be produced internally. This observation reveals a strong predilection for contractors to use market processes to procure any and all possible components. Defense contractors in the aerospace industry would, by preference, produce nothing themselves. The normal market processes allow them to procure possible components as cheaply as possible from least-cost producers, identified through competition and bidding for contracts.

This predilection for market procurement carries over to items that are complex but not specific. The probability of producing such items internally was identified as .02. It is normally possible to write contracts with existing subcontractors specifying the necessary characteristics of even complex components.

Components that are highly specific but not complex have a somewhat larger chance of being produced internally – .31. Even though such items do not involve a large degree of production interdependence with other components, the threat of being at the mercy of a monopoly supplier forces defense contractors to produce these items through an internalized hierarchical production process about one-third of the time.

The striking and central result is the interdependent effect of complexity and specificity. Components that have *both* characteristics are, with a high probability (.92), produced internally. Aerospace firms find that the combination of a highly complex and specific component makes it unsatisfactory to rely on a subcontractor. Not only would a supplier have a degree of monopoly power as a result of the lack of competitive suppliers for a specific item, but the necessity of coordinating a highly complex item with the producers of other parts would add to the bargaining power of the subcontractor. Aerospace firms evidently are not confident of their ability to get the necessary degree of cooperation from producers of highly complex parts when those producers also have the market power that goes with the production of a specific component. As Masten (1984) summarizes, "The hazards of incomplete contracts in complex environments appear to be much greater when specialized designs are involved, increasing the likelihood of internalization from 31 percent to 92 percent" (412). Hierarchies are most likely to exist because of the inability of parties to negotiate mutually satisfactory contracts in the presence of information asymmetry, monopoly, and production interdependence.

Bargaining failure

SUMMARY

Coase's argument is double-sided (Rutten 1990). In the absence of trans-action costs, there would be little reason to impose a hierarchical solution on individuals who could easily achieve efficient outcomes by means of voluntary contracts. In the presence of transaction costs, however, reliance on voluntaristic negotiations of efficient contracts could be disastrously expensive.

When negotiators have both the capacity to veto contracts that leave them individually worse off and the ability to misrepresent their private val-uations of the negotiated commodity, there can be no guarantee that vol-untary negotiation will achieve efficient outcomes. Information asymmetry has the capacity to undermine efficient negotiation, especially when each side has some market power with respect to the other. In situations of high mutual interdependence and information asymmetry, it is better to have a hierarchical institution that can impose solutions to policy conflicts on po-tentially unwilling participants.

Hierarchical firms, then, are more than the nexus of voluntary contracts. They partake of "political" authority to impose solutions without the in-efficiencies of constant bargaining among participants. Employees submit to this authority because they realize that, in the long run, they will be bet-ter off in a system that has the authority to impose outcomes on everyone. Of course, in such a hierarchical system, a central concern to all is just how these authoritative decisions are made. This is the topic of the next chapter.

3

Voting failure
Social choice in a dictatorial hierarchy

> If we exclude the possibility of interpersonal comparisons of utility,
> then the only methods of passing from individual ordering to social
> preferences which will be satisfactory and which will be defined for
> a wide range of sets of individual orderings are either imposed or dic-
> tatorial.
>
> Arrow (1963: 59)

Steven Cheung (1983) tells of prerevolutionary Chinese coolies pulling
barges along canal towpaths. The problems of shirking evidently plagued
the Chinese workers; each person was aware that as long as everyone else
was presumed to be shirking, he should shirk as well. But the group as a
whole could not produce as much or get paid as much as it could if all
worked with a will. The coolies' response was to create the role of supervisor. The job of the supervisor, who was selected from among the coolies
themselves, was to punish shirkers and "whip" the workers into greater
effort.

The image of the man with the whip brings into sharp focus the issue of
the Leviathan as the solution to market failure. In the preceding chapter, it
was argued that hierarchy is a mechanism for imposing solutions on actors
when self-interested behavior and bargaining both lead to inefficiency. But
once hierarchical political authority is created, the constitutional question
remains – who shall make authoritative decisions for the firm?

Indeed, it is possible to imagine that political authority in the firm could
be wielded through democratic means. Municipalities and school districts
tax themselves by some kind of majority rule procedure every year. The decisions they make are no less coercive and binding on individuals for being
democratic in origin.

The same thing could conceivably be true within a team production process. Why shouldn't the team members use some form of democratic

decision-making process to achieve coercive solutions for team shirking? The nature of decision making within Leviathan is a completely open question – whether we are concerned with governments solving public goods consumption problems or firms solving team production problems.

This brings us to the question that forms the basis of social choice theory: What characteristics should we require of an authoritative group decision-making body? If we have to belong to municipalities that have the authority to tax us for the provision of public goods, or to firms that have the authority to require cooperative team effort in the interest of greater firm profits, how should those municipalities and those firms make these authoritative decisions? This chapter reviews arguments showing that, in order for group decision making in the presence of externalities and public goods to be satisfactory, the group must be not only coercive, but dictatorial – responsive to only one person's tastes.

THE DISADVANTAGES OF DEMOCRACY

A major theme of this book is that interactive teams must (if they are to resolve inefficiencies resulting from mutual incentives for shirking) constitute themselves as a political organization. That is, they must take unto themselves the authority to make binding decisions about distributions of jointly generated revenue and about mandated levels of individual effort. Like any other authoritative political organization, they must have a way of aggregating individual preferences about group decisions themselves. The social decision process can thus be conceptualized as a function that takes all possible combinations of individual preferences as inputs and provides a social preference ordering as an output.

There are many ways in which this can be done. For instance, imagine that two members have to decide on a mutually mandated high, moderate, or low level of effort. Each person can rank these three alternatives in three different ways; this means that there are thirty-six possible combinations of rankings for the two of them. A well-defined social decision process must provide a fixed social preference ranking for each of these. What desirable characteristics should the social decision function have?

In 1951, Kenneth Arrow stipulated a set of desirable characteristics for social choice. He then demonstrated conclusively that *no social choice function can simultaneously guarantee all of these characteristics.* This means that every social organization, including markets, states, and hierarchies, exists in a world of trade-offs. In order to ensure one desirable characteristic of social choice, an organization must give up other characteristics. For this "impossibility theorem," Arrow quite deservedly won the Nobel Prize in economics.

Arrow's theorem provides insight into the nature of the trade-offs that must be taken into account in social decision making. These trade-offs are just as binding in hierarchies as they are in markets or legislatures. The trade-offs implied by Arrow's impossibility theorem occur even in the presence of ideal information conditions. In the presence of information asymmetry (to be discussed in the next chapter), then, the problem of designing a hierarchy that makes satisfactory authoritative group decisions becomes even more complex.

Designing a democracy

The problems of designing authoritative team decision rules can be most clearly illustrated by an example. Suppose that a group of five shoemakers discover an interdependent team production process that will enable them to produce many more shoes together as a team than they ever could as individuals. The advantage is based on specialization: Two individuals cut out the uppers, two cut out the soles, and one stitches them together.

Recognizing an unfortunate tendency for each of them to shirk, they agree to form a coercive group decision-making rule for punishing any individual who fails to conform to group decisions. They then search for a voting rule by which they can make authoritative group decisions, such as decisions allocating the revenue generated by their joint effort.

Each of these shoemakers is a rational and consistent decision maker; that is, each has a well-defined set of preferences. By this we mean two things. The first is that the preferences of each are *transitive*. If an individual prefers alternative x to alternative y and alternative y to alternative z, then she must prefer x to z. Furthermore, her preferences for any two alternatives x and y are assumed to be *independent* of the presence of any other alternatives.

It is to be hoped that the team of shoemakers can find a voting rule that makes decisions with the same minimal rationality properties that characterize each of the members. That is, the team is looking for a decision rule that will result in transitive group references and in which group preferences for pairs of alternatives would be independent of irrelevant alternatives.

Problems with majority rule

An obvious rule for making group decisions is majority rule. Majority rule is a procedure by which alternatives are voted on in pairs. Alternative x defeats alternative y (xPy) if x gets more votes than y in this two-way vote.

The five shoemakers may try to use majority rule to allocate the revenues generated by their more efficient team production process. Suppose there are $100 in profits to be divided among the five. The two sole cutters feel that, while the stitcher's job requires the most skill, their own role is the most arduous; they therefore propose the following split:

	Sole cutters (2)	Upper cutters (2)	Stitcher
Proposal X	$20 each	$15 each	$30

The upper cutters feel that, while their work may be less arduous, they have taken on many additional administrative tasks such as buying raw materials and keeping customers happy. They have put in a good many more hours than the other three team members, and that encourages them to offer the following proposal:

	Sole cutters (2)	Upper cutters (2)	Stitcher
Proposal Y	$10 each	$22.50 each	$35

The stitcher feels that, while his work is less arduous and time-consuming than the other tasks, it requires the skill of a highly specialized and scarce training. If he were to quit, the team would be unlikely to find anyone to replace him, so he offers proposal Z:

	Sole cutters (2)	Upper cutters (2)	Stitcher
Proposal Z	$15.00 each	$12.50 each	$45

Table 3.1 summarizes the preferences of the five team members for these three allocations of the team's revenue. It can be verified that each team member has preferences that are transitive and that each member's ranking of X and Y (for example) does not depend on the presence or absence of Z.

Using majority rule to determine the outcome, the shoemakers find that one majority (upper cutters and stitchers) prefers proposal Y to proposal X. A different coalition (stitcher and sole cutters) prefers Z to Y. Yet a third majority coalition (sole cutters and upper cutters) prefers X to Z. While each of the individuals has a transitive preference ordering for the three alternatives, the group as a whole has intransitive preferences. For any alternative they might settle on, there would always be a majority coalition that always preferred something else.[1]

In the presence of such a majority rule cycle, the order in which alternatives are considered is vital. If proposal X is pitted against proposal Y, with the winner being pitted against proposal Z, then proposal Z will be the winner. Two other agendas (allowing X and Y the last spot in the voting agenda) will result in two other outcomes being chosen. The power to determine the agenda is equivalent to the power to determine the outcome. It is because of this that membership on the House Ways and Means Committee and the

[1] Majority rule will always result in such intransitive group preferences on any distributive question such as this. Given any proposed distribution, a majority will always support an alternative distribution that takes some of the resources from a minority of the voters and distributes it among the remaining majority (Ward 1961).

Table 3.1. *Majority rule and Borda count rankings of three alternatives*

Three alternative allocations of $100 of team revenue:			
Proposal	Sole cutters (2)	Upper cutters (2)	Stitcher
X	$20 each	$15 each	$30
Y	$10 each	$22.50 each	$35
Z	$15 each	$12.50 each	$45

Transitive individual preference rankings of three allocations:			
Ranking	Sole cutters (2)	Upper cutters (2)	Stitcher
First	X	Y	Z
Second	Z	X	Y
Third	Y	Z	X

Intransitive majority rule preference:
Y beats X, X beats Z, Z beats Y

Borda count ranking of {X, Y, Z}	Borda count ranking of {X, Y}
X = 11	Y = 8
Y = 10	X = 7
Z = 9	

Rules Committee (which together determine the tax agenda for the House of Representatives) in such a sought-after position. Agenda control allows for the imposition of a politically sustainable outcome on the essential arbitrariness of majority rule distributive decision making.

Nor is it only distributive questions that are subject to majority rule intransitivity. Whenever there are three or more alternatives, majority cycles may occur, and they are more likely to occur the larger the number of voters, the larger the number of alternatives, and the more dimensions along which voters evaluate alternatives. The instability of majority rule makes it unacceptable as a mode of decision making in most firms.

Problems with the Borda count

Given this flaw in majority rule, some voting bodies turn to voting rules that guarantee a transitive group preference ordering. Such a voting rule was devised two centuries ago at the time of the French Revolution and is called the Borda count.

Unlike majority rule, the Borda count does not rely on a series of pairwise votes. Instead, each voter casts a ballot that consists of a complete, transitive ranking of the alternatives being considered. Each person's last-ranked alternative gets one vote, each person's second-to-last-ranked alternative gets two votes, and so on up to the top of the rankings. The alternative with the most votes wins. The Borda count may therefore result in a tie, but it cannot result in a majority rule cycle.

If the five shoemakers vote on the three alternatives in Table 3.1, the Borda count winner is proposal X. It gets three votes from each of the sole cutters, two votes from the stitcher, for a total of eleven votes. In next place is proposal Y, with ten votes. In last place is proposal Z, with nine votes. Thus, the Borda count neatly yields a transitive social preference ranking, unlike majority rule.

However, the Borda count is manipulable in another way. Suppose the upper cutters demand a runoff election between the top-ranked proposals X and Y, without Z. A Borda count between these two alternatives yields only seven votes for X (two each from the sole cutters and one vote from the upper cutters and the stitcher). Proposal Y earns eight votes (one vote from each of the sole cutters and two votes each from the upper cutters and the stitcher). As a result, the relative ranking of X and Y *depends on whether alternative Z is on the agenda.*

The point, of course, is that the Borda count is a voting procedure that makes the relative ranking of any two alternatives dependent on the presence of a third alternative. As a result, it is subject to a variety of strategic manipulations, either by misrepresentation on ballots or manipulation of the alternative set that is to be considered. If instituted as the decision rule in a firm, it would put a premium on politics of the most debilitating sort – backdoor politics, bureaucratic manipulation of the agenda, and lying. Worse, the Borda count would result in a kind of inconsistency that would seem to bode ill for economic performance. Like the restaurant customer who prefers pot roast to chicken unless fish is on the menu, a firm using the Borda count could prefer one manufacturing strategy to another unless it considered a third losing alternative. The coherent decision making that is necessary in firms would be lacking.

The necessity of dictatorship

Majority rule and the Borda count are just two of the many ways that the members of a democratic production cooperative could make decisions about the distribution of profits or other policy decisions. Each is flawed. But surely there are other voting rules that provide transitive group preference rankings in which the rankings of any two alternatives are independent of how people cast their ballots for a third alternative.

In particular, we are looking for a mechanism that satisfies both independence of irrelevant alternatives and transitivity. Furthermore, we are seeking to resolve the inefficiencies generated by market failure, so we will stipulate that the mechanism satisfy a minimal condition of social efficiency: Pareto optimality. This condition will require that, *if* every member

63

of the group prefers x over y, then the group should not select y. This is the requirement that teams, for example, do not satisfy in the case of individually determined levels of effort: The team reaches a level of mutual shirking despite the fact that everyone would prefer an outcome in which all worked harder. The condition of Pareto optimality is a weak condition because it makes no requirements of group choice between pairs of alternatives for which all the members of the group are *not* unanimous.

In addition, we would like the function to be defined for every possible set of individual preferences; that is, the hierarchy should not fail to reach any decision because of a particular configuration of individual preferences. This condition is known as "universal domain." (That is, the *domain* of the social choice function is all possible sets of individual preferences.) Universal domain does not require that every person's vote count equally, or that every person's vote count at all. It simply specifies that the group choice be well defined no matter what combinations of individual ballots are cast.

Arrow asked if there were any social choice functions that satisfied these four conditions. His answer was: only one, a dictatorship. In order for a group to make efficient choices that exhibit the consistency of any rational individual decision maker, the group must make one such individual a dictator. This makes the choice rather stark. If a team does not make one of its members a dictator, the team will (1) be subject to inefficiencies, (2) be subject to instabilities like majority rule, (3) be subject to manipulation like the Borda count, or (4) be indecisive in the case of certain combinations of individual preferences.

HIERARCHY AND DICTATORSHIP

The Arrow theorem suggests that a firm's manager who permits other employees to share in the decision making of the firm could create organizational instability, indecisiveness, inefficiency, or manipulability. Firms that seek to realize the efficiency potentials in specialized, interdependent team production processes not only must create authoritative group decision structures, but also must centralize power. The inevitable result is hierarchy. This is consistent with the highly centralized decision-making style in firms in the early part of this century, both in the day-to-day operations of the manufacturing plant and in the philosophy of decision making articulated by leading business figures of the times. The institutional evolution of twentieth-century firms has been marked by the search for unity and coherence through dictatorship.

Early industrial firms began with small, family-held operations. As Alfred Chandler (1977) has documented, as late as 1840, "nearly all top managers were owners; they were either partners or major stockholders in the enterprise they managed" (3). Because of this, the notion was prevalent that decision making within the business firm was rightly limited to a single owner or family. Within the original family firms,

the personal leadership and appeal – the charisma, to use Max Weber's word – of the capitalist himself served to motivate workers. . . . While some workers held supervisory responsibility for others, nonetheless the actual exercise of power was concentrated in the capitalist's hands. Ultimately all workers were equal because all were quite powerless; the owner had all the power. (Edwards 1979: 26)

As small family firms burgeoned into modern corporations, the owners attempted to retain as much of this dictatorial style of management as possible. They tried to maintain their authority over personnel, marketing, operations, and capital decision making. They resisted threats from government, labor unions, and their own managers, but (as we shall see) ultimately to no avail.

One family that made the transition for a family-owned enterprise to a corporate bureaucracy was the Vanderbilt family. Commodore Cornelius Vanderbilt made a fortune in shipping and set out during the Civil War to become a railroad magnate. After buying the New York & Harlem and then the Hudson River Railroad, he set his sights on the New York Central. In 1865 he broke connections between his railroad and the New York Central in Albany, forcing state legislators and others to walk their baggage across the Hudson River bridge in the state capital. When the public protested, he complained, "Can't I do what I want with my own?" (Josephson 1934/1962: 71). Vanderbilt and other entrepreneurs of the era felt that their organizations must be operated as a dictatorship.

Voluntaristic market contracts versus employer authority

It is one thing for owners to want to assert full authority over their firms as they expand; it is another thing to determine how to achieve that kind of asymmetric authority, for the labor contract is voluntary on both sides, constrained by the forces of competition. The economics of competitive markets would seem to place definite bounds on the ability of employers to assert anything like the level of centralized authority that might be necessary to achieve coherence and consistency in a large, increasingly diverse complex organization.

There is a recent tradition in organizational economics that emphatically asserts that the employment contract is no different from any other. Alchian and Demsetz (1972) rigorously reject the image of the firm as a kind of private Leviathan:

It is common to see the firm characterized by the power to settle issues by fiat, by authority, or by disciplinary action superior to that available in the conventional market. This is delusion. The firm does not own all its inputs. It has no power of fiat, no authority, no disciplinary action any different in the slightest degree from ordinary market contracting between any two people. I can "punish" you only by withholding future business or by seeking redress in the courts for any failure to honor our exchange agreement. That is exactly all that any employer can do ... To speak of managing, directing, or assigning workers to various tasks is a deceptive way of noting that the employer continually is involved in renegotiation of contracts on terms that must be acceptable to both parties. (777)

The voluntaristic nature of the employment contract at Ford was apparent and was strictly constrained by market competition during its earliest years. The labor market was competitive, which meant there were multiple employers and multiple employees. As is normally the case in competitive markets, the labor market in Detroit at the time reached an equilibrium wage level at which the quantity of labor demanded by employers was equal to the quantity of labor supplied by employees. As a result, there was minimal unemployment – no stable excess supply of labor.

Competitive forces thus tended to undermine employer authority. Individuals who did not like the heavy-handed style of a particular employer could (and did) leave at a moment's notice. One observer of the Detroit labor market claimed that automobile workers "are continually on the alert for 'better pay,' and a difference of five cents per hour in favor of a new job will lead them to 'throw up' an old job without delay." Or they may quit for a variety of other reasons:

It may be the opportunity for overtime in the next few weeks, or less bossing, or a larger or shorter noon-hour, or less standing on their feet, or cleaner work, or any of a dozen slight personal reasons that prompt these truly "independent" laborers to transform their names to other pay-rolls so frequently. (Meyer 1981: 81)

Changing jobs was relatively costless for employees because the market-clearing competitive wage guaranteed that they would neither have to take a cut in wage nor have to stand in line for a new job. One visitor at the Ford plant said that the competitive labor market in Detroit allowed a worker "to quit his job in the morning and find employment in another factory at noon" (Meyer 1981: 84).

While competitive market equilibria guaranteed that turnover was costless for employees, it was not costless for employers. Annual turnover in Detroit in the early years of the automotive industry was 100 to 200 percent, and in 1913 Ford had a turnover rate of 370 percent. "This meant that Ford managers had to hire more than 52,000 workers to main a workforce of about 13,600 persons" (83). Seventy-one percent of these turnovers were "five-day men," who were presumed to have quit when they failed to show up five days in a row. The direct costs of this high level of turnover were staggering. One contemporary expert figured the cost at $35 for each new employee, although estimates went as high as $70 (84). In 1913, the monetary cost of labor turnover was $1,820,000.

What worried Ford most were the limitations on productivity that this turnover rate implied. The high rate, combined with an absenteeism rate of

10 percent, meant that practically all of the workers were relatively new at their jobs. Even though the new assembly line jobs were relatively unskilled, it was debilitating to start a new person at each job several times a year and to have that person be absent one day in ten.

Furthermore, the unskilled jobs were of little intrinsic interest, and shirking was rampant, despite Ford's bitter invectives against "soldiering." Ford complained that "the undirected worker spends more time walking about for tools and materials than he does working; he gets small pay because pedestrianism is not a highly paid line" (Meyer 1981: 88). Ford's supervisors could have tried to get tough on shirking, but given the fluid labor market, this would have simply exacerbated the problem of turnover and absenteeism.

The net result was that the productivity gains of Ford's assembly line and other technological advances were not as great as anticipated; "in practice, productivity fell short of expectations" (Meyer 1981: 71). In 1909, an average of 1,548 workmen produced an average of 0.70 cars per worker per month. Exponents of the technological innovations at Ford hoped for a 100 percent increase in productivity, but this proved difficult. In 1913, production had increased enormously, but due mainly to an increase in scale: 13,667 workers produced an average of 1.12 cars per worker per month; "Ford worker productivity increased only 60 percent" (72). Thus, by 1913, Ford Motor Company was focusing directly on the problem of improving the productivity of the individual worker.

The efficiency wage: creating political authority

It seems clear that a great degree of political authority on the part of the employer would have been inconsistent with the fluid labor market that characterized Detroit in 1913. In order for managers to acquire asymmetric authority, a firm must create some barrier between itself and the fluidity of the labor market. One mechanism for doing so is described by the "efficiency wage" hypothesis (see Akerlof and Yellen 1986). This hypothesis maintains that a good many firms typically pay *more* than the market-clearing wage in order to increase the loyalty and productivity of employees. This has the unfortunate effect of causing involuntary unemployment, but it also has the effect of greatly increasing the cost to an employee of quitting. When firms are paying an efficiency wage, an employee has to give up a larger wage in order to quit, and even more important, the employee must face the strong possibility of not being rehired by a different firm.

The empirical fact that labor markets, unlike other markets in the United States, do not clear means that the employer has a great deal more authority than the purchaser does in other contractual relationships. That is, the employer has an asymmetric ability to dictate the behavior of employees in the presence of unforeseen contingencies in incomplete contracts.

Undoubtedly, this increases the ability of the firm to impose nonnegotiated, low-transaction-cost solutions to market failures caused by team production processes.

This seems to have been very much the intention of Henry Ford when he made the dramatic and celebrated managerial innovation described in the Introduction. In 1914, the daily wage at Ford Motor Company was roughly $2.34. Ford was in the process of replacing a large number of skilled craftsmen with unskilled assembly line workers. These workers had low morale and low commitment to the firm. In that year, Ford announced that wages would go up to $5 a day. This was a huge gamble on Ford's part, since the resulting increase in labor costs would eat up half the firm's expected profits in the coming year. The explicit reason for taking this gamble was to increase the authority of Ford Motor Company to enforce higher productivity standards on individual workers, without simply increasing turnover.

The authority-enhancing quality of the plan was accentuated by the way it was implemented. The $5 day was not an increase in the daily wage; the daily wage remained at about $2.50. The increase came in the form of a profit-sharing plan with strict rules regarding eligibility. The rules mandated an extensive series of worker behaviors intended to increase worker efficiency and malleability. Workers had to prove their worthiness for participation in the plan by demonstrating thrift, sobriety, good morals, and good work habits.

In order to monitor these behaviors, Ford created the large Ford Sociology Department, staffed by investigators who made frequent home visits. On these visits, they would ask to see employees' bank books to document their savings habits; they would make recommendations about improved housing; and they would check up on marital happiness and alcohol abuse. Workers who were found wanting could have their checks turned over directly to their wives or could be dropped from the profit-sharing plan. The latter was an especially effective sanction, because a worker who was not on the plan would do the same work as his colleagues and get only half the pay. Furthermore, the company would not have to find and train a replacement, as it would if it fired the employee.

The results were startling. The turnover rates in 1915 dropped from 370 percent to 16 percent. Productivity increased by about 50 percent (Raff 1988: Table 1). There was a long waiting list for Ford jobs, despite the fact that the jobs themselves were notoriously boring and unmotivating. Ford, who was known as one of the most autocratic managers of his time, seemed to have been making a Machiavellian deal with his workers: "I will pay you enough to make it worth your while to accept my dictates on the job." Once employees had accepted a $5 a day contract, they had necessarily accepted the broad grant of concentrated discretionary authority that went to Ford.

Voting failure

Ford became a national celebrity as a result of the $5 day. What is more, there is evidence that Ford created a pattern that has persisted in U.S. industry. While firms do not have sociological departments that formally investigate the private lives of their employees, the simple payment of a wage that is greater than the market-clearing wage performs the essential function of making it costly to quit one's job. Contrary to Alchian and Demsetz, firms became vested with authority that exceeds that of voluntary market exchange. The existence of involuntary unemployment provides the opportunity for political authority in the firm.

Political authority and the employment contract

Thus, while it is correct to say that the employment relationship is contractual, this ignores the fact that the "contract" is a flexible instrument capable of being more or less specified, more or less broad, more or less authoritarian. While economists view "contractual" relations as essentially voluntary and symmetric, Hobbes and others have used the "contract" as a metaphor for the institutionalization of the absolute monarch.

The contract will embody a more voluntaristic, economic relationship to the extent that each party has symmetric alternatives to it. It will embody a more political and hierarchical relationship to the extent that one party in the contract has no low-cost alternatives to the relationship and must accept a contract that grants broad discretionary authority to the other. Hobbes pictured people being forced by the dismal "state of nature" to accept a contractual relationship that allows the ruler to dictate virtually anything. Subjects have the right to resist the ruler only if the ruler's actions directly deprive them of life. In a limited sense, this contract, like a labor contract with a firm, is voluntaristic. But the Hobbesian contract is in effect forced on subjects by the dismal alternative represented by the state of nature; the voluntary labor contract may partake in some part of the authority of the Leviathan insofar as the alternative facing the employee is equally dismal.

What does an employee provide in exchange for her salary? In large part, what she provides is a willingness to accept the employer's resolution of intrafirm conflicts as definitive. In Alchian and Demsetz's (1972) own terminology, if two members of a team production process differ as to the inputs each is required to provide, they must regard the employer's arbitration as final. This can obviously go a long way toward saving on the transaction costs of nonhierarchical negotiations over team production efforts.

How willing will the employee be to accept an unfavorable employer decision? Of course, the employee's willingness will have its limits; and that is the primary point of the Alchian and Demsetz quote given earlier in this chapter. But the long-term nature of the employment contract increases the willingness of the employee to accept any given unfavorable decision. This, too, distinguishes the employment contract from other contracts. In a negotiation over a contract to buy a used automobile, I will be unwilling to accept a mediated resolution that leaves me paying more for the automobile than it is worth – I would rather walk to the next used-car lot. But every employee has had the experience of having to live with an imposed solution to a given dispute that is totally unacceptable in the short run; the employee is constrained to "average" that unfavorable decision with a long-term expected set of interactions within the firm. It is only when the employee finds herself the loser time and again that she begins to think about alternative employment.

The persistence of unemployment and the pattern of paying a wage that is greater than that which would equalize demand and supply results in economic conditions that will allow for an asymmetric grant of authority to the employer. The employer pays for the political authority to specify behaviors in broadly incomplete contracts. The coercive nature of this authority is observed in the "driving" supervisors.

The "driving" method of supervision

As mentioned in the preceding chapter, the "internal contracting" system of plant coordination that existed in the last part of the nineteenth century was gradually replaced by a system of foremen supervising employees on a daily wage. The method of supervision in these workshops was quite different from the autonomy that characterized the contractors. The system was known as "driving" – "a combination of authoritarian rule and physical compulsion" (Nelson 1975: 43). Driving was "most apparent in industries where the management controlled the manufacturing process and the foreman's principal responsibility was to insure that the workers did not reduce the machines' potential . . . 'the agent drives the superintendent, he drives the overseer, and the overseer drives the operative' " (44).

There were few constraints on the foreman's power. Only 6 percent of manufacturing employees were unionized in 1900 (Nelson 1975: 47). The foreman's authority extended to hiring, training, and disciplining employees. He was responsible for enforcing the manager's policies regarding hours of work, pace of work, standards of behavior, and personal services on and off the job. Employees who complained were told to quit or were fired. "Nor did the manufacturer often contradict the foreman's decisions, no matter how arbitrary or unfair they may be" (44), for the foreman was simply the visible manifestation of the authoritarian philosophy of management at the turn of the century, and after.

The driving system at Ford

The link between the $5 day and Ford's autocratic style is clear. Ford felt that employees worked for two reasons only: "One is for wages, and one is for fear of losing their jobs." He told a journalist, "I have a thousand men who if I say 'Be at the northeast corner of the building at four a.m.' will be there at four a.m. That's what we want – obedience" (Halberstam 1986: 93–4).

The assembly line that Ford perfected at his famous Highland Park plant was quite compatible with the driving system of foremanship. It simplified each worker's task, so that it was not necessary to hire skilled workers who had to be in some part internally motivated. According to one observer:

The Ford company has no use for experience, in the working ranks anyway. It desires and prefers machine-tool operators who have nothing to unlearn, who have no theories of correct surface speeds for metal finishing, and who will do what they are told, over and over again, from bell-time to bell-time. (Meyer 1981: 52)

The assembly line made it easy to spot shirkers, because shirkers simply "did not have the same rhythmic movements as the other members of the shop" (59). The uniform rhythm was set by the assembly line itself. The standard output per machine, or "machine rating," made it unnecessary to provide much internal motivation for the worker. As one journalist of the time noted, "Equipment obviously sets the pace in the Ford shops. That is why Ford needs no highly refined method of wage payment to furnish an incentive to put. They must very nearly do a standard day's production whether they wish to or not" (37). The foremen were instructed as to the desired output of the crew, and the foremen "forced" the desired output by a combination of physical threats and the threat of firing – the physical threats being more efficacious because any objection would necessarily result in firing. "There is mighty little chance for the shirker to persist in the Ford plant, even though the entire force is paid a daywork basis" (62). After the plant was mechanized and the $5-day policy was implemented, foremen were increasingly "chosen for physical strength. If a worker seemed to be loitering, a foreman simply knocked him down. The rules against workers talking to each other were strict" (Halberstam 1986: 94).

The scope of Ford's authority extended farther and deeper than that of a great many other top managers. The Ford Sociology Department gradually evolved from a welfare agency into a spying organization intent on determining whether employees drank at home or supported a union – both offenses punishable by firing (Halberstam 1986: 93). The man who eventually became Ford's chief assistant – and the person Ford claimed was the greatest man he ever knew – was Harry Bennett, long-time chief of security at Ford. A former sailor and former boxer, Bennett did not know a great deal about autos, but he did not hesitate to use violence on recalcitrant employees. Bennett's staff of boxers and ex-convicts intimidated the workforce and kept unions out (101).

But it was not just the assembly line workers who were kept powerless. Ford also failed to heed the advice of engineers, dealers, accountants, and

71

even his own son, resisting all attempts to improve his famous Model T until market share had been irretrievably lost to General Motors. When Chrysler switched to a six-cylinder engine in 1929, Edsel Ford increased pressure on Ford to develop his own version. Edsel and the company's chief engineer spent six months working on a six-cylinder engine. Then Ford invited them to observe his new scrap conveyor. The first item they saw going up the conveyor was their six-cylinder test engine (Halberstam 1986: 94). It was not until 1936 that Ford finally entered the market with a six-cylinder engine.

Ford also resisted pressure from dealers. When they tried to tell him that customers wanted changes in the ignition system, Ford replied, "You can have them over my dead body. That magneto stays on as long as I'm alive." He felt the same way about changing the color of the Model T. "You can have them any color you want, boys, as long as they're black" (Halberstam 1986: 90).

Accountants, who need a degree of professional autonomy in order to perform their function credibly, were treated in the same way. Ford regarded them as potentially placing constraints on his independent authority. To keep them subservient, he would periodically walk into their office and say: "I want them all fired. They're not productive, they don't do any real work. Get them out of here today" (Halberstam 1986: 99). The result, as might be imagined, was financial chaos. One new financial officer was amazed to find, as late as 1946, a room full of bookkeepers trying to estimate the value of a foot-high stack of currency so that they could estimate how many millions of dollars were in the immense piles of cash lying around the room. When the new officer asked for the profit estimates for the next month, he was told that the estimates could be any figure that was desired (100).

Even stockholders were relegated to a similar degree of subservience. In 1917, Ford was sued by the Dodge brothers, who owned a great deal of Ford's stock and were complaining about the lack of dividends despite Ford's huge profits. During the trial, Ford said that he didn't like giving profits to stockholders because it wasn't any fun; the real fun was in putting profits back into the plant. When asked about the size of the profits, he said they were so large they were just "awful." "We don't seem to be able to keep the profits down" (Halberstam 1986: 80). Ford lost the suit and was required to pay out $19 million in dividends. His reaction was to take control of as much company stock as possible so that as little discretion as possible would be lost to "greedy" stockholders who would spoil his fun.

Throughout the internal management of the firm, Ford was careful to stop anyone who might be a competing source of authority. "Anyone who might be a threat within the company, because of superior leadership ability, was scorned as often and as publicly as possible." Bill Knudsen, one of Ford's most talented production men, was an advocate of modifying the

Model T to allow changing of gears. Ford publicly humiliated Knudsen until he was forced to resign. He became a leading figure at General Motors during the years that that company caught up with and surpassed Ford (Halberstam 1986: 89–90).

After Knudsen left, Ford's son Edsel was the only person who could tell Ford anything that Ford didn't want to hear. "It was Edsel's job to tell his father that sales were down, Edsel's job to represent the six-cylinder engine, which the company desperately needed, Edsel's job to speak for better suspension systems" (Halberstam 1986: 92). Ford responded by publicly humiliating him frequently. "In 1942 Edsel got undulating fever from drinking milk from his father's dairy; Ford disapproved of pasteurization. The old man blamed his illness on Edsel's bad habits" (95). Edsel died in 1943.

Summary: political authority in a hierarchical firm

It is true that the employment relationship is a voluntary one and that exit is available to those who prefer an alternative. However, the policies at Ford were clearly designed to make exit costly. In implementing these policies, Ford Motor Company clearly created a degree of asymmetric, open grant of authority for itself vis-à-vis its employees. Contrary to the claims made by Alchian and Demsetz (1972), Ford created "the power to settle issues by fiat, by authority, [and] by disciplinary action superior to that available in the conventional market" (777).

The result was a hierarchy that resembled a political system much more than it did a market. Ford's employees were "in" the labor market only briefly. After signing an employment contract, they found themselves in a political institution in which Machiavelli would have been completely comfortable. Indeed, Ford seems to have taken to heart Machiavelli's answer to the question:

[Is it] better [for a ruler] to be loved than feared or feared than loved? It may be answered that one should wish to be both, but, because it is difficult to unite them in one person, it is much safer to be feared than loved, when, of the two, either must be dispensed with. (Machiavelli 1513/1952, 24)

Ford's autocratic style served the company well during its early years, when Ford's innovations seemed to be exactly the right ones at exactly the right time, every time. The advantages of this dictatorial style were exactly the ones suggested by Arrow. The choices were certainly transitive and consistent – the company did not cycle from four-cylinder engines to six-cylinder to eight-cylinder engines again. The choices made also satisfied the independence of irrelevant alternatives – if Ford preferred the four-cylinder engine over the six-cylinder engine, that ranking was unaffected by whether or not the eight-cylinder engine was on the agenda. If the company had been run by majority rule or a plurality, one of these characteristics would have been a problem.

Were the choices Pareto optimal? Yes, because all of the decisions reached were Henry Ford's first choices. No changes could therefore have been made without making Ford himself more dissatisfied. It is clear that the organization was created and maintained to make sure that Ford always got his first choice.

And yet something was unsatisfactory about the decision making at Ford Motor Company. Although Ford always got his first choice, one must wonder if he himself was best served by this pattern of decision making. If he had availed himself of the information that Edsel and his engineers had, would he have insisted on vetoing the six-cylinder engine for as many years as he did? One might well suppose not, because, by finally allowing the six-cylinder engine to be produced, Ford later admitted that he had made a mistake.

This example suggests why dictatorship, despite the fact that it alone combines the favorable decision-making characteristics listed earlier, is nevertherless not the social choice mechanism in business firms. While dictatorship provides the unity and coherence needed in a firm, it seems to fail because of one of the same problems that causes markets to fail—information asymmetry. The very authority of a dictatorship serves as an obstacle to obtaining the information needed to make wise decisions.

It would seem easy to conclude that firms adopt centralized, hierarchical decision-making styles if and when the potential for market failure makes them desirable. But the theme of the rest of this book is that it is not as easy as that. Information asymmetry, monopoly power, and team production externalities confound market processes, bargaining, and voting institutions. They also present managers with day-to-day dilemmas that endanger the health and well-being of the hierarchies they control.

PART II

Managerial dilemmas

When Edsel Ford died in 1943, many wondered who would step into his role as heir apparent to the Ford Motor Company. A leading candidate was security chief Harry Bennett, who had had close personal ties to Henry Ford. However, Edsel's son Henry managed to gain control of the company (with the aid of his mother and grandmother) and fire Bennett and his cronies.

This left Henry Ford II in the astounding position of having inherited complete control of a large and famous, if failing, organization. He knew he had to turn the organization around. He put up signs saying "Beat Chevrolet" all around the River Rouge plant. But he realized very soon that this was easier said than done. Dictatorial power over a large number of people was not enough. As he told one of his aides, "Clearly, I just don't know enough . . . to run this damn place" (Collier and Horowitz 1987: 214).

He hired the rising star of the General Motors system, Ernie Breech, who was a disciple of the great Alfred Sloan. Breech had the management expertise that Ford lacked. But this first appointment presented Ford with the dilemma that will occupy the next several chapters of this book: how to control subordinates who have the expertise that you lack. He initially offered Breech the presidency at Ford, then backed away at the last minute, fearing that he was giving away too much authority. He made Breech executive vice-president with the "authority to make decisions" subject to veto by Ford (Collier and Horowitz 1987: 220). Immediately after this appointment, Ford panicked again, telling his closest adviser, "My lawyer says I'm abdicating by making Ernie vice-president." His adviser responded: "You can't give him the power. You must make it understood that you are to retain the power" (220).

The problem facing Henry Ford II was one that every leader of a modern organization confronts: maintaining authority while recognizing one's own informational deficiencies. Attila the Hun may not have had to deal with subordinates who knew more than he did. He may have gained his position because he was smarter and stronger than any other person in the army. But modern leaders have to deal with the problem of information asymmetry.

In the first chapters of this book, market failure was explained in terms of information asymmetry, which provided a prima facie case for hierarchy. However, information asymmetries do not disappear just because a hierarchical organization is created. The dilemma for those at the top of hierarchies is to use the expertise of multiple subordinates without allowing the organization to fall into disarray. As Chapter 4 discusses, Henry Ford II was able to resolve this problem only in part. Even in the context of hierarchy, the pulling and tugging of individuals with informational advantages relative to other actors can result in Pareto inefficiencies. This notion is concisely captured in social choice theory by the "Sen paradox" (Sen 1970, 1976).

Economists would naturally look to the creation of an appropriate incentive system to resolve the problem facing Henry Ford II. They would propose that he write a contract with Breech that offered incentives for Breech to work in Ford's best interests. What would such a contract be like? This question is pursued in some depth in Chapters 5, 6, and 7. Of course, incentives are used in every organization, and often with great effectiveness. However, there are a number of disturbing results in the literature on incentive design that portray the limits of pursuing efficiency through hierarchical incentives. Briefly, information asymmetries and team production externalities produce the same kind (although not necessarily the same degree) of inefficiency in hierarchies that they produce in markets. The specter of hierarchical failure, I will argue, is a day-to-day concern of business managers like Henry Ford II, a concern for which incentive design poses no easy or ultimate answers.

In Chapter 8, the possibility of hierarchical failure leads full circle back to markets. The failure of internal incentive systems is, after all, no news to students of socialist economies. The argument is made in economics and finance that it is the external incentives posed by the market economy in which hierarchical firms are embedded that effectively discipline managers and employees. If that is the case, it appears that, paradoxically, markets correct hierarchical failure. This is the inverse of the story told by economists, who seek to explain the existence of hierarchies as corrections for market failure. And if markets are necessary to correct hierarchical failure, then the question is still open – why have hierarchy in the first place?

4

Horizontal dilemmas
Social choice in a decentralized hierarchy

> If there is any sort of "discretionary power" left to individuals restricting outcomes, we must either give up Pareto optimality or acyclicity.
> Aldrich (1977: 16)

If every individual had complete and perfect information about the effects of alternative outcomes on his or her own well-being, the problem facing society would simply be that of aggregating the differences among individuals. But social decisions also serve the purpose of combining the judgments of individuals, each of whom may have only incomplete and faulty information about the effects of an alternative on his or her own well-being.

Despite the technical advantages of dictatorship as a means of aggregating conflicting individual preferences, dictatorship may do very poorly when the problem is one of making collective judgments about difficult problems. Machiavelli understood that even an absolute prince has to get accurate information and advice from others; hence, the prince has to avoid "flatterers," or advisers we would call "yes men": "There is no other way of guarding oneself from flatterers except letting men understand that to tell you the truth does not offend you" (1513/1952: 33).

The simple fact is that no one person can know enough to program the behavior of all the other members of the firm as if they were robots. As a result, the expertise of specialists becomes a political resource within the firm, one that inevitably results in a dispersion of political power within the organization. The purpose of this chapter is to understand why the delegation of decision-making authority is inevitable within a hierarchical structure and what implications delegation has for the efficiency and unity of hierarchical decision making. The analysis will show that delegation to experts leads to the potential for social dilemmas within a hierarchy, a potential that is the central problem facing the managers of any modern firm.

77

THE USE OF KNOWLEDGE IN ORGANIZATIONS

In the first half of the twentieth century, one strand of rational economic analysis led to optimistic forecasts regarding the possibilities of centralized planning and decision making under socialism. Just as the "economic theory of the firm" conceived of decision making as the centralized, efficient allocation of resources by the satisfaction of marginality conditions, the planning of the economy was seen as one large optimization problem. Indeed, the theory of the firm was seen as a model for planning under a socialist economy, and the socialist economy could be thought of as a giant firm. If the information conditions could be satisfied, a centralized planner could guarantee a centralized, efficient solution to resource allocation problems in ways that markets plagued by monopoly or externalities could not.

The Austrian economist Friedrich Hayek criticized this faith in centralized decision making. While his criticism was directed at centralized decision making in society, it applies equally well to dictatorial decision making in a firm. In a classic article entitled "The Use of Knowledge in Society," Hayek (1948) begins by criticizing the economic theory of the firm (as applied to socialist planning):

If we possess all the relevant information, *if* we can start out from a given system of preferences, and *if* we command complete knowledge of available means, the problem which remains is purely one of logic. . . . This, however, is emphatically *not* the economic problem which society [the firm] faces. . . . The reason for this is that the "data" from which the economic calculus starts are never for the whole society [firm] "given" to a single mind which could work out the implications and can never be so given. (77)

While in the social choice view of dictatorship a single actor's preferences "count," in social decision making no one actor can even know what he or she "wants" without information supplied by other actors. The head of a firm may "want" to make profits, but preferences over any of the action alternatives available to him depend on information that other people must supply. Should Ford Motor Company make a front-wheel-drive car? As Hayek (1948) says:

The peculiar character of the problem of a rational economic order is determined precisely by the fact that the knowledge of which we must make use never exists in concentrated or integrated form but solely as the dispersed bits of incomplete and frequently contradictory knowledge which all the separate individuals possess. (78)

These bits of incomplete information include information about the popular response to front-wheel drive, from marketing; information about the costs, from production; and information about the availability of capital, from finance. "To put it briefly, it is a problem of the utilization of knowledge which is not given to anyone in its totality" (78).

Horizontal dilemmas

Even if the dictator manages to combine the technical expertise of marketing, production, and finance, that is insufficient, as Hayek points out:

> Today it is almost heresy to suggest that scientific knowledge is not the sum of all knowledge. But a little reflection will show that there is beyond question a body of very important but unorganized knowledge which cannot possibly be called scientific in the sense of knowledge of general rules: the knowledge of the particular circumstances of time and place. It is with respect to this that practically every individual has some advantage over all others because he possesses unique information of which beneficial use might be made, but of which use can be made only if the decisions depending on it are left to him or are made with his active cooperation. (80)

Here is the nub of it. Even the most autocratic executives find that they must depend on subordinates with the knowledge of "particular circumstances of time and place." This information monopoly, though of the most trivial kind, makes necessary some degree of delegation or sharing of decision-making authority. This delegation becomes even more essential as conditions shift rapidly:

> If we can agree that the economic problem of society [the firm] is mainly one of rapid adaptation to changes in the particular circumstances of time and place, it would seem to follow that the ultimate decisions must be left to the people who are familiar with these circumstances, who know directly of the relevant changes and of the resources immediately available to meet them. We cannot expect that this problem will be solved by first communicating all this knowledge to a central board which, after integrating all knowledge, issues its orders. We must solve it by some form of decentralization. (83–4)

The advantages of independence in problem solving

We have Jonathan Bendor to thank for the clearest mathematical exposition of the problems that information asymmetries produce for dictatorial hierarchy. Suppose that a dictator has the ability to make every subordinate in the organization perfectly submissive; why would such a dictator ever grant one or more of those subordinates independent status? If the dictator knew everything there was to know about every problem she faced, there would seem to be no self-interested reason to create an independent (and therefore potentially competitive) force. But without omniscience, omnipotence might be dangerous.

Bendor (1985) begins by assuming that a problem must be solved by finding some critical value s. He wonders whether two people working separately on the problem (call them I and J) would be more likely to find a successful solution than two people working together (call them T and U). He assumes that each of the four has an equal chance of finding the critical value:

$$p(T > s) = p(U > s) = p(I > s) = p(J > s).$$

79

In his fascinating treatment, Bendor assumes that "success breeds success," which would seem to be an argument in favor of two people working together. That is, the conditional probability of one member of a pair coming up with a second successful solution, given that the other member of the pair has come up with one successful solution, is *greater* for the *interactive pair* than for the two people working separately:

$$p[(T > s)\backslash(U > s)] > p[(I > s)\backslash(J > s)].$$

This assumption captures the notion of independence; that is, a person who is working closely with a successful other is more likely to be successful himself.

From this Bendor derives the counterintuitive result that the *independent pair* is *more likely* to find some outcome that meets the critical value than the interactive pair. As Bendor (1985) notes, "Two relatively independent heads are better than two relatively dependent heads" (47).

Bendor uses the laws of probability to deduce that the independence notion implies that one of the interactive pair is *less* likely to have a good idea if his team member does not have a good idea. Thus, if what is important is that at least one good idea occur, the pair working separately is unambiguously more likely to meet that criterion of success. For this reason, the dictator may be driven to creating independent actors, just for the problem-solving advantages that independence provides. A jealous dictator will no doubt seek ways to gain the advantages of independence while creating as small a political threat as possible; and therein lies much of the basis for Machiavellianism. However, a dictator who needs good information and good ideas must create the basis for independence inside the hierarchy.

The subordination of hierarchical authority

Bendor's analysis suggests that independence in problem solving increases the likelihood that a successful solution will be found. However, suppose two alternatives are generated by two independent units in a bureaucracy, and there is a difference of opinion about which of the solutions is superior. The existence of these independent "brain-storming" units within a hierarchy does not necessarily lessen the authority of the would-be dictator. Surely the dictator will refer to her own judgment in deciding the merits of the alternatives generated by her problem-solving staff.

But the same kind of analysis that justifies the existence of independent problem-solving agents within the hierarchy also requires the outright subordination of the dictator to others' judgment; for the possibility of human error can best be corrected by subordinating the judgment of the dictator.

This result was first formally established by the Marquis de Condorcet in an attempt to ascertain how groups could best make choices. In what became known as the "Condorcet jury theorem," Condorcet assumed that each citizen has a probability of choosing the alternative that is better for the organization as a whole. As long as the average probability of making the right choice is greater than .5, the probability of the group majority being correct increases to 1 as the group gets large (Grofman and Feld 1988).

It is advisable to limit dictatorial authority even if a dictator's advisers are no more expert than himself. Suppose, for example, that a dictator and each of his two subordinates independently have a 60 percent probability of making the correct judgment. All three individuals would be better off if the correct judgment were made. Why should the dictator ever defer to his subordinates, who are no more expert than he? If the dictator agreed to be bound by majority rule, the correct judgment would be made 65 percent of the time; that is, the majority judgment would be a 5 percent improvement over any one of them making the decision autonomously. In particular, on those occasions in which the dictator had a different opinion than his two subordinates, the two subordinates would be correct 60 percent of the time, and he would be right only 40 percent of the time. As the number of independent advisers increased (each with a 60 percent chance of being correct), the probability of the majority being correct would come as close to 1 as necessary.

The implications of this result for hierarchy are enormous. Not only will a smart dictator, it seems, have to rely on staff to generate alternatives from which to choose, as Bendor argues; in matters of judgment, the dictator will be better off deferring to group opinion in choosing among those alternatives. Furthermore, the benefits of deferring to majority opinion occur only if the voters are truly independent and not mimicking the dictator. This suggests that subunits of a hierarchy not only must be regarded as brainstorming offices, but should often have real power in the selection of alternatives.

The case for deferring to subordinates is even stronger if the subordinates are true experts. Suppose the dictator and one assistant each have a 60 percent chance of being correct in matters of marketing, but the marketing assistant has an 80 percent chance of being correct in such judgments. Because of the subordinate's expertise, majority rule is an even greater improvement over dictatorial decision making; a majority will be correct 74.4 percent of the time, instead of 65 percent of the time. However, majority rule can be improved on: The dictator would do better to defer to the expert alone and get a correct judgment 80 percent of the time. As variations in the ability of the individuals became more pronounced, the majority judgment of the group would be likely simply to water down the quality of decision making by the expert.

For these reasons, as problem solving and decision making in an organization become much more complex, those individuals who have expertise not only will be called on to exercise this expertise, but will increasingly manage to secure a real share of decision-making authority. With complexity comes delegated decision making.

The political challenge to dictatorship

The mathematical arguments against dictatorial judgments have been anticipated by the behavioral literature on organizations, which for much of the twentieth century has documented the emergence of pluralist decentralization in hierarchies. The primary explanation of the phenomenon of pluralist, decentralized decision making in hierarchies has been the notion of "dual authority" – whereby formal, hierarchical authority is challenged by the authority of expertise.

Mary Parker Follett (1940), one of the earliest critics of monocratic hierarchy, asked, "How can you expect people merely to obey orders and at the same time to take that degree of responsibility which they should take?" Implicitly, she was arguing that, when one delegates the responsibility of implementing a decision in a given dimension, the price a superior has to pay for cooperative and conscientious implementation is some deference to the wishes of the subordinates. Suddenly, the door is opened to bargaining between superiors and subordinates.

Max Weber (1946) also argued that hierarchical authority does not lead to dictatorship when he pointed out that "the 'political master' finds himself in the position of the 'dilettante' who stands opposite the 'expert,' facing the trained official" (232). That this expertise becomes a power base, carefully guarded by the experts, is obvious to Weber: "Every bureaucracy seeks to increase the superiority of the professionally informed by keeping their knowledge and intentions secret" (233).

THE HISTORICAL LIMITS OF DICTATORSHIP
IN HIERARCHY

Thus, despite the most serious intentions of autocrats like Henry Ford, the U.S. firm has been transformed from a centralized to a decentralized hierarchy. The firm is thoroughly embedded with nests of specialists, each slowly leveraging its own brand of expertise into positions of shared authority and power.

Impetus for delegation: engineers and scientific managers

The pioneers in this movement toward expertise and shared authority were professional managers who felt that many of the firm's decisions should be delegated to them. Foremost among these, of course, was Frederick Taylor. Taylor was an engineer who became convinced that the high-flying entrepreneurs and capitalists who ran the late-nineteenth-century firms made abominable managers. They were, he believed, wasting a good deal of the firm's resources through sloppy management and a loose reliance on "traditional" and commonsensical manufacturing procedures.

His experiments on metal cutting demonstrated the "one best way" of performing that vital manufacturing operation and won him worldwide acclaim. Taylor felt that careful, methodical experimentation could reveal the "one best way" of performing any task that a firm might face, from stoking coal to administering a personnel system. He formulated his ideas under the title "scientific management" and soon had a devoted following of engineers who were trained in his techniques.

Taylor placed the blame for inefficiency on management and implied that any failure to adopt his system was a sign of selfish bullheadedness on the part of short-sighted owners. Owners quite clearly and accurately perceived that their authority and discretion as entrepreneurs were being challenged by engineers, who, after all, had no capital at risk and were supposed to be their employees.

One of the areas in which Taylor was most insistent that authority be transferred was personnel administration. Traditional practice included virtually no careful selection of applicants, no training, and no statement of employee responsibilities and rewards. In many establishments, people seeking jobs simply appeared at the gates in the morning and evening, and a foreman needing more help would select someone from the crowd and give him a chance to demonstrate his abilities on some task.

Taylor felt that scientific management required the identification and selection of the right person for each job and that one of management's primary responsibilities was adequate training. This concern became increasingly popular as the old "driving" method of foremanship resulted in growing labor problems and as the necessity of finding and training a labor force for a more technologically complex physical plant increased (Taylor 1911, 1947).

As an example, the driving foreman of the brass foundry at National Cash Register fired union molders in his shop, precipitating a strike and then a lockout in 1901. After the dispute had ended, Chief Executive Officer (CEO) John Patterson appointed personnel reformer Charles Carpenter to create the "first modern personnel department in American industry" (Nelson 1975: 109). One of the first acts of the Labor Department, as it was called, was to deprive foremen of the ability to fire employees unilaterally or arbitrarily. By systematizing labor contracts and handling disputes over wage inequities, it also destroyed the authority of foremen over their subordinates' compensation.

All of this was done with the intention of "strengthening management," and it was sold to Patterson and other bosses at National Cash Register in this way. However, the management that was strengthened was no longer a single, unconstrained boss at the head of a simple linear hierarchy, but a multifaceted "administration" composed of production experts with their stopwatches, personnel experts with their wage contracts, and lawyers, marketing specialists, and numerous other staff members. The CEO, sometimes without even knowing it, was gradually put in the position of being told by various staff experts what was "impossible," "illegal," "inappropriate," or "bad policy."

Thus, despite the fact that Taylorism was widely seen to be strengthening management, it was also responsible for transforming management into a modern team in which power was delegated to and shared by a variety of specialists. It was for this reason, no doubt, that Taylorism was ignored or heartily condemned by many business leaders of the day. Even when scientific management was given a trial in a plant, management often decided it didn't like what it did to its own prerogatives. Where it was tried,

the experts encountered more opposition from managers than workers. In some cases it came from the highest levels. Scientific management was often introduced in the course of a power struggle between the younger and older members of the management group or as a part of a larger reform program after the younger men had taken over. (Nelson 1975: 75)

The superiority of expert, delegated management became the basis for a constitutional shift in power relations, replacing the dictatorship of the entrepreneur.

Accountant autonomy

A striking example of the increasing constraints and decentralization in the firm was the rise of independent accountants. During the first part of the century, accountants had been regarded as mere bookkeepers whose job was to supply the figures the boss wanted, even if they were "cooked":

Because their profession had labored for years to escape the tight grip in which corporate management held it, most accountants ardently wanted to exercise, in fact, more of that "independence" they claimed to be essential to good accounting practice. Corporate managers, lacking respect for such independence, often tried to dictate to the auditors, encouraging them to shade the truth or even to misrepresent the state of a company's financial health. (McCraw 1984: 190)

Even more than labor and social legislation had increased the independence and authority of personnel experts, the securities legislation of the New Deal gave accountants an opportunity to guarantee an autonomous position in the firm. When regulator James Landis indicated a willingness to grant the accounting profession a large degree of self-regulation, the profession quickly joined the coalition of those supporting securities legislation. One accountant wrote that, because of the new legislation, "no longer must the public accountant single handed strive against the prejudiced desire of the officers of clients for what he believes to be fair and correct presentation of the facts in the financial statements." Another wrote: "The control function of accounts takes on a new and quite different form. Instead of being merely a tool of control by business enterprise they become a tool for the control of business enterprise itself" (McCraw 1984: 190). The accountants, along with the production experts and personnel managers, became another center of autonomous, delegated political authority in the hierarchical firm.

The multidivisional firm

The examples presented thus far confirm that top-level managers were constrained to delegate decision-making authority to engineers, personnel administrators, accountants, and other technical staff members. But even more fundamental than this, managers were eventually forced to make wholesale grants of authority to subordinate line officers – officers with general operating authority and responsibility for a large proportion of the firm's core production activities.

The classic account of this devolution of authority is Chandler's *Strategy and Structure* (1962). Among other cases, Chandler cites that of Du Pont, which by early in the twentieth century had developed a very strong, centralized hierarchy with functional departments for production, purchasing, sales, and so on. During the First World War, Du Pont embarked on a strategy of diversification, moving from the traditional base in ammunition and explosives into dyes, paints, and other chemicals. As it turned out, the imposition of a standard marketing strategy for these very different kinds of products was ineffective. Du Pont discovered it was losing money in these products, even though less diversified competitors were making money. As Chandler (1962) noted, "The marketing of consumer goods demanded a new and more extensive type of advertising 'with a direct appeal to the consumer' and the creation of an enlarged national distributing organization including, possibly, even retail outlets" (93).

Coordination along product lines, but across the functional departments, was proving impossible. "The activities of each line within each functional department were effectively managed, but no one was responsible for administering them so as to assure a profit on each individual line of products" (96). This was especially the case since the peak of the functional hierarchy was serving as a bottleneck to cross-functional coordination. Furthermore, the top executives did not have the information they needed to invest capital across different product lines. The functional lines gathered accounting information in such a way that it was impossible to determine return on investment for different product lines.

As the crisis worsened, a group of young executives drew up a proposal for creating two or more "practically self-contained" divisions. The divisions would handle sales, purchasing, production, and accounting separately. Lines of accountability were drawn from the divisional managers to the president; however, the delegation of authority to these divisional managers was great. For instance, the proposal stated that the divisional manager should give monthly financial reports to the president. Certainly this degree of accountability would leave the president in a position to fire inadequate managers; however, this reactive stance was quite different from the conception of the president as first decision maker in the firm. The president was put in a position of having to approve or disapprove of an unknown number of decisions made by someone with substantial delegated authority.

Delegation and interest aggregation

The creation of personnel offices, the development of autonomous accounting staffs, and the spread of multidivisional firms are just some of the more striking examples of the delegation of authority to experts in organizations. With the acceleration of technological change in industry, firms have found it necessary to incorporate pockets of specialists in engineering, biology, advertising, finance, and virtually every other discipline – and to vest these specialists with decision-making authority.

This would pose no problems if each specialist simply used his or her expert judgment to advance the firm's best interests. But experts end up having different preferences than the rest of the firm, as well as different levels of expertise. The authority that is delegated to experts inevitably gives them some opportunity to advance their own interest. For the firm, this means that the advantages of dictatorship so clearly captured by the Arrow theorem – coherence, efficiency, and consistency – will be at risk. As pockets of delegated authority spread within the decentralized firm, keeping the firm on a unified coherent course will become ever more difficult.

THE SEN PARADOX: TRADE-OFFS IN A DELEGATED HIERARCHY

What kinds of trade-offs must be made in decentralized hierarchical decision making? Another impossibility result, known as the Sen paradox, will provide a good deal of insight about the nature of trade-offs in hierarchies (Sen 1970, 1976, 1983). Loosely paraphrased, it says that any organization that delegates decision-making authority to more than one subset of individuals must suffer from either incoherent behavior or inefficiency for some combinations of individual preferences.

In practice, all large organizations involve some degree of delegation. Chief executives find it necessary to grant authority to a large or small number of specialized subordinates to make some decisions for the organization. In a more centralized firm, these delegated decisions are fewer and

Table 4.1. *Decentralized choice at Apex, Inc.*

	Apex must choose one of four alternatives:	
	Production technology I	Production technology II
Marketing strategy A	*x*	*y*
Marketing strategy B	*z*	*w*

Organizational decision procedure (minimal delegation):

Marketing specialist Smith is decisive for the pair (x,z); the boss, Ms. Doe, is decisive for all other pairs

Transitive individual preference orderings:

Mr. Smith	Ms. Doe
y	*x*
z	*w*
x	*y*
w	*z*

Intransitive social preference ordering:

z beats x (Mr. Smith is decisive)
y beats z (by Pareto optimality)
w beats y (Ms. Doe is decisive)
x beats w (by Pareto optimality)

more trivial than they are in other firms, but delegation exists in any large firm. The decisions of the subordinates with delegated authority contribute to the final organizational decision.

As an example, let us consider Apex, Inc. Apex has to decide between two possible production technologies and two possible marketing programs. Any production technology can be combined with any marketing program, so there are four possible overall strategies. These choices are shown in Table 4.1. Everyone in the firm has his or her own opinion about the relative merits of the four strategies. In particular, let us suppose that there are two individuals in the organization. Because of his superior expertise, the marketing vice-president, Mr. Smith, has been delegated the authority to rank-order outcomes x and z; that is, if production technology I is chosen, Mr. Smith gets to decide between marketing strategy A and marketing strategy B. The boss, Ms. Doe, gets to rank-order all other pairs of alternatives.

Managerial dilemmas

This organization, then, is not a complete dictatorship. It is minimally decentralized in that one person other than the boss has the authority to make decisions about some aspects of the group choice. From a social choice perspective, the problem with delegated hierarchies is that, because they are not complete dictatorships, they logically violate some other desirable characteristic of social choice. The Sen paradox reveals that hierarchical delegation requires trade-offs between the following characteristics:

Universal domain. As with the Arrow theorem (Chapter 3), the organization should be able to make choices for all possible combinations of individual preferences. No combination of individual preferences should leave the organizational choice undefined.

Pareto optimality. For all pairs of alternatives x and y, the organization should choose x over y if everyone in the organization prefers x over y. Once again, this is a weak requirement that says nothing about what the organization should decide in the case of disagreement. It simply says that unanimous agreement should be reflected in the final outcome.

Transitivity. If the organization prefers x over y and y over z, then it should prefer x over z. Once again, this seems to be a minimal requirement for any kind of consistency or meaning in group choice. This requirement is also known as acyclicity.

Minimal delegation. There are at least two individuals or discrete subgroups in the organization, each of whom has the authority to rank-order at least one pair of outcomes. The Apex corporation has minimal delegation because Mr. Smith, in addition to Ms. Doe, has the authority to determine one pair of rankings.

The Sen paradox states that these four minimally desirable characteristics in a hierarchy are mutually inconsistent. That is, in any organization with minimal delegation, there will be some combinations of individual preferences that lead to either inefficiency or intransitivity in group choice.

As an example, suppose that Mr. Smith and Ms. Doe have the preferences shown in Table 4.1. The hierarchy's social preference must be as follows: By Pareto optimality, y must beat z, and x must beat w; the reason is that both actors agree on these rankings. By minimal delegation, z is ranked higher than x because Mr. Smith's expert opinion in this area is determinative. And finally, Ms. Doe has the authority to rank w over y. Putting these four outcomes together, we have a set of circular (intransitive) preferences for the hierarchy: Apex believes x is better than w, which is better than y, which is better than z, which is better than x.

Because the hierarchy has intransitive preferences, there is no single choice the organization can make that is consistent with its "constitution" or rules of procedure. If it chooses outcome z or w, then it is choosing an

88

outcome that both members of the organization can agree is inferior. If it chooses outcome y or x, then it is violating the organization's allocation of decision-making responsibilities – such a choice would be "illegal" given the organization's structure.

For any possible organizational delegation of decision-making power, this problem will necessarily arise for *some* possible set of individual preferences. But the universal domain condition requires us to ask what would happen under every possible set of individual preferences. And the overwhelming fact of the Sen paradox is that, as long as there are two subgroups in the organization that specialize in separate aspects of the organization's decision problem, there must *always* be some sets of individual preferences that require a choice between Pareto optimality and transitivity.

HORIZONTAL SOCIAL DILEMMAS: PARETO SUBOPTIMALITY IN DECENTRALIZED ORGANIZATIONS

Every delegated hierarchy must violate Pareto optimality, transitivity, or universal domain. Each possibility carries with it a set of unpleasant organizational problems. Organizational design in delegated hierarchies necessarily involves trade-offs between various kinds of unpleasantness (Hammond and Miller 1985).

One possible outcome is simply a violation of Pareto optimality: That is, each of those actors with authority over some set of decisions facing the organization makes what he or she thinks is the best choice for the organization, but the net result is an outcome that no one likes. For instance, boss Doe chooses production technology I, and marketing specialist Smith chooses marketing strategy B, and the result is outcome z. Each has acted in a way that is consistent with his or her own preferences, and yet both can agree that some other alternative (e.g., y) would be better. The outcome z is stable, but inefficient. Because of delegation, individual self-interest will be inconsistent with the firm's best interests.

This is, of course, an ironic outcome, since the purpose of the hierarchy, as discussed in Chapter 1, is to "solve" social dilemmas in nonhierarchical teams. Hierarchy may make efficiency gains *relative* to nonhierarchical teams, but the meaning of the Sen paradox is that no specialized hierarchy (satisfying universal domain) can be immune to the kind of social dilemmas it is intended to solve. The empirical literature on hierarchies – especially the literature of sociology and social psychology – is full of examples of inefficiencies, often called "bureaucratic dysfunctions." While the behavioral literature on bureaucratic dysfunctions does not often describe it this way, the inefficiency generally arises when various subunits of the organization pursue their own interests within their traditionally defined spheres of delegated authority.

89

Managerial dilemmas

Inefficiencies in multidivision firms

A classic example of self-interested subunit behavior aggregating to inefficient bureaucratic behavior, as predicted by the Sen paradox, can be found in the multidivision firms created in the mid-twentieth century. Chandler's discussion of these firms, referred to in Chapter 3, shows why the creation of a division structure in large firms was virtually an inevitable result of the inability of centralized executives to coordinate product lines across functional departments. The multidivision firm solves this problem neatly, but opens the door to other kinds of problems.

Chandler describes the vigorous decentralization of Sears under General Wood in the thirties and forties. The Sears stores were divided among five regional divisions – virtual fiefdoms – that were granted complete operating autonomy:

In the spirit of decentralization, each vice-president in charge of one of the five sovereign territories developed his own administrative procedures. Each had authority to design and "drop" his own new stores. They could take out bank loans at will. They protected the right of local store managers to price the goods and select the things they wanted to carry from the warehouses. They could structure a staff around themselves in whatever way they liked, and even after the territories each employed over fifty thousand people, the territory kings preferred to dole out raises and bonuses personally to even the most junior executives. The territories had gained so much control over company communications that corporate directives from Chicago were rewritten when they weren't thrown away. Muscle flexing in the form of subverting the slightest hint of administrative control from the Parent organization became a regular Field pastime. (Katz 1987: 17)

This attitude was passed down to individual store managers as well.

Decentralization was pursued even within the central organization. The buyers handling different product lines were expected to develop an intuitive feel for what would sell in middle America and were granted a great deal of autonomy in pursuing "hunches" that the central staff would not presume to second-guess. Sears buyers were known to sign enormous contracts with small-time entrepreneurs – turning them overnight into huge manufacturing enterprises like Schwinn Bicycles and Whirlpool (Katz 1987: 33). When one buyer invested in kerosene refrigerators that turned out to heat rather than cool food, he thought he would be fired. Instead, General Wood assured him: "A buyer has to venture. I hope you don't lose such a sum again, but I don't want this experience to inhibit you. You have to venture. A good Sears buyer has to assume the risks" (34).

This grant of operational autonomy in the field and among the central buyers encouraged a vigorous pursuit of profits at each of these levels. However, it was not clear whether the pursuit of profits in each store, region, and buying line would necessarily be efficient for Sears as a whole. By the early seventies, profits and market share were dropping in the face of competition from chain discount stores and even from the small shops in the shopping malls that Sears anchored. A share of Sears stock fell from $90 in 1974 to $60 in 1975.

The problem that began to emerge in the seventies had the common feature that some eminently rational behavior by a subunit carried large negative externalities for the firm as a whole. For instance, individual store managers were frequently tempted to use illegal "bait-and-switch" marketing techniques in which customers were lured into a store by advertised low prices on individual items, only to be told that the store was "temporarily sold out" of those items and offered higher-priced goods. Because of the company's long-term reputation for integrity, customers were willing to believe that individual Sears stores were operating in good faith. However, that reputation was an exhaustible good that could ultimately be used up by the self-interested actions of some of the managers. Individual store managers were free-riding on the Sears reputation for integrity, and the cumulative effect was to erode the value of that asset. The result was a bait-and-switch scandal in the fall of 1973, culminating in a complaint by the Federal Trade Commission.

At the same time, Sears was charged with racial and sexual discrimination in hiring; the hiring procedure, like individual store advertising policy, was highly decentralized: "Over a thousand people spread all over the country [could] hire people as they each saw fit" (Katz 1987: 24). The central executives were embarrassed, in no small degree because of their own powerlessness:

They also knew that despite government threats, they could do little to stop the practices. So much power had been ceded downward from level to level, from territory to group to store, that no officer in Chicago or even the territory kings could make local store managers do much of anything at all. (24–5)

The same decentralization was creating inefficiencies in the central staff units. Sears was among the last retailers to move into the use of computers simply because the vice-president of operations had complete authority to make the decision, and he wanted nothing to do with the "goddamned newfangled things" (28). The delegation of authority in Sears was resulting in a firmwide "social dilemma" in which self-interested, protective actions by a variety of store officials were aggregating to outcomes that all could agree were disastrous.

Horizontal conflict at Sears

Both the field and the buyers' organization had an enviable record in socializing their members. The field members were convinced that they were the lifeblood of Sears, the people who hustled the goods and brought in the money. They believed that sales personnel needed a free hand if their instinctive feel for the territory and its customers was to be fully effective. The field valued the "merchant" –

a sales soldier with wings, a sort of retail mystic, who could see a sale coming a mile off. A great merchant could look at an item and know in a glance how many Americans would want to buy it – and the best of the great ones wouldn't ever be able to tell you why. (Katz 1987: 31)

The merchants of the field considered themselves superior to the buyers in the Sears Tower. In the decentralized world of Sears, there was no hierarchical relationship between the field and the buyers – the merchants in the different regions were not forced to carry the goods purchased by the buyers. Theirs was essentially a horizontal, market relationship. But the buyers on the other side of the internal market had a different set of values and beliefs:

If the store runners of the Field saw themselves as foot soldiers, . . . then the Sears buyers were like hunters. Discipline and conformity were subsumed in an appreciation of atavistic instincts, hunches, and tour-de-force gestures. Badges were won less for big dollar profits at the end of the year than for brilliantly conceived buys. (Katz 1987: 34)

As the last phrase suggests, the buyers were motivated in large part by the need to establish and enhance their professional reputation within the association of buyers – and this was not necessarily the same as doing what was best for Sears as a whole. For decades the buyers resisted the introduction of sophisticated market research, because their organization valued those who were gutsy enough to take large risks based on an instinctive "feel" for the industry.

Moreover, the tribal conflict between the field and the buyers did not always result in smooth communication, coordination, or planning between these two core subunits. For instance, the buyers, who exercised great market power in their purchases from Sears suppliers, were able to obtain many goods at very low prices, which meant that Sears stores could obtain goods cheaply, sell them at very low profits to a large number of customers, and still make large profits. The buyers looked good when they purchased goods that were sold in large quantities. However, the Sears field men often marked up the prices in the hopes of making greater profits (which made them look good), and sometimes this resulted in slow sales, making the buyers responsible for those purchases look bad. Thus, there was a long-standing and very costly conflict: buyers trying to force field men to "push the goods" through prolonged and low-priced sales, field men trying to keep local revenues as high as possible by marking up prices.

Eventually, the buyers contrived an ingenious way to obtain power over the field. They arranged with Sears suppliers, with whom they had very close relationships, to "overbill" the store managers. That is, the store managers were charged more than the Sears purchase price; the suppliers got the true purchase price and the difference went to the buyers in Chicago. For example, if Sears was buying a hammer for $10, the Sears store manager might have on his books a purchase at $12, and the Sears buyer would have the sum of $2, in what was known as a "599" account. The buyer would then distribute this money to different Sears store managers as he saw fit. Because the buyer controlled the distribution of this profit, however, he could use it to "bribe" store managers to put the goods that he was purchasing on sale, to advertise them heavily, and to keep them on sales for a prolonged period of time (Katz 1987: 54).

In effect, this represented a monopoly distortion of the market relationship between Sears buyers and stores. There was absolutely no guarantee, or any special reason to think, that this bribe money would be used by the Sears buyers to pursue profit-maximizing marketing strategies. It was simply used to enhance the prestige of the buyers within their professional domain. The buyer for washing machines might have a large "599" account as a result of his market power with respect to purchasers; he would use that account to promote advertising for washing machines, despite the fact that the advertising money would be much better spent on a less saturated market.

In fact, the "599" account was a major reason that decentralization came to an end at Sears. In the midseventies, the central office realized that Sears was losing market share to discount stores and mall boutiques and that Sears had no systematic or effective marketing response to this threat. Because the advertising and promotional budget in the field was supplemented in an unknown way by the "599" accounts, the center did not even have the information necessary to engage in effective planning. The vice-president of planning, Phil Purcell, found that the system

made it impossible to see which items were selling well in the Field or which buyers were buying well, because 599 dusted everyone's tracks. Purcell couldn't locate the real promotional costs of the goods or the costs of markups or markdowns. . . . He couldn't draw a bead on market share. Every numerical indicator was tainted by politics and history and held close to the vests of guys named Doc and Charlie. (Katz 1987: 85)

The "599" account system and the decentralized autonomy of the field and buyers were rooted out during a long and painful process by a centralizing management in the late seventies and early eighties.

Inefficiency, transitivity, and decentralization

Given problems of this kind, the "bite" in the Sen dilemma is very real. At Sears, delegation had resulted in subunit vigor, but overall inefficiency. Restoring efficient practices would involve changing the pattern of delegation and decentralization that had been valued by the company for years.

93

Managerial dilemmas

The central executives obviously needed to intervene in the operations of the stores, to stop discriminatory hiring, and to bring to a halt the destructive bait-and-switch practices. This would require a constitutional change in corporate governance that would effectively eliminate local control over hiring and advertising practices. The process of implementing this constitutional change was begun with the appointment of reformer Ed Telling as the new chairman of the board in 1977. Telling undertook a "palace coup" that effectively eliminated the old autonomy of the field vice-presidents. He did this before he was even officially installed, by taking the unheard-of action of deposing the vice-president in charge of the Pacific division.

Dictatorship versus delegation

The analysis so far seems to leave us with two equally unacceptable choices: Centralized dictatorship is untenable because of its failure to generate sufficient diversity or sufficient problem-solving strategies; decentralized delegation is untenable because of free riding and destructive externalities. Is there any way out?

The Sen paradox offers one way – which will be explored in the remainder of this chapter and in succeeding chapters. The trade-off between delegation, efficiency, and transitivity occurs for only *some* of the combinations of individual preferences that may exist when members of an organization are allowed to articulate any of their individual preferences. It is the universal domain condition that necessitates this all-encompassing acceptance of individual preferences. For instance, if every individual in a firm always had identical preferences, then making decisions for the firm would be easy. Any set of decisions could be delegated to any subordinate with the assurance that efficient, transitive preferences would always result. If members of a hierarchy could be prevented from having problematic differences of opinion, there would be no dilemma: Hierarchies could resolve public goods inefficiencies, information asymmetries, and other market-confounding dilemmas with ease.

Of course, the same thing could be said of markets. They, too, could operate efficiently if we could be assured that people would not bring the "wrong" combinations of individual preferences to the marketplace. But the whole purpose of a market is the sovereignty of individual tastes: The market exists to respond to the preferences of the customer. The hierarchy, in contrast, does not operate on the basis of a philosophical dictum that employees' preferences, no matter how diverse, are inviolate.

Seen in this perspective, it is clear that in terms of efficiency, the advantage of the hierarchy over the market (if it in fact exists) exists because of the superior ability of the hierarchy to shape and mold individual preferences into patterns that are mutually consistent. We will explore the possibilities inherent in violating the condition of universal domain – that is, constraining or changing the preferences of the actors involved so that self-interested, decentralized action will not result in inefficient or intransitive group choice.

So far, in all of the discussion about inefficiency and intransitivity in decentralized organizations we have assumed that the condition of universal domain is not violated. That is, we have assumed that the organization's decision rule is defined for all possible sets of individual preferences. But what if the organization somehow violates this condition, by screening out the problematic sets of individual preferences? Does such a violation of the condition of universal domain offer hope for reconciling efficiency, stability, and delegation in hierarchies?

Restricting individual preferences is in fact the only way to combine the advantages of delegation in a hierarchy with the requirements of Pareto optimality and transitivity. The most obvious means for doing so is selection: choosing people who will have the "right" preferences.

Selection and adverse selection

In markets and electoral bodies, assuming such restrictions on individual preferences is simply inadequate if the assumption turns out to be false. If a consumer happens to object to another consumer's cigarette smoke or a voter happens to have multipeaked preferences, there is nothing to be done but give up on the certainty of efficient, stable equilibria. Neither a market nor a legislature can require its members to change their preferences.

In a hierarchy, however, restrictions on individual preferences are a frequent element of organizational design. Hierarchies take it upon themselves to select members who have compatible preferences. For instance, firms try to identify highly motivated, competitive individuals; such people, it is assumed, will be less likely to engage in the shirking that threatens to produce a social dilemma in every firm. The more the employee is expected to work autonomously, as a salesperson operating in the field, the more important such selection processes become.

The ability to select people who have a high preference for work, initiative, and loyalty is limited by the information asymmetries that were discussed in Chapter 1. The problem, of course, is the market-for-lemons problem. Let us assume that there are a large number of applicants for the position of sales representative for a firm. For some, such a job has great psychic costs. For others, not only are the psychic costs low, but many aspects of the job, including making a sale, are enjoyable.

By hiring people of the latter type, the firm gets more effort for the same pay. It would like to be able to identify such people with certainty; however, the information is in some sense internal to the applicants and undetectable. Hard-working applicants would like very much to prove their worth; however, any statements they might make regarding their enjoyment of work could as easily be made (falsely) by lazy applicants.

The result is that the market failure in the market for lemons is re-created in labor market failure. The firm would be willing to pay more for highly motivated workers or more productive workers, but cannot do so. As Spence (1974) has shown, the employer will pay each kind of employee the *expected* marginal product, which is the same for productive and nonproductive applicants – as long as there is no way of distinguishing one from the other.

Overcoming the information asymmetry: signaling and certification

Consequently, businesses would like very much to be able to overcome the information asymmetry that keeps them from selecting people with desirable utility functions. To the extent that they can identify the "hidden" types – hard workers and loyal employees – they can more confidently delegate authority to subordinates *without* triggering the Sen paradox results of inefficiency and/or intransitivity.

Just as a mechanic can offer his services to certify the value of a used car, thus ameliorating the information asymmetry problem in that market, there are various signals by which job applicants can certify their "type." Perhaps first and foremost is education. The salary that a graduate of an MBA program can secure is much higher than that which a high school graduate earns. Part of what is being paid for is training; but part is certi-fication of initiative and motivation. Similarly, previous work experience, even when irrelevant to a new job, demonstrates the capacity of an applicant to show up at work regularly and perform a minimum amount of work.

In the labor market for lemons, the psychologist is the closest analogue to the car mechanic. A psychological test, the Thematic Apperception Test, or TAT, is used to isolate a high need for achievement (n-ach) (McClelland 1961). Other tests have been developed to isolate a variety of desirable traits in employees. Sears, for example, gave a $50,000 grant to the famous University of Chicago psychology professor L. L. Thurstone to develop an examination for applicants. The examination tested for intelligence, but also for a "schedule of personality traits," asking "Do you like to hunt? Do you like to wrestle? Do you swear? Are you fidgety? Do you yell at games along with the crowd? Do you have trouble giving orders to servants?" (Katz 1987: 318).

The test was designed in part to decrease the effect of the adverse selection problem by identifying what would otherwise be "hidden" traits – laziness, dishonesty, disloyalty. The organization wanted employees who would work hard and would take the initiative for the good of the company. Tests such as this are quite simply a way of restricting individual preferences in order to reconcile decentralization, efficiency, and transitivity. If people with strong preferences for shirking are not allowed into the organization, problematic preference profiles will presumably not appear. Some work role autonomy can be granted to these individuals without automatically creating a social dilemma.

These certification devices, like the services of the auto mechanic, are expensive; their use represents the efficiency cost of solving the information asymmetry problem. As Spence points out, if education is costly, its use as an effective signal of positive attributes may make both highly motivated and undermotivated applicants worse off. It can make undermotivated employees worse off because they are now exposed as being what they are, but it can make highly motivated employees worse off because in equilibrium the cost of procuring an education is greater than the extra wages they can earn by being differentiated from undermotivated employees (Spence 1974: 20).

Ironically, however, selecting industrious, loyal individuals solves only one level of the Sen paradox. If two different subunits of an organization each select industrious individuals who are loyal to *subunit* goals and values, the Sen paradox can reemerge at a higher level in the organization, as the phenomenon sometimes called "tribal warfare" (Neuhauser 1988).

TRIBAL WARFARE

One of the most widespread phenomena in large-scale organizations is known as "tribalism" – conflict among organizational subunits having different sets of goals. Tribalism in organizations generally results in resources being wasted in the pursuit of conflict, lost opportunities due to forgone opportunities for cooperation, or instability as each organization responds in a self-interested way to other subunit actions.

Clearly, these are all manifestations of the Sen paradox writ large. Energetic pursuit of subgoals results in outcomes that are inefficient for the organization as a whole. And unfortunately, the organizational use of techniques of "restriction of individual preferences" does not solve this problem. Because it is the subunits of the organization that control the selection, recruitment, and socialization processes, it is these very processes that allow the subunit goals to be pursued vigorously and "selflessly" by subunit actors. Because the subunit recruitment and socialization are so successful, each subunit can be seen as a self-interested, maximizing rational actor with sufficient decentralized authority to bring about inefficiency and/or instability in organizational decision making.

Tribal conflict at Ford

After the young Henry Ford took over Ford Motor Company from his grandfather, he realized that he needed to hire subordinates with expertise. He managed to hire a good many talented individuals. Within a few years, however, those experts had evolved into warring factions whose energetic pursuit of subunit goals put the firm at risk.

Ford's executive vice-president, Ernie Breech, wanted to pursue a policy of decentralized, semiautonomous divisions, as had existed at General Motors. The first step in implementing this structure was to create a semiautonomous Ford Division, to which would later be added Lincoln–Mercury and other divisions. The man named to head the Ford Division, which originally constituted almost the entire Ford Motor Company, was Lewis Crusoe, a semiretired General Motors executive who was less a numbers man than a real car man, a man with gasoline in his veins, as they said in Detroit.

Within three months of setting Crusoe up, Breech realized that Crusoe's operational authority was almost as great as his own, and that Crusoe therefore posed a considerable challenge. At a meeting of the Product Planning Committee, with both Ford and Crusoe present, Breech tried to reclaim some of his authority. Crusoe immediately defended his terrain. He told the Planning Committee that he would accept advice but that he intended to "guard the independent thinking of the division as though it was an entirely separate company" (Collier and Horowitz 1987: 240). Since Crusoe by then had impressed Ford, and since Ford had himself been worried about how to control Breech, Crusoe succeeded. In the wake of this decision, Breech worriedly offered the analogy of football, suggesting that he would be coach and that Crusoe would be the quarterback calling his own plays. But Ford, as owner, had effectively created a competition between coach and quarterback in an attempt to retain his own control of the team. Whenever there was a conflict between Crusoe and Breech, Crusoe would appeal over his head to Ford, and generally win.

Breech, worried about the growing power of Crusoe, recruited Robert McNamara, future secretary of defense for the Kennedy administration, as his ally. McNamara was one of a group of "whiz kids" who had used sophisticated management and control techniques to oversee wartime production and been hired by Ford to help fill the expertise gap. Breech and McNamara had a shared interest because McNamara was trying to demonstrate the usefulness of advanced financial and accounting management techniques in the automobile industry, and Breech was looking for some way to contain Crusoe's power.

By contrast, Crusoe was the head of a growing group of old-time auto producers who hated the financial analysts like McNamara. They correctly pointed out that McNamara and his sort didn't know anything about cars or their appeal to the mass public. These subgroups tended to recruit entirely different kinds of employees. The production "tribe" under Crusoe contained the old-time engineers, craftsmen, and "car men" who had created the industry, and they tended to recruit engineers with similar orientations. The core belief of this group was that producing a well-made car and advancing the technology were the company's most important jobs.

The financial and accounting staff felt that holding costs down was the secret to making large profits. Therefore cost minimization, rather than technological advancement or automotive excellence, was the core value of this group. Scorned by the old-time production men as simple "bean counters" and "paper pushers," they nevertheless advanced rapidly to a position of strength at Ford under the leadership of Breech and McNamara.

Henry Ford delegated broad authority in the financial control area to Breech and the whiz kids, and he delegated operational control of the production of the postwar line of Fords to Crusoe. The problem was that these delegations of authority conflicted, as in the following case: Crusoe wanted to compete against the sportier and higher-priced lines of General Motors cars with a new car called the Thunderbird. McNamara and the finance people in the central office "said that the new car couldn't make money and tried to kill it by holding back funds for tooling" (Collier and Horowitz 1987: 245).

In this case Crusoe won; in other cases the whiz kids won. The point is that, as predicted by the Sen paradox, there was no guarantee that decisions optimal for the company as a whole would result from delegating financial and operational authority to two quite separate and committed subgroups. The conflict was always a source of instability and, often, inefficiency. Ford did not try to stop the conflict, because he felt that pitting one side against the other increased his own shaky authority.

One disaster produced by the conflict was the Continental Mark II. The original idea behind the Continental was that it would not necessarily make money itself, but that it would facilitate the marketing of the entire line of Ford cars. The Continental was to be such an attractive top-of-the-line car that it would draw people into Ford dealerships, and they might then end up buying a Ford instead of a Chevrolet.

But the Continental became identified with the Crusoe faction at Ford, and it became fair game for the Breech–McNamara faction. Breech made a series of decisions – for instance, refusing, in the name of cost cutting, to allow a four-door version of the car to be made – that made it much less attractive to the high-income families who were the intended buyers. The net result was that just enough money was invested in the Continental to make sure that it would be a big loser, but not enough for it to serve the marketing purpose for which it was intended.

For several years, Crusoe's authority grew as he continued to make money for the firm. As his authority grew, he became bolder, and Henry's support for Crusoe against Breech became more enthusiastic (Collier and Horowitz 1987: 247). As a sign of Crusoe's increasing authority, he developed what came to be known as the "Big Plan," a scheme for creating several new divisions at Ford to compete with the more expensive lines of General Motors. Some divisions would create new Mercurys, Lincolns, and Continentals, while another one would create a totally new car. Crusoe was careful to get Ford excited about the plan and to make sure that everyone in the company knew that Ford supported it before it came up for general discussion. Because Ford was known to favor the plan, all of the people who would normally have voiced reservations about it turned into yes men. At the meeting of the Product Planning Committee in 1955, Breech was the only person to raise his hand against it. The result was the Edsel, which turned out to be a financial disaster for Ford. Once again, enthusiastic pursuit of "tribal" goals shattered coherent planning and limited overall efficiency.

CONCLUSION

The approach taken in this chapter suggests that, as long as hierarchies have more than one subordinate unit in an organization, each capable of determining some aspect of the organization's behavior, they may be subject to the same problems of inefficiency and incoherence that have been more extensively studied in voting, committee, and legislative contexts.

Nondictatorship, efficiency, and transitivity can be reconciled, but only if unrealistic assumptions are made regarding restrictions on individual preferences. As long as individuals value leisure or have their own policy preferences, shirking or "deviationism" will have the potential to produce inefficiencies or instabilities in otherwise homogeneous teams or in simple hierarchies. Multiple specialized subordinates and experts compound the problem by building in additional pluralism of values within the organization and by reinforcing the decentralized decision rules that give subordinate units the ability to determine aspects of the organization's overall behavior. Each of the traditional Weberian elements of bureaucracy – hierarchy, specialization, and expertise – presents a new manifestation of the Sen paradox.

Hierarchy seems to offer no magic solution to the problems that have been studied extensively in legislatures regarding the collective consumption of goods with externalities. In bureaucracies, as in other social choice mechanisms, there must be a trade-off between desirable characteristics. In particular, if we want any degree of decentralization in hierarchies, we cannot guarantee that stable choices will be efficient, or that efficient choices will be stable.

As the structure of the Sen paradox reveals, the only way around this problem is to violate the condition of universal domain. Substantively, this means that, in order to have stable, efficient, delegated decision making, organizations must guarantee that individuals do not present problematic combinations of individual preferences to the organization. In other words, individuals must present "coherent" preferences. Individuals with preferences that will create problematic preference profiles must be eliminated from the organization or convinced to change their preferences.

As a result, organizations use selection and socialization to screen out individuals with problematic preferences. There is no doubt that these techniques allow for a greater degree of coherence and efficiency in organizational decision making than would otherwise be the case. However, there is also little doubt that these techniques are insufficient by themselves to eliminate the problematic preference profiles. For one reason, "adverse selection" problems make it difficult to measure the most important characteristics of potential recruits.

Just as important, however, the selection and socialization processes are for the most part conducted by organizational subunits. As a result, large organizations must still concern themselves with the Sen paradox.

What tools does this leave the central hierarchy of a large, specialized organization? Probably the most fundamental tool is the incentive system. In terms of the Sen paradox, an incentive system may be thought of as a violation of the condition of universal domain for the purpose of reconciling transitivity, efficiency, and delegation. That is, an incentive system is intended to permit delegation without creating disunity or inefficiency. Rather than allowing people to articulate any set of preferences in an organization, an incentive system is used to shape and mold the "natural" preferences of risk-averse or lazy members and to control the centrifugal tendencies of autonomous subunits. The following three chapters will examine the possibilities and limits of incentives as ways of reconciling decentralization, coherence, and efficiency in organizations.

5

Vertical dilemmas
Piece-rate incentives and credible commitments

WITH JACK KNOTT

> The important result is the moderate level of reward and compliance in equilibrium, even though both individuals would be better off with a high degree of reward and a high degree of compliance. The Pareto optimal result is not achieved because both superior and subordinate have an incentive to break away from it. The supervisors quite naturally have an incentive to give less than the maximum reward to the subordinates, and the subordinates quite naturally have an incentive to float through their work situation with less than 100 percent effort.
>
> Miller (1977: 50)

While it is necessary to delegate authority to individuals with specialized knowledge, that very delegation opens the door to incoherent organizational action. What is needed, therefore, is an incentive system that will encourage organizational specialists to use their knowledge in the coherent pursuit of organizational goals. An ideal incentive system will overcome information asymmetries and team production externalities, transforming an organizational social dilemma into an organizational "invisible hand." An incentive system should harness individual self-interest in pursuit of organizational goals.

Most hierarchies make little attempt to use their compensation systems to overcome the temptation of team members to shirk. Only 22 percent of U.S. workers feel that there is a direct connection between their effort and how much they are paid, despite the fact that 61 percent want their pay to be tied to their performance (Lawler 1987: 69–76). Most U.S. employees are paid on the basis of a flat wage fixed on the basis of seniority, rank, education, or another nonperformance variable; and firms that supposedly link pay to performance do a very poor job of establishing the link. Studies of "merit-based" compensation show that most people are ranked "above average" and that the differences in pay for superior performance are neglible (Lawler 1971; Baker, Jensen, and Murphy 1988).

How do rational individuals respond to an absence of a pay–performance link? Clearly, a wage system creates no special incentive for employees to increase their productivity. Individuals on a flat wage get no extra earnings when their output increases. Why do most profit-maximizing firms fail to establish a clearer link between pay and performance?

This chapter and the next two chapters will address this question in depth, arguing that the most fundamental reason for the failure to use incentives is the inevitable limits of any incentive system. Information asymmetries, monopoly, and team externalities make it impossible to reconcile hierarchical dilemmas by means of incentives. Self-interested behavior by employees in responding to incentives, and by employers in creating incentive systems, leads to inefficient firm outcomes. Incentive games in hierarchies constitute what I call a "vertical dilemma."

COSTLY EFFORT AS INFORMATION ASYMMETRY

Many conflicts in organizations stem from the fact that individual employees bear some private costs. Economists typically assume that each individual has an upward-sloping marginal cost-of-effort function in which earlier units of effort are less costly than later units; the individual finds that installing the first hub-caps on automobiles is less painful than installing the thousandth or millionth.

Why should additional units of labor be more costly to the individual? Effort involves the expenditure of energy; we have all been programmed by evolution to seek high-energy inputs (such as those with a high sugar content) and to avoid high-energy outputs (such as twenty-four hours of wind sprints). If individuals found wind sprints as intrinsically rewarding as sugar consumption (and vice versa), they would run an energy deficit and die. The first levels of effort, like jogging the first three or four miles, may be less costly, or even enjoyable. Nevertheless, any activity undertaken for a long enough time becomes monotonous, tiring, and eventually painful. Consequently, the assumption of upward-sloping marginal effort supply curves is probably the safest assumption economists make.

Although we may assume that unit effort costs are increasing, they cannot be directly observed by anyone other than the individual, any more than can the benefits of consumption. The unobservability of effort costs constitutes an information asymmetry in the market of labor. The latter part of this chapter deals with the strategic importance of this information asymmetry.

Managerial dilemmas

The forcing contract

Assume that one employee, with an upward-sloping marginal effort cost function, is employed by one employer. What would happen if the employer *knew* precisely the nature of the employee's effort cost function? This knowledge would be of great value to the employer. With it, he could calculate the level of subordinate effort that exactly maximized the potential profit: It would be the level of effort that maximized revenue less the effort cost of the employee.

As a simple illustration, suppose that the employee's marginal effort cost (MC) in the production of a certain number of units of some good Q were as follows:

$$MC = c + 2dQ.$$

The good could be sold by the employer at a fixed market price of p. Then the profit available to the firm would be maximized at the quantity at which $p = c + 2dQ$. In the absence of external job opportunities, the manager could conceivably achieve almost the entire surplus by means of a forcing contract. The forcing contract would pay the employee a total salary slightly in excess of the employee's total cost of effort at the efficient quantity, if and only if the employee supplied the efficient quantity of the good; otherwise, the employee would be paid nothing and would be fired. Presented with this choice, the employee would barely prefer to provide the efficient quantity of effort and would leave the employer with almost all of the surplus generated by that effort.

If the employee did have alternative job opportunities, as a result of a relatively free labor market and low job mobility costs, the minimum payment in the forcing contract for efficient levels of effort would have to be just larger than those available alternative payments, corrected for the costs of quitting and moving to another job. These alternatives would cut into the amount of profits available to the employer, without changing the form of the forcing contract.

Despite the fact that employee effort costs are ultimately private information, employers can, in stable situations, make educated guesses about what they are. Many firms hire a large number of industrial engineers, or time-and-motion study experts, who make educated guesses about what the efficient levels of effort must be. The more stable the technology and the more well known it is, the better these guesses will be.

As a result, those firms with the best information about employee effort costs may use something like the forcing contract. When the employee comes on the job, she is given a detailed description of the tasks that are expected of her. She is also told that if she fails to perform the task as described, she will be fired.

Limitations of the forcing contract

This kind of forcing contract works reasonably well when a given set of conditions apply. First, the costs of monitoring the detailed behavior of each subordinate must be reasonably low. Since the subordinate is in no way internally motivated to perform the task, it is to be expected that he will shirk at every opportunity.

Second, the job must be relatively stable. If the job changes frequently, the employee must be assigned a new set of detailed instructions, and perhaps trained to perform them, again with little or no motivation. Even more important, every time the task changes, the employee's personal effort cost function may have to be recalculated to determine exactly the optimal level of effort. This last point reemphasizes the fact that employees' effort cost functions are ultimately unknowable.

For the vast majority of tasks in real-world organizations, the conditions just stated do not hold. For any skilled job, it is impossible to specify ahead of time the exact order and technique involved. This is certainly true of white-collar jobs such as teaching and engineering, where the required technology is "inside the head" of the person hired to do the task. This is also the case for most skilled blue-collar jobs, for the same reason. Welding, dye making, carpentry, and plumbing are all tasks in which the technology is intrinsic to the individual job holder, rather than handed to the job holder in the form of an extensive job description.

Even for jobs in which the basic requirements can be specified, firms normally require of employees exceptional behaviors at appropriate times. Even the most elaborate contract for a welder or a salesperson cannot specify the appropriate response in all contingencies. Local conditions change, and employees must be able to respond instantaneously with the appropriate adjustment of the machinery or sales pitch.

This fact makes it is necessary to motivate, rather than program, the worker. In some organizations, an "incentive" contract, which is keyed to the performance of the worker, is the customary solution. This requires less extensive monitoring, less specification of expected behaviors, less coercive hierarchy, and less information by superiors about subordinate effort costs.

THE PIECE-RATE CONTRACT: THEORY AND EXPERIENCE

The piece-rate contract pays the employee an amount based on the number of units, or pieces, the employee produces. Under such a contract, the supervisor is largely freed from the burden of enforcing detailed rules and regulations on increasingly resentful employees. Rather, the supervisor is, ideally, a neutral person who measures individual output and pays accordingly. If the employee's performance drops, the supervisor need make no comment — the drop in performance carries its own punishment. If the employee deviates from standard operating procedures, he can himself determine whether such innovation was worthwhile or costly in terms of his own performance and pay. The theory of the piece-rate system is that it should align the self-interest of employees with organizational goals.

An incentive wage system has been advocated for a long time. Frederick Taylor, the father of scientific management, wrote an article titled "A Piece Rate System: A Step Toward Partial Solution of the Labor Problem" (1895). Ironically, it was advocated as a system that would make both workers and owners better off, but it was opposed by both sides (Nelson 1975: 53). Unions felt it would be an insidious way to get more work out of employees for less pay, while owners felt it diminished their authority. Overall, it was one of the least frequently adopted features of scientific management at the turn of the century (74–8). Nor has its use increased dramatically over this century. One reason for this has been the recognition that piece-rate systems often do not work as planned.

Most research on the piece-rate contract has revealed that implementing the system is fraught with problems. The problems were first, and perhaps best, illustrated by the cases discussed in sociologist William Whyte's classic study *Money and Motivation* (1955).

Whyte detailed the experiences of a graduate student named Donald Roy, who worked in a steel fabrication plant as a drill press operator. The incentive system at the plant was a standard variation of the piece-rate system. For each job, there was a "price" set by the industrial engineers, or "time-study men." Workers' individual earnings, in the upper range, were fixed by how many "pieces" they produced at this price. However, they were guaranteed an hourly rate of $.85 an hour, which set the lower bound of compensation. If the pieces they produced did not yield a level of pay that was greater than their guaranteed minimum, that was termed "not making out." If the pieces they produced yielded a level of pay that was greater than the minimum, that was known as "making out."

As might be guessed, this resulted in a great deal of strategic behavior on the part of the employees. If they felt that the "price" for their particular task was so low that they could never "make out," they had no incentive (beyond the threat of being fired) to produce anything at all. This was known as "goldbricking."

Goldbricking was, of course, a result of the guaranteed minimum pay rate. More interesting was a phenomenon known as "quota restriction," which was widespread within piece-rate organizations. Quota restriction occurs when a price is set high enough that it is relatively easy and in the self-interest of the employee to make out, earning more than the guaranteed minimum. But employees were very careful to limit how much they earned because of the widespread understanding that, if they earned too much, the time-study men would reevaluate the job and lower the price. Roy reported the following interaction:

Jack warned me that the Methods Department could lower their prices on any job, old or new, by changing the fixture slightly or changing the size of drill. According to Jack, a couple of operators (first and second shift on the same drill) got to competing with each other to see how much they could turn in. They got up to $1.65 an hour, and the price was cut in half. And from then on they had to run that job themselves, as none of the other operators would accept the job. (Whyte 1955: 23)

Similar social pressure to restrict output exists in a great many piece-rate organizations. Nor was Jack's warning unfounded. Managers habitually gave in to the temptation "to cut the rate so the wage earners, though producing more, would earn approximately what they had under day work" (Nelson 1975: 45). The problem was such that employers themselves urged one another to exercise self-restraint in cutting piece rates, so that employees would have no reason to engage in quota restriction. "Employers who gave the situation serious thought soon came to the conclusion that the solution lay in two areas: more care in rate fixing and a guarantee against rate cutting" (45).

The piece-rate system, which was intended to bring the simple rationality of market exchange inside the firm, now seems much more complicated. Employees threaten one another so that they do not work as hard as they can; employers warn one another not to engage in self-interested profit maximization. What role do threats and warnings have in what is supposed to be a simple payment scheme that relies on individual self-interest to motivate employees? Is this kind of behavior rational?

A MODEL OF PIECE-RATE GAMING

The inefficiencies and gaming of the piece-rate system can easily be understood in the context of a simple Stackelberg game. A Stackelberg game, unlike other games, assumes that one player, the leader, "moves" first, after which the follower chooses a maximizing, self-interested response.

In the piece-rate game, the leader may be thought of as management, which selects a piece-rate level. After this, the employee (follower) decides how many pieces to produce. These two decisions can be charted on the vertical and horizontal axes of a graph, as presented in Figure 5.1. What are the preferences of the two sides for the outcomes in this space? Figure 5.1 shows sample "indifference curves" for both employer and employee. That is, a given indifference curve for the employer connects sets of outcomes (outputs and piece rates) that produce exactly equal levels of profit for the employer, assuming that the employer can sell any quantity produced at a constant market price p. For simplicity, we assume that the only variable cost is the wage of the employee. Therefore, the profits of the leader are simply $(p - w) Q$, where w is the piece rate and Q is the quantity of pieces produced. This yields indifference curves (or, more properly, iso-profit curves) like those shown in Figure 5.1. As the lines indicate, the leader gets

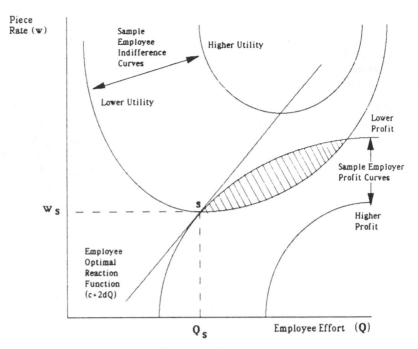

Figure 5.1. The Stackelberg equilibrium in a piece-rate game.

the most profit in the lower-right-hand corner, where she is able to sell a large number of pieces that are procured at a low piece rate.

Similarly, a given indifference curve for the employee connects all those points that generate a constant level of net benefit, where net benefit is defined as total wages less the (psychic) cost of production. The employee is assumed to have an increasing marginal cost of effort given by

$$MC(Q) = c + 2dQ.$$

The follower's net benefit, then, is the difference between the wages earned (wQ) and the total cost of effort (which is $cQ + dQ^2$). These assumptions yield indifference curves in the effort–wage space as shown. The employee is best off working moderately hard at high wage rates.

For any given piece rate, the follower can easily determine the optimal number of pieces to produce by producing until the marginal cost of effort exactly equals the wage. This means that the employee reaction function shown in Figure 5.1 indicates the employee's optimal number of units to be produced for any given wage rate. For any point on this line, the employee's indifference curve will be tangent to the horizontal line (piece rate), indicating that the employee can achieve no higher level of net benefit by producing more or less.

108

If the employer chooses any possible piece rate, the employee will therefore select the level of effort given by the effort supply curve in the graph. The employer's maximization problem is therefore constrained by this line. Which point on the effort supply curve yields the most profits? The leader's maximizing choice will be determined by the point of tangency between the reaction line and the highest possible iso-profit line. This is shown as point *S* in Figure 5.1.

This outcome is a Stackelberg equilibrium. Given the wage rate associated with point *S*, the employee has no incentive to produce more or less. The employer has no incentive to change the piece rate, as any other piece rate will result in lower profits. It is a stable outcome. However, is it efficient?

Clearly, it is not. The employee's indifference curve through *S* is tangent to a horizontal line, while the employer's indifference curve through *S* is tangent to the upward-sloping marginal effort cost line. Therefore, the two players' indifference curves through *S* must cross that point. There must be a region in which both the employee and the employer can be better off. The region is given by the shaded area interior to both indifference curves through *S*. This area consists of outcomes in which the employee works harder than he has any incentive to do, given the employer's piece rates, and in which the employer sets a higher piece rate than she has any reason to do. In other words, every such Pareto-preferred point is unstable. The fact that both the employee and the employer can perceive that there are piece-rate–effort level combinations that would make both sides better off accounts for the frustrating feeling of underefficiency that permeates the literature on piece rates.

Employee misrepresentation

What theoretical possibilities are open to employees under such a system? One possibility is strategic misrepresentation of the employee response curve. Suppose, for instance, that employees decide not to work as hard, at any piece rate, as they would if they were to maximize their net benefit. This would seem, by definition, to be irrational. But such a strategy, systematically and uniformly held to, would force the employer to respond to quite a different reaction function, as shown in Figure 5.2.

If the employer were forced to respond to the reaction as shown in the figure, her profit-maximizing response would be to set wage rate w_T rather than w_S. This would result in a (pseudo-) Stackelberg equilibrium of point *T*. This would not necessarily be more efficient than the original Stackelberg equilibrium; in fact, it would be less efficient in this case. However, it would result in a sizable redistribution of surplus from the employer to the employee.

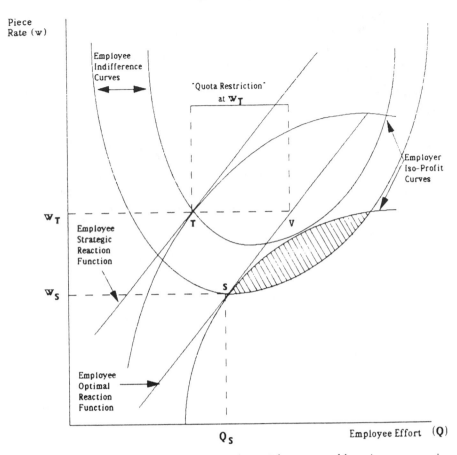

Figure 5.2. Redistribution of gains in employees' favor caused by misrepresentation of the employee reaction function.

What would it take to achieve outcome T instead of S? It would require employee self-control because, at the higher "pseudo-equilibrium" piece rate, individual employees could benefit by producing off the misrepresented reaction curve at point V. Doing so, however, would reveal to the employer that the false reaction function was in fact false and would encourage the employer to cut piece rates. Outcome T could not be maintained without quota restriction.

Group norms and quota restriction

The employees who were trying to engage in quota restriction in order to maintain outcome T, especially those working different shifts on the same machine, would realize that any one person's demonstration of productivity could spoil the strategy for all. Consequently, the individuals in a work group would be in a prisoners' dilemma, in which each worker would, in the short run, face a temptation to work *harder* than the level of effort indicated by the misrepresented reaction function; the group benefits of outcome T could be maintained only through the sanctions available to the small work group. These norms are clearly illustrated by Donald Roy's experience:

From my first to my last day at the plant I was subject to warnings and predictions concerning price cuts. Pressure was the heaviest from Joe Mucha, a day man on my machine, who shared my job repertoire and kept a close eye on my production. . . . Joe Mucha advised: "Don't let it go over $1.25 an hour, or the time-study man will be right down here! And they don't waste time, either!" . . . Jack Starkey spoke to me after Joe left. "What's the matter? Are you trying to upset the applecart?" (Whyte 1955: 23)

At Roy's plant, group norms sanctioning quota restriction were 100 percent effective. The distribution of the earnings made by different individuals during Roy's time there was truncated, with more than 60 percent of the employees making out and more than 50 percent earning in the range of $1.25 to $1.34. However, *no one* dared to earn more than the socially acceptable $1.34 rate. There were no "rate busters"; "such behavior was distinctly frowned upon and men who violated the group's standards would at least be ostracized from the group if not more severely punished" (Whyte 1955: 21–4).

The effort bargain

Not only could quota restriction be used to maintain favorable piece rates, but the strategies described in the Stackelberg game were used to raise unfavorable prices. One such situation involved Jack Starkey and Ed Sokolsky, who were assigned the task of making hinge bases. This task was known as a "stinker," with a price of twenty-three cents. As a result Ed, Jack, and the other workers on the task engaged in a deliberate slowdown in an attempt to raise the price. "Ed and Jack asked for a price of 38 cents. Ed said that they could turn out 3 an hour, but, until they got a decent price, they were turning out 2 an hour" (Whyte 1955: 24). The techniques used to enforce this slowdown were imaginative:

Ed seems to have constant trouble with his jig, a revolving piece attached to the side of the table. Two disks seem to stick together, and Ed is constantly (every day or so) using the crane to dismantle the jig (a very heavy one). He sands the disks and oils them, taking several hours for the cleaning operation. Steve [the foreman] saw the dismantled jig again tonight and bellowed, "Again?" Steve does not like it. (Whyte 1955: 25)

The slowdown, which began in December, was wearing on the individuals involved by May. One worker complained that Jack had turned out twenty-eight hinge bases in one day. "That's too many, nearly 3 an hour. He'll have to watch himself if he expects to get a raise in price." It was not until August that the workers won a raise in piece rate from twenty-three cents to twenty-eight cents. At this rate, they still felt they could not make out and continued to restrict output. In the end, the final price was thirty-one cents per unit, and the employees turned in almost four pieces an hour, for hourly earnings of $1.20 (Whyte 1955: 25–6).

Management's resources

Management, of course, was not powerless in this effort bargain. First of all, it tried to encourage individuals not to give in to social pressure, so that effort costs could be more accurately determined. One new man, Orvis Collins, reported that the introductory talk the factory superintendent gave each new employee was basically intended to encourage competition among the workers, as a way of fighting quota restriction norms. "He told us about how the piecework system was set up so that nobody could hang on anybody else's shirt tail. He said it was every man for himself" (Whyte 1955: 11).

In addition to this basically exhortatory technique, management has another method for fighting effort restriction norms – time and motion studies. The strategic importance of this is to provide independent information about the levels of output workers should be able to achieve. In Whyte's study, group norms for misinforming the time-study man were fully as important as group norms concerning goldbricking. Starkey, an old hand, briefed Tennessee, a newcomer:

"If you expect to get any kind of a price, you got to outwit that son-of-a-bitch! You got to use your noodle while you're working, and think your work out ahead as you go along! You got to add in movements you know you ain't going to make when you're running the job! Remember, if you don't screw them, they're going to screw you!"

"I don't see how I could of run it any slower," said Tennessee. "I stood there like I was practically paralyzed."

"Remember those bastards are paid to screw you," said Starkey. "And that's all they got to think about. They'll stay up half the night figuring out how to beat you out of a dime. They figure you're going to try to fool them, so they make allowances for that. They set the prices low enough to allow for what you do."

"Well, then, what the hell chance have I got?" asked Tennessee.

"It's up to you to figure out how to fool them more than they allow for." (Whyte 1955: 15)

Consequently, Starkey was one of the heroes of the plant; he was a man who knew how to burn up a drill whenever the time study men asked him to pick up the speed (he used touched-up drills):

Ray knew all the tricks! I used to have to laugh at the way he got up a sweat when they were timing him. He'd jump around the machine like a monkey on a string, with the sweat just pouring off him! His shirt used to get soaking wet, and he'd have to wring it out afterwards! And when they finished timing him, he'd stagger away from the machine a little, like he'd given everything he had in him. . . . I never did see Ray sweat a drop when he was actually running a job; he was always about 40 pounds overweight, the laziest guy I ever did see. (Whyte 1955: 17)

The gaming in the piece-rate system thus centers on the issue of information asymmetry, with managers never being quite sure what the employee marginal cost of effort functions are and employees systematically trying to protect that information asymmetry (Kilbridge 1960). As Starkey told Tennessee:

"Remember those guys don't know their ass from a hole in the ground as far as these machines are concerned. When they tell me to speed up to about what I figure I can run the job, I start to take my apron off, and tell them, 'All right, if you think it can be run that fast, you run it!' They usually come around." (Whyte 1955: 16)

This kind of strategic misuse of information is not unusual. On the contrary, as psychologist Ed Lawler (1987) has noted:

Employees engage in numerous behaviors in order to have rates set in such a way that they can maximize their financial gains relative to the amount of work that they have to do. They engage in behaviors such as working at slow rates in order to mislead the time study expert when he or she comes to study their job. They hide new work methods or new procedures from the time-study person so the job will not be restudied. In addition, informal norms develop within the organization about how productive people should be with the result that the workers themselves set limits on production. Anyone who goes beyond this limit may be ostracized or punished. . . . In summary, piece-rate plans often result in an adversarial relationship between those on the plan, and those designing and administering the plan. The result is that both sides often engage in practices designed to win the game or war at the cost of organizational effectiveness. (70–1)

This description by a psychologist is of interest because he is clearly trying to portray the piece-rate game as a social dilemma. Employees are, he believes, engaged in "maximizing" behavior; both sides try to "win the war at the cost of organizational effectiveness." The simple piece-rate system engenders the kind of conflict between individual rationality and group well-being that hierarchies were designed to eliminate.

WHEN DO PIECE RATES WORK? A COMMITMENT MODEL

The reality of piece-rate hierarchies often bears little resemblance to the ideal — motivating employees to high levels of effort and providing employers with the valuable information about effort costs necessary to make efficient decisions. Are there any instances of piece rates working the way they are supposed to? What conditions might allow that to occur?

The basic problem with piece rates is that employees believe that employers will inevitably adjust piece rates downward in response to high salaries. Employers are aware that this is the problem, and consequently are aware,

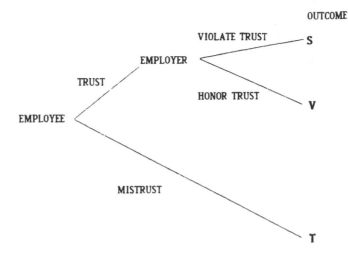

Figure 5.3. The piece-rate game as a commitment problem. Employer's outcome ranking: $S > V > T$. Employee's outcome ranking: $V > T > S$. (Refer to Figure 5.2 for a graph of these outcomes; T represents a Pareto-suboptimal Nash equilibrium.)

at an abstract level, that the solution is to make a credible commitment not to lower piece rates to keep payments comparable to the going day rate – in other words, to offer "a guarantee against rate cutting" (Nelson 1975: 45).

But visualizing the solution to the piece-rate dilemma is not the same as implementing it. The problem is captured by a simple game-theoretic model called the "commitment problem," due to Kreps (1984). In the commitment problem, as shown in Figure 5.3, an employee has a choice of trusting or not trusting the superior. In the piece-rate context, to "trust" means to reveal fully the employee reaction function rather than engage in quota restriction. To "mistrust" means to engage in quota restriction, which in terms of Figure 5.3 would result in outcome T.

If the employee trusts the superior, the superior has a choice of honoring or violating that trust. Again, in the context of the piece-rate game, to "violate trust" means to use the information revealed by the employee to cut piece rates to a minimum, while firing excess employees generated by the full effort of employees. This can be regarded as outcome S. To "honor trust" means not to lower piece rates in response to a good effort by employees and to provide some security against employees working themselves out of a job, which is pictured in Figure 5.3 as outcome V.

The superior has an incentive to violate that trust, which would leave the subordinate worse off than if he failed to trust the superior. Consequently, the subordinate refuses to trust the employer, which results in outcome T. But this leaves both worse off than outcome V, the outcome available if the subordinate were trusting and the superior were trustworthy.

In this game, the superior could visualize that both would be better off if she could commit herself to honoring the employee's trust. However, such a commitment would not be credible since it would not be in the superior's self-interest to keep the commitment once the employee had chosen to give the superior the opportunity to live up to the commitment. The problem is how to produce a commitment that is credible.

In the context of the piece-rate game, employers may realize that both sides could be better off if they, the employers, could credibly commit themselves to not cutting the piece rates. But the difficulty is finding an appropriate way to bind themselves to that commitment, since employers inevitably have an incentive to lower piece rates once employees trust them by revealing effort costs. Labor contracts cannot be written to specify piece rates for specific jobs, since the jobs themselves are constantly changing. Roy reported, "Jack warned me that the Methods Department could lower their prices on any job, old or new, by changing the fixture slightly or changing the size of the drill" (Whyte 1955: 23). Thus, there is no outside agency like the courts to enforce a commitment by the employer to a specific piece rate.

Furthermore, not only would a legal challenge to a change in piece rates be expensive, but it would have little chance in the courts, where the "business judgment" rule protects the rights of employers to make such adjustments based on their responsibility to shareholders to use their best business judgment.

Even if the commitment problem with respect to particular piece rates were solved, the same general problem would arise with regard to long-term employment. If employees were to exert themselves under a given piece-rate system, productivity would increase; employees could then expect that employers would have an incentive to fire a proportion of the employees as a result of these productivity increases. It would seem that, for piece rates to have the desired effect on productivity, employees would need assurances about continued employment.

A failure of commitment

One striking example of the strength of the pressures generating a "no trust – no honor" equilibrium is provided by Alex Bavelas and George Straus in their classic work *Money and Motivation* (1955). The Hovey and Beard Company manufactured toys, and one group of women had the job of painting them. At one point, the firm switched from hand painting to a technology based on an endless chain of hooks, from which individuals would remove toys, spray paint them, and replace them on the hooks. This change in technology was accompanied by a piece-rate bonus and a learning bonus, which was intended to motivate an eager and effective response to the new technology. However, production levels were far below those the company had anticipated. The women complained about the speed of the chain of hooks, the messiness, and the poor ventilation.

The foreman, with encouragement from a consultant, agreed to a meeting with the eight workers. After hearing their complaints, the foreman had several talks with engineers and the plant superintendent, who were skeptical of the women's complaints. After a while, however, the foreman succeeded in obtaining fans to alleviate the ventilation problem. The women were elated and spent a great deal of time deciding on the right locations for the fans. Their morale and production went up, and discussions with the foreman continued.

Encouraged, the foreman continued the process of negotiation on other issues and finally managed to get permission for an experiment in which the women would control the speed of the hooks. The women experimented with varying the speed, making it somewhat lower early in the morning, for instance, and setting it at its highest point in the middle of the morning. Once again, morale went up and production increased. After the women got control of the speed of the hooks, their production was up to 50 percent above that expected before the new technology went into effect. Their earnings were higher than expected due to the piece-rate bonus and the learning bonus. In fact, the women were earning more than some of the skilled workers in the plant, who complained vigorously to management. Cost accountants were no doubt complaining that the wages paid to these women were way out of line with those the firm paid for comparably skilled jobs and were much higher than the women could get for comparable jobs in different firms.

The plant managers now faced the common temptation of all managers who use a piece-rate bonus plan to increase output. Now that the women were working hard, their earnings were up. The information that was needed about possible production levels had been obtained. Profits would be even higher if production were kept at the current level and the piece-rate bonus reduced. This would not only increase profits, it would also decrease the political hassle caused by paying the women more than the skilled male workers in the plant.

As a result, the managers revoked the learning bonus and the workers' control over the speed of the hooks. Production dropped immediately, and within a month six of the eight women quit. The foreman, who had in effect represented the management to the workers, felt aggrieved and left for another job as well.

Piece-rate success through commitment: Lincoln Electric Company

The short-term temptation to use information gained from highly motivated employees under the piece-rate system to keep wages low can be overwhelming. Nevertheless, a few tantalizing cases of successful piece-rate management suggest that the problems of credible commitment are not impossible to overcome.

The Lincoln Electric Company is a highly successful manufacturer of arc welders located in Cleveland. It is a small company with a record of constant productivity improvements that allowed it to squeeze General Motors out of the arc-welding business and maintain a large market share in an old-fashioned, low-technology industry (Baldwin 1982: 50).

The key to Lincoln's success is that its employees, unlike those at most other piece-rate companies, are convinced that their employers will neither lower piece rates nor fire excess workers if they work their hardest, earn high wages, and increase productivity. The managers of Lincoln Electric know that this is the key to their own success. One said:

When we set a piecework price, that price cannot be changed just because, in management's opinion, the worker is making too much money. Whether he earns two or three times his normal amount makes no difference. Piecework prices can only be changed when management has made a change in the method of doing that particular job and under no other conditions. If this is not carried out 100 percent, piecework cannot work. (Fast 1975: 4–5)

The employees at Lincoln Electric, unlike those at Roy's piece-rate company, accept that policy as a fact, and are highly motivated and productive. Productivity has been twice that of other manufacturers since 1945. Wages (including bonuses) averaged $44,000 in 1981 (Baldwin 1982: 50); by 1988, individual earnings were more than $80,000 for hard workers who didn't mind working overtime (Posner 1988: 95). Employees engage in little or none of the strategic misrepresentation of effort cost functions that is typical of most piece-rate plants, and there are no reported norms against rate-busting.

On the contrary, it is generally recognized that workers have an incentive to improve the technology in small and large ways:

If he can re-arrange his work space or tasks to get a job done faster, he is free to do so – and will pocket more money. The company doesn't object if someone figures out a way to beat the times figured into the piecework rates, since the higher volume will spread overhead costs over more pieces. The worker will get rich, but so will the company. Or the worker could turn in a suggestion for restructuring the job, losing the piecework windfall but gaining bonus points in return. Bonuses, awarded for teamwork and reliability, average something close to 100% of base pay in most years, but vary widely from worker and worker. (Baldwin 1982: 52)

The management constantly has to withstand a temptation that other firms give in to. For example, when the economy heads down, there is pressure to reexamine whether employees are getting paid too much. This pressure is likely to be accentuated by the fact that the employees have nice cars, earn more income than comparably skilled employees in the same urban area, and at times even make more than managers. Shareholders can point out that, in any given year, dividends could be higher if piece rates were simply adjusted downward to make salaries more comparable to those of other firms in the region. But all of these pressures are steadfastly withstood by Lincoln Electric, unlike Hovey and Beard.

Furthermore, employees have a job guarantee, despite the fact that demand for arc welders is highly responsive to business cycles. Founder James Lincoln clearly understood the incentive effects of this guarantee:

Laying off the worker because of slackening of business is death to efficiency. No worker will strive for efficient production when his very efficiency will throw him out on the street that much sooner, and no sane man would expect him to do so. Naturally, he will strive to spin out the job as long as he can, by any means he can think of. Anyone else in his place would do the same thing, including the manager, who now, because of habit, follows the program of laying off when work is slack – or whenever it is more convenient for the manager than accepting responsibility would be. (Lincoln 1961: 80)

During the deep recession in the early eighties, this policy was strained to the limit, when every market the company sold in collapsed and overall revenue fell 40 percent. The company trained some production people to sell, and put others on maintenance crews, and refused to fire anyone. Hourly earnings were cut in half, but the company managed to make a profit even during the worst year of the recession, and so the company paid dividends as usual and paid bonuses to employees that averaged 55 percent of salaries (Posner 1988: 96).

The managers at Lincoln Electric are in effect honoring the trust that employees have vested in them by revealing private information about maximal effort levels. How a firm like Lincoln Electric manages to commit itself credibly not to exploit this trust, and how it manages to convey this commitment to the employees, is the primary topic of the last third of this book. For now, it is sufficient to point out that solving this problem of commitment goes far beyond the simple mechanical process of setting incentives and monitoring effort.

CONCLUSION: BEYOND PIECE-RATE
INCENTIVE CONTRACTS

The piece-rate story is a simple one, but it nevertheless provides insight into the effort bargaining that characterizes labor–management relations at a good many firms. It raises the possibility that the Alchian and Demsetz solution to team shirking – efficiency through hierarchical monitoring and incentives – will not be easily achieved. Even though managers may have the expertise of time-and-study engineers at their disposal, the self-interested behavior of employees and managers under the institution of the piece-rate contract leaves them far short of the potential efficiency gains from hierarchy. Both subordinates and superiors could be better off if subordinates worked harder and superiors fixed higher piece rates than either side has an incentive to do on its own. Self-interested behavior in the hierarchy leads to a vertical social dilemma.

While the analysis of piece rates is a valuable way to introduce the question of efficient incentive setting, the next step is to ask whether there is not a more efficient incentive system. The next chapter undertakes a more general review of incentives and contracts. The fundamental discovery is that information asymmetry, monopsonistic behavior by employers in labor markets, and team production externalities combine to confound the search for hierarchical efficiency in incentives.

While it is easy to construct an incentive system in the absence of information asymmetry, monopoly pricing, or team production externalities, this simply tells us that hierarchies work well under the same conditions that promote market efficiency. The problem is discovering incentives that insulate hierarchy from the deleterious effects of team production externalities, monopolistic exchange, and information asymmetry.

6

Hidden action in hierarchies
Principals, agents, and teams

> As long as we insist on budget-balancing [in our system of incentives]
> and there are externalities present, we cannot achieve efficiency. Agents
> can cover improper actions behind the uncertainty concerning who was
> at fault. Since all agents cannot be penalized sufficiently for a deviation
> in the outcome, some agent always has an incentive to capitalize on this
> control deficiency.
>
> Holmstrom (1982)

If hierarchies are going to reconcile efficiency, transitivity, and minimal delegation in their decision making, they can do so only by manipulating individual preferences. The piece-rate system discussed in the preceding
chapter is one example of an incentive system that attempts to manipulate
individual preferences in such a way that crafts persons with specialized
skills can be delegated autonomy with regard to many production
decisions.

The piece-rate system seems to perform that function only partially, at
best. The use of individual incentives of this sort seems only to dramatize
and enhance the underlying conflict of interests in hierarchy. Theoretically,
there is very good reason for this – the piece-rate system is a vertical manifestation of the Sen paradox within hierarchy. The subordinate chooses
how hard to work, and the superior chooses the piece-rate wage – this constitutes sufficient "delegation" to kick off the Sen paradox. As long as individuals have upward sloping supply functions for their individual effort,
the resulting game will be inefficient or unstable.

But perhaps the problem with the piece-rate system is the limited nature
of the contracts available. After all, the piece-rate system is based on a fixed
payment per unit of output; this sharply constrains the set of incentive
systems that one can imagine. Perhaps a more creative incentive system
could reshape individual preferences sufficiently to reconcile individual

self-interest and group efficiency. Is there some unconstrained incentive system that will guide individually self-interested actors to efficient outcomes? Is there an incentive system that will create an invisible hand in a hierarchical organization? The answer, as one might expect, is that it depends. The nature of the qualifying conditions will shed a great deal of light on the nature of hierarchical decision making.

PRINCIPAL–AGENCY THEORY

Piece-rate incentives are intended to address two problems, which have been called the "hidden action" and "hidden information" problems. Piece rates are meant to encourage individuals to take costly efforts on their own initiative, especially when the effort may be difficult for supervisors to monitor; in other words, they are an attempt to address the hidden action problem. Further, piece-rate incentives are meant to encourage individuals to reveal something about themselves – namely, the nature of the private cost functions involved in given tasks. The hidden action and hidden information problems will be dealt with separately in the next two chapters.

Risk in the production process

Assume for the moment that the employer in a piece-rate game as shown in Figure 5.1 knows the subordinate's true reaction function. The employer is then able to calculate the level of subordinate effort that exactly maximizes the potential profit: It would be the level of effort that maximizes revenue less the effort cost of the employee. However, even with this perfect knowledge about the employee's type, it might be impossible to infer the degree of effort actually made by the employee, because the observable output may be affected by variables other than the unobservable individual effort.

Even in a hierarchy, a supervisor can rarely observe the amount of employee effort directly. Instead, what she observes is some output that is determined by factors that include the employee's effort, but also a variety of uncertain other events – the weather, general economic conditions, or just luck. Hence, the employer and employee cannot write a contract that is based on the amount of input, but only on the amount of output.

Examples of such situations are numerous. A salesperson may devote hours of time and effort to the job in a given month, only to find that the product is not selling due to unforeseen moves by the competition or bad economic conditions. These effort levels are not generally observable – only the final sales can be measured by the salesperson's supervisors. Similarly, a research and development office cannot contract over effort levels: All that a supervisor can observe might be mysterious activities in the lab or brainstorming around a chalkboard. The observable differences between the R&D activities of the staff and "goofing off" may be marginal. All that can be observed are outcomes: new product ideas and patents. Nor can a supervisor deduce anything "backward" from the number of patents to staff effort levels – there is a large random element that, along with the staff effort, codetermines product levels.

The question, for the sales problem and for the R&D problem, is: Who shall bear the risk that is associated with the random element in the production function?

Insurance and market failures

People are assumed to have different levels of tolerance for risk. Entrepreneurs may be relatively risk neutral; that is, they might just as soon have a 10 percent chance of losing $1,000 as pay $100 for sure. Most people, however, are assumed to be risk averse most of the time. They would prefer to pay $100, or even slightly more, rather than bear a 10 percent chance of losing $1,000.

Because of these differences in risk preference, it is possible to have trades that make both a risk-averse and a risk-neutral person better off. This is the origin of the insurance industry. A risk-averse person can pay a risk-neutral person to bear risk, and both can be made better off. Economic analysis of the insurance industry, however, has made it apparent that there are certain problems that can make it impossible for some of these Pareto-optimal trades to take place. Mathematically, these problems are the same as those that firms face in trying to provide incentives for employees. A simple example from the insurance area provides a perfect analogy, in fact, to the problem of risk bearing in firms.

Assume a homeowner who derives utility from wealth and from smoking. His utility from smoking is .005 utile, and his utility from wealth is $U = \ln(\text{wealth}/\$100K)$. He owns $100,000 in gold and $100,000 in a home. His home has a 10 percent chance of burning down if he smokes, and a 5 percent chance of burning if he does not smoke.

The utility he derives from total wealth is

$$U(\$200K) = .69315 \text{ utile.}$$

The utility he would derive from his gold alone is

$$U(\$100K) = \ln 1 = 0 \text{ utile.}$$

Therefore, the expected utility of smoking is

$$EU(S) = .9(.69315) + .005 = .62884 \text{ utile.}$$

When he does not smoke, he loses the utility from that source (.005) but his probability of retaining the $200,000 worth of wealth increases to .95:

$$EU(NS) = .95(.69315) = .65845 \text{ utile.}$$

Overall, therefore, he would prefer *not* to smoke.

Can the homeowner and an insurance company make a trade that makes them both better off, given that the company is not risk averse and he is? The minimum price of insurance if he does not smoke is $5,000. If he pays that price, he will get (risk free) the utility

$$U(\$195,000) = .66783 \text{ utile.}$$

In fact, he could be better off paying even $6,000 for insurance:

$$U(194,000) = .66269 \text{ utile.}$$

Both he and the insurance company would be better off if the insurance company agreed to take $6,000 and he would not smoke.

However, the insurance company could not agree to insure the homeowner even though both sides would be better off. The reason is that, once insured the homeowner would have no incentive to refrain from smoking. This is called the "moral hazard" problem. As long as he was not insured, the potential loss of his home would serve to keep him from smoking. Because he would have no way of documenting to the insurance company that he did not smoke, the insurance company would have to assume that he would give in to the temptation; this means that the minimum payment for insurance would be at least $10,000. But the utility of $190,000 is only .64185 utile, so the homeowner would not want to pay what the insurance company would have to charge, even with the additional pleasure of smoking. Therefore, as long as the information asymmetry about the homeowner's smoking existed, he could not afford to pay the premium it would take to make it worth the insurance company's while to bear his risk. The result would be an inefficient failure to shift the risk to the efficient bearer.

Moral hazard in hierarchies

The story of moral hazard in hierarchies is structurally just the same as the story of moral hazard in insurance. In both cases, the ability of a relatively risk averse individual to hide risk-increasing action makes it impossible for efficient contracts to be written.

Assume an employee who derives utility from income and from shirking (Figure 6.1). Her utility from shirking is .005 utile, and her utility from wealth is

$$U = \ln(\text{income}/\$100K).$$

As an employee, if she does not shirk, she has a 95 percent chance of generating an amount of revenue equal to $100,000 + R$ and a 5 percent chance of generating simply R. If she does shirk, she has a 90 percent chance of generating $R + \$100,000$ and a 10 percent chance of generating just R. Her income comes from a flat salary of $100,000; in addition, the company has agreed to pay her the entire $100,000 in additional revenue as a bonus if she generates it. The utility she derives from her flat salary would be

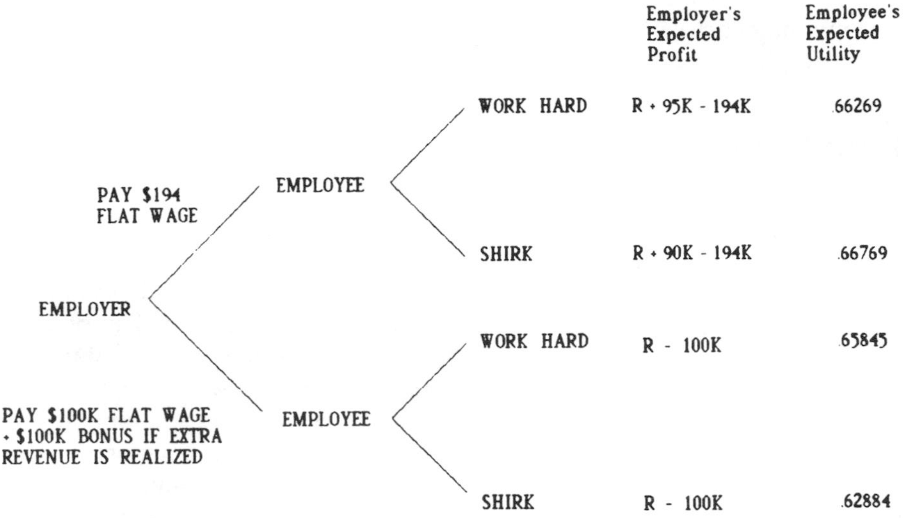

	Employer's Expected Profit	Employee's Expected Utility
WORK HARD	R + 95K - 194K	66269
SHIRK	R + 90K - 194K	.66769
WORK HARD	R - 100K	65845
SHIRK	R - 100K	.62884

PAY $194 FLAT WAGE — EMPLOYEE

EMPLOYER

PAY $100K FLAT WAGE + $100K BONUS IF EXTRA REVENUE IS REALIZED — EMPLOYEE

Figure 6.1. The inefficient Nash equilibrium in the principal – agent problem.

$$U(\$100K) = U(\ln 1) = 0.$$

The utility she would derive if she received her bonus is

$$U(\$200K) = .69315 \text{ utile.}$$

Her expected utility of shirking is therefore

$$EU(S) = .9(.69315) + .005 = .62884 \text{ utile.}$$

Her expected utility of *not* shirking is therefore

$$EU(NS) = .95(.69315) = .65845 \text{ utile.}$$

Therefore, she would prefer *not* to shirk, just as the uninsured houseowner would prefer not to smoke. The possibility of losing her bonus effectively disciplines her on-the-job behavior.

Can she and her employer make a Pareto-optimal trade? Her employer would like to pay her less and does not mind bearing risks. She, however, would be willing to take a smaller fixed salary in order to avoid the risk of losing her bonus. A trade should be possible. If she could be guaranteed not to shirk, her employer could pay her a flat salary of $194,000, and both would be better off. Her utility would be

$$U(\$194,000) = .66269 \text{ utile.}$$

which is greater than the utility with the risky bonus. Her employer would be better off, as long as she did not shirk; the employer would have a 95 percent chance of earning the additional $100,000 in revenue, while paying out only an additional $94,000 in wages.

124

Hidden action in hierarchies

However, this efficient trade could not be transacted. The reason is that the employee would have no incentive to refrain from shirking once she received a flat wage. The employer would be worse off if she gave in to the incentive to shirk than if he simply let her have the $100,000 if it was generated. This can be called the "moral hazard" of a flat wage. Furthermore, the employee would have no way of documenting to the employer that she was not shirking.

Therefore, the employer would have to assume that she was shirking, making it impossible to pay her more than an additional $90,000 in flat wage. But

$$U(\$190,000) = .64185 \text{ utile.}$$

Even if the employee then shirked, her utility would go up to only .64685 utile, which is still less than bearing the risk and not shirking. Therefore, as long as the information asymmetry about her shirking existed, she could not afford to accept the flat wage that would make it worth the employer's while to bear the risk. The result would be failure to shift the risk to the efficient bearer. The employee would have to continue to accept the risk of losing the bonus; the company would have to continue to pay her the larger bonus instead of the smaller flat wage. The inefficient Nash equilibrium of the game would be for the employer to pay a risky wage and the employee to work hard.

Risk bearing and inefficiency: empirical evidence

The economist Joseph Stiglitz (1987), looking at employment contracts, is concerned that firms do not find efficient solutions to the problem of risk bearing; in general, he says, firms ask employees to bear risks that they could more efficiently bear themselves. The foremost example, as he points out, is the risk associated with economic cycles. If employees could be insured against that risk, they would (being risk averse) be willing to work for much smaller salaries. (Witness the reluctance of tenured faculty members to give up the security of academe for higher, riskier salaries "outside.") Firms could earn more profits by paying those smaller, safer salaries if it were not for the negative incentive effects of guaranteeing employment. Furthermore, firms should pay training and moving costs and should index salaries "so that the firm, not the individual, bears the risks associated with inflation. None of these predictions conform to what is actually observed" (Stiglitz 1987: 50). Firms force employees to bear risk, even though employees and firms would both be better off if employees could be paid smaller, more certain salaries. Firms have to use the inefficient punishment of risk bearing in order to maintain employee incentive effects.

Indeed, as foreign competition increases, firms become more concerned about increasing the productivity of their employees and are consequently

125

forced to press more and more risky "incentive" plans on employees. Nancy Perry (1988) documents the increasing use of various plans: "Most of these programs share two characteristics: They put more of each employee's pay at risk, and they link that pay more closely to performance" (51). This can result in higher average pay for employees, but unionized employees worry about the downside of the risk involved.

Du Pont's recent, highly publicized "incentive pay plan" illustrates the costs associated with shifting risk from the firm to employees. A *Wall Street Journal* (1988a) article indicated the theme with its first line: "Du Pont's fibers division is raising the stakes for its employees." It is doing so by tying pay to profits. The workers in that division will be given smaller raises than those in other divisions, in exchange for a chance to earn a share of profits. In five years, their fixed salaries will be 6 percent less. If profits are less than 80 percent of the profit goal by that time, they will earn no bonus, and above that level they will earn a bonus depending on the size of profits. If profits are 150 percent of the goal, their take-home pay will be 12 percent greater than that of employees in the riskless divisions. The article cites disagreement among employees on the desirability of the plan:

Many employees, distrustful of management, say the plan is a gamble they'd rather not contend with. They worry that officials can decide to take a write-off and sacrifice a year's profit goal. . . . "There are so many loopholes for management," says Wayne Jefferson, a spinning-machine operator and union representative at the Seaford, Del., nylon plant, which approved the plan. "How do we know if we've reached our goal?"

The central problem, of course, is that the profits generated at Du Pont are not determined solely by the effort levels of the employees. The other determinants of profit, including the state of the economy, regulatory decisions, competition from domestic sources, political decisions affecting trade barriers, and shifts in consumer attitudes, are outside the control of both management and employees and constitute the risk that is being shifted to the employees for the sake of incentives. But as the article notes:

Many employees feel powerless to influence profits. Some, too, say they have a hard time devising ways to work more efficiently. . . . If a recession should strike, many employees say they would consider a pay cut unfair, as they have no control over the economy. "We're talking about an investment where I can lose money, and it may not be my fault."

Of course, that is precisely what risk sharing means.

Management naturally hopes that the incentives effect of this shift of risk will more than pay for the increased expected labor costs. According to the article, some signs of this are already apparent:

Jean Tanner, a marketing specialist for Dacron, likens it to "becoming a homeowner rather than a renter." She adds: "You care more about keeping it up. I think more about what's best for the business." Miss Tanner says she would consider turning back 10% to 20% of her 1989 advertising budget if it seems she can do as well with less. Where she might have looked twice at expenses before the plan, she says, she'll now go over them a third and fourth time. She's also planning to concentrate efforts on video news releases and on getting talk-show coverage instead of spending money to buy ads.

This incentive effect is purchased at a significant cost. The expected payout in wages is greater under the incentive system. If the company has underestimated the risk aversion of the employees, it may begin to experience labor shortages as risk-averse employees seek jobs elsewhere; it might have to increase the incentive bonuses to keep a constant labor supply. If a recession hits, the company could pay the price in terms of lower morale.

Whether or not Du Pont is making a smart move by imposing this incentive plan, the point is that both Du Pont and the risk-averse employees would be better of if the employees could be trusted to engage in the desired profit-boosting activities with a flat salary. In general, because employees are perceived as not being trustworthy, both sides are driven to a less efficient outcome, in which managers pay incentive bonuses that are more costly to the firm, and worth less to the risk-averse employees, than the flat salary.

TEAM SHIRKING

The Du Pont example illustrates the second problem of hidden action as well as the first. Up to this point, we have been assuming that productivity is a function of employee effort and exogenous, random variables:

$$\text{Output} = Q(\text{effort} \times R),$$

where R is a random variable associated with varying economic conditions, raw material quality, customer receptiveness, market competitiveness, and so on. The manager's problem is to disentangle employee effort from the observed level of output; the employee's temptation is to shirk to the degree that effort is hopelessly confounded with that random element.

But as Alchian and Demsetz noted in their original explanation of hierarchy, employees are often in a team production function; for example,

$$\text{Output} = Q[\text{effort}(i) \times \text{effort}(j)],$$

where i and j are the members of a two-person team. In such a setting, the confounding of the efforts of the various team members may be just as profound as the confounding of overall team effort with the exogenous random variables. One individual's marginal productivity is itself a function of how hard other team members are working. One team member's efforts are more productive if other team members are themselves working hard.

127

Thus, at Du Pont, one problem envisioned by employees operating under the group bonus plan is that no one individual in the fibers division will feel that her efforts contribute very much to the overall profits that will determine the size of her bonus. If marketing specialist Jean Tanner turns back 20 percent of her advertising budget – say, $10,000 – profits might increase by $10,000. But only a fraction of that $10,000 – say 50 percent – goes into the bonus pool for the employees. And that $5,000 is divided among the twenty thousand employees who work at the division, which means Ms. Tanner will get perhaps $0.25 in additional bonus as a result of her $10,000 contribution to profits.

Thus, a reasonable figure for the amount each employee might receive is only 0.000025 of every dollar that she saves the fibers division. Jean Tanner evidently found that motivating enough to turn back 10 to 20 percent of her advertising budget. But one wonders if it is going to dawn on her that it would be worth a quarter of a dollar to do things the easy way. Ms. Tanner likened the incentive plan to being a homeowner instead of a renter; but how much care would she give to a house that she and twenty thousand other people shared ownership of? How eager would she be to undertake costly repairs?

Team production and incentives

At one time, the craftsman might well have been independent – the number of shoes that could be made by a shoemaker in a day did not depend on how hard anyone else worked. But with the advent of the division of labor and specialization, interdependencies became much greater. The number of shoes created now depends on the interactive efforts of workers in a number of specialized roles.

In general, in a multiplicative production function of this sort, overall output goes to zero as any one team member's effort goes to zero. This fact captures the observation that workers on the line are dependent on the efforts of those who keep the raw materials flowing, on maintenance workers who keep the machinery running, and on a series of designers and supervisors who have to perform hundreds of tasks to keep the line moving. And as the auto industry has learned, any one of the workers may be able to keep production down by sabotage or simply by performing a task in such a way that it has to be redone.

The problem is that interdependence of team members can obscure individual effort in the same way that uncertainty due to random variables does. If output decreases in a given month, who is responsible? Each individual team member can blame any other team member. The supervisor is once again apt to have good information about output, but may have much less valid information about the effort levels of every individual team member and about the way that interdependencies among team members aggregate to total output.

A logical impossibility. This poses a logical problem for the supervisor – one that has been studied by economist Bengt Holmstrom of Yale. To the extent that a supervisor is uninformed about individual effort levels in a team production situation, there is no way for a manager to divide the revenues generated by the efforts of the team members in such a way as to motivate the appropriate levels of effort. A brief sketch of Holmstrom's proof is instructive.

Holmstrom assumes that there are n agents whose actions determine a level of revenue x. The actions taken are unobservable and are costly to each of the agents. In particular, we assume the production function is a team production in which the productivity of each individual's action is determined by other individuals' levels of effort.

Holmstrom points out the desirability of three characteristics of an incentive system – and then shows that they are logically inconsistent. First, Holmstrom examines the *Nash equilibrium* outcome of an incentive system. At such an equilibrium, each individual will find that he or she could not do better by choosing a different effort level, as long as all others do not change their effort levels. Simple marginal analysis tells us that, in such an equilibrium, each person will find that his or her marginal cost of effort is exactly equal to marginal gain; otherwise, the individual could be better off by working harder or not as hard. Second, Holmstrom stipulates that the outcome be *budget balancing* – that is, the incentive system should exactly distribute the revenues generated by the actors among the actors. Third, Holmstrom examines *Pareto efficiency*. This means that the outcome should be such that the individuals in the organization could not find a different outcome that would make them all better off.

Holmstrom shows that no budget-balancing system can create a Nash equilibrium that is also Pareto efficient. In other words, every budget-balancing incentive system will induce a social dilemma among its participants. The reason is that individuals will bring their own marginal cost of effort into equality with their own marginal gain. This means that each individual will not undertake an additional unit of effort that will produce less individual gain than individual cost – even if that extra unit of effort produces more gain for other individuals on the team.

As an example, suppose there is some individual who has a marginal revenue productivity of $12: Each unit of her own effort generates an extra $12 for the team. According to Pareto optimality, she should exert additional effort as long as the cost to her of that effort is less than or equal to $12; each such unit of effort generates more revenue for the team than it costs her as an individual. The only way to motivate her is to make sure that she gets *all* of the marginal revenue from her last unit of effort. In a team, it is impossible for this to be the case for every individual, as long as the incentive system is budget balancing. If everyone gets all of the last dollar produced, the team will have to pay out more in incentives than it generates. But if the individual gets only one-third of the marginal revenue from her actions, she will work only as long as her effort costs her less than $4 per unit.

Thus, team production causes a social dilemma in hierarchies as well as in the nonhierarchical teams described by Alchian and Demsetz. The team production function implies production externalities that result in the same fundamental schism between individual and group benefit that consumption externalities produce. No budget-balancing incentive system can overcome the problem.

Team production as a cover for shirking. Intuitively, this proof shows that team production externalities create just as much of a "cover" for shirking by employees as do environmental uncertainties. This is true whether or not the employees want to shirk; industrious employees are incapable of proving, in a team production setting, that a decline in team productivity was not due to their own effort instead of shirking of lazy employees. And as Holmstrom points out in the quote that begins this chapter, an incentive system that would give everyone an incentive not to shirk is too expensive to impose.

Interdependence among large subunits: transfer pricing

The analysis of shirking in interdependent teams suggests the inevitability of strategizing and conflict. This is most apparent in hierarchical firms, not at the level of the small work group, but among larger subunits of the organization and at higher levels of the hierarchy.

For instance, organizations often discover interdependencies between production and sales divisions. The ability of the sales division to develop and retain happy customers may depend on the flexibility of production with regard to customer requirements for delivery. At the same time, efficient production processes can be disrupted by constant demands from sales regarding rescheduling of high-priority customer orders. It is easy to imagine that both divisions would be better off with a degree of cooperation from the other; however, many organizations discover that these two divisions spend a great deal more time waging war than cooperating.

Similar interdependencies may exist between R&D and sales, engineering and production, and R&D and engineering. As organizations become very large, the problem of coordinating these interdependencies across the major divisions may be a substantial obstacle to organizational success. That is in fact one of the main reasons for the development of decentralized, product division form for firms in the second quarter of the twentieth century. The inability to coordinate across multiple functions and multiple products created such inefficiencies that it became easier to separate product lines into autonomous divisions.

The product-line division works very well as long as interdependencies across products do not exist. To the extent that interproduct interdependencies exist, however, organization by product-line divisions can provide incentives for individual division managers that discourage, rather than encourage, the necessary cooperation.

The most common interdependency that can exist among product lines occurs when one division manufactures a product that can be used as an input into another division's manufacturing process. It is just this kind of synergy that makes it desirable to have the two divisions in the same firm. The presence of a dependable, high-quality, low-cost input is valuable to the user division, and reciprocally the presence of a dependable market is valuable to the supplier division.

Ironically, however, the interdependencies between such divisions often become a major political headache for multidivision firms. The reason is that the executives in each division are normally compensated on the basis of their own division's book profits. Therefore, the user division has every incentive to try to obtain the other division's product for as little as possible or to go to another source that is cheaper, of higher quality, or more dependably supplied. Similarly, the supplier division has every incentive to charge the other division as much as possible for its product and to insist that the user division be denied the opportunity to shop around.

Thus, the divisions often end up engaging in hostilities around the set of issues known as "transfer pricing." If the user division manages to secure a policy that allows it to pay less than the market price for the other division's products, the supplier division will rationally respond by serving its other customers first. The user division will then be hampered by a nondependable flow of its necessary inputs that will hurt its own ability to produce and market its product. At the same time, if the supplier division secures a policy of market pricing of its sales to other divisions, the other divisions will have every incentive to shop around, thus depriving other divisions of its market and depriving the overall firm of the synergies that led to vertical integration in the first place.

These problems may be pervasive in firms with autonomous, but interrelated divisions. Of course, the problems become more serious as the degree of interdependency increases. In his book *The Transfer Pricing Problem* (1985), Eccles cites the case of one firm he calls Milton, Inc., in which the interdependencies were not too great, but the degree of conflict was intense. Milton had several autonomous groups, including a semiconductor group and a retail electronics group. One was a natural supplier and the other a natural customer, but both groups preferred to do business with competitors rather than with one another. One manager said: "The internal guy, whether as supplier or as user, is never treated as well. I've been on both sides. It's sad but understandable" (126). Another manager pointed out that the very interdependencies that create the opportunity for mutually beneficial gain also create the potential for politically damaging blame sharing:

An in-house guy may say not to supply for three weeks. He would be much more careful to do this with an outsider due to cancellation charges. Conversely, an in-house guy may say he needs more, and if he doesn't get them he complains to his boss. Guys will say they could be doing better if the other guy was doing better. Hence, people are reluctant to do business in-house. (126)

Or as a marketing vice-president agreed, "If managers sell inside, they are only doing what they are supposed to. If they screw up, they get in trouble" (126).

The bottom line was that self-interested behavior by managers of various divisions could hurt the company as a whole. One of Eccles's examples is Locke Chemical Company, where the Fine Chemicals Department purchased a raw material from the Consumer Division of the same company. The transfer price on this raw material gave the Consumer Division a healthy profit. Because of deteriorating demand, the Fine Chemicals Department was losing money by selling the product, known as PNB, for which it needed the raw material. However, the Consumer Division was making more on selling the product to Fine Chemicals than Fine Chemicals was losing on PNB. From the standpoint of corporate profits, the company would be better off the more PNB that Fine Chemicals could sell. However, the head of Fine Chemicals noted, "there is no motivation for our line managers . . . to secure additional volume on PNB since for every pound we sell, we lose more money" (Eccles 1985: 197). He could see that it made corporate sense to sell more PNB, but it hurt the indicators of divisional profit on which his own pay depended:

From a corporate point of view, I'm under self-imposed pressure to stay in PNB. And it would never serve the corporate interest to let me buy (the raw material) outside. However, if I keep selling more PNB, I just lose more money and it negatively impacts my performance income. When it comes time to decide how to allocate resources, I wonder why I should put people on PNB. Why should I spend a lot of money on it? I remind my boss constantly and he says, "Wear your corporate hat." (198)

Whether the direction "to wear your corporate hat" provides enough motivation to get division managers to pursue organizational efficiency over self-interest is doubtful. Eccles notes that there was the belief in the firm that "this kind of transfer pricing problem had led to suboptimal corporate performance, because some businesses had not been pursued aggressively enough" (199).

Whether or not it led to suboptimal performance in Locke Chemical, it is clear that this is the kind of interdependency problem in which the distribution of revenues generated by interdependent team efforts does not guarantee the right amount of self-interested motivation at all points in the firm. Indeed, according to Holmstrom, there can be no budget-balancing way to allocate revenues optimally. Since the allocation of full costs in such transfer pricing is regarded as a basic accounting constraint, the overwhelming evidence of widespread transfer-pricing conflicts in multidivisional firms is simply a manifestation of the mismatch of individual self-interest and organizational efficiency. We are also led, with Holmstrom, to examine whether it is possible to reconcile individual self-interest and organizational efficiency by sacrificing this budget-balancing constraint.

EFFICIENCY, BUDGET BALANCING, AND CREDIBLE COMMITMENT

Holmstrom demonstrates not only that efficiency is inconsistent with budget balancing in team production processes, but that there is an efficiency-generating incentive system that creates an imbalance, that is, a residual profit or loss that must be owned by someone who is not an active member of the production team. Holmstrom offers one such example; however, this example raises once again the issue of credible commitments by employers. The ownership of the residual by the employer creates an incentive for the employer to violate the efficiency of Holmstrom's efficient incentive system. How, then, can the employer make a credible commitment to efficiency?

An efficient, residual-generating incentive system for teams

Because the requirement of budget balancing seems fundamentally inconsistent with efficiency in team production or in the revelation of team member types, Holmstrom proposes an entirely novel solution to the problem of team shirking. He proposes that the fundamental advantage of a hierarchical firm is precisely that it does not have to balance a budget. He argues that the primary responsibility of the owner of a firm is to absorb the residual generated by members of the team, thus allowing incentives that promote efficiency among the members of the team.

Holmstrom's proposed solution is a form of forcing contract, as discussed at the beginning of Chapter 5. Instead of an individual forcing contract, it is a joint forcing contract for the team as a whole. This contract gives every team member a "take-it-or-leave-it" offer that he or she (just barely) cannot refuse. The team members make a contract with the entrepreneur that will allow them to share the revenue generated by their efforts if it is as great as the Pareto-optimal outcome; if they fall short of the efficient outcome, *all* of the revenue will go to the entrepreneur. The entrepreneur's responsibility is not to monitor, chastise, or sanction subordinates; it is simply to serve as a "sponge" for the surplus (Hammond 1984).

Such an arrangement would eliminate the moral hazard problem among team members. It would make every team member's full effort essential to anyone (and everyone) getting paid. The incentive for shirking would disappear because every team member would realize that shirking would deprive everyone (including oneself!) of all benefit of effort.

The residual owner's ex post incentive to renege

Holmstrom's residual-generating joint forcing contract works well as long as the "profit sponge" – the noninvolved owner who absorbs the residual – remains outside the firm. The problem is that the entrepreneur as sponge has an incentive to intervene in a way that increases the size of the profits that she owns, even at the cost of efficiency for the firm.

Eswaran and Kotwal (1984) argue that any one with a stake in the size of the residual would attempt to change the subordinates' incentives with a bribe. The owner of the residual realizes that getting one of the subordinates to shirk absolves her of any contractual obligation – under the joint forcing contract – to pay any of the other workers. Then she would get the revenue generated by the efficient level of effort from all but one of her employees and would not have to pay any of them. This outcome could be achieved by changing the incentive system. By bribing just one of the employees *not* to work at the efficient level, she could greatly decrease her payroll and thus increase her profits.

The implications of Eswaran and Kotwal's argument go beyond the joint forcing contract. The major implication is that there must be a fundamental tension inside any hierarchy; there *must* be a conflict of interest between profit maximization for the owners and efficiency for the firm as a whole. That is the point of demonstrating that the joint forcing contract, which Holmstrom shows to be an efficient incentive system, would not be chosen by anyone interested in maximizing profits *net* of payments to subordinates. From the standpoint of economic efficiency, the payments to subordinates are part of the surplus generated by team effort, which is to be maximized. From the standpoint of owner profits, the payments to subordinates are a cost, just like the cost of raw materials or land, and therefore something to be avoided. It is not surprising that an incentive system that encourages the team members to maximize their joint surplus is not one that would be chosen to maximize residual profits net of incentive payments to team members.

Indeed, the most fundamental implication of the Holmstrom impossibility result is that the inevitability of a surplus generated by any efficient incentive system necessarily creates a conflict with profit maximization. This is the case not just for the joint forcing contract, as shown by Eswaran and Kotwal, but for any efficient incentive scheme. If we were to suppose that there was no such tension, we would reach a logical contradiction.

Suppose that the N members of a team are acting under an efficient incentive system, like Holmstrom's joint forcing contract, which creates an efficient Nash equilibrium for the N team members. We know from Holmstrom that the team must be generating a residual that goes to an owner. We ask whether the owner can increase profits by switching to an inefficient incentive system (by a bribe or any formal change in the contract with team members). Suppose he cannot. If the employer has no incentive to change the incentives facing the subordinates, the $N + 1$ actors (team members and residual owner) would collectively constitute a budget-balancing, efficient Nash equilibrium – something Holmstrom showed was logically impossible. One of the $N + 1$ actors *must* have a reason to take a different course of action. If the team members are operating under an efficient incentive system, the incentive for inefficiency cannot tempt any of them; consequently, the incentive for inefficiency must be facing the owner himself, in his choice of incentive systems.

The conclusion is that any owner must find that the efficient incentive system for team members is not the one that maximizes the size of the residual. Efficiency must require committing the owner not to pursue profit maximization in contract negotiations with team members.

Credible commitments

The problem, then, is not that efficient incentive systems do not exist. Holmstrom has shown that a joint forcing contract would generate an efficient Nash equilibrium for the game. The problem is that the owners of the residual generated by the efficient incentive system could do better with an inefficient incentive system. By changing the incentive system (bribing an employee), the owner can create more residual profits.

Eswaran and Kotwal appropriately term this problem the "moral hazard of budget breaking" to show the parallelism with the moral hazard problem of shirking by subordinates. Holmstrom's solution is only a quasi-solution; it demonstrates that the incentive to shirk cannot be eliminated altogether, but only shifted from employees to owner. Holmstrom has thus articulated a dilemma without any neat answers. The distribution of revenues generated by team efforts necessarily creates incentives for inappropriate behavior – if not by the employees, then by the manager or the owner of the "residual" profits. There will always be incentives for individuals to shirk, cheat, or follow their own preferences in ways that cumulate to organizational inefficiencies.

Once again, as with the piece-rate system of the last chapter, the fundamental dilemma in incentive systems is the tension between employer self-interest and firm efficiency. If the members of a team were offered the joint forcing contract proposed by Holmstrom, it would seem on first glance to be an advantageous solution to the shared problem of team shirking: Everyone would know that every other member of the team had every incentive to work instead of shirk. However, the far-sighted employee would not accept the joint forcing contract, simply because he would expect that the owner of the firm would violate the terms of the contract with a hidden bribe to one of the members. The employee would not sign a joint forcing contract without knowing that the employer was altruistic or forcibly constrained from engaging in the opportunistic behavior that a joint forcing contract would offer.

A necessary condition for the success of the joint forcing contract proposed by Holmstrom (or any other scheme for inducing efficient levels of effort from subordinates) is a credible commitment by the owner of the firm not to engage in such a hidden bribe; it would be hard to imagine how such a commitment could be made. This theme will be pursued with regard to hidden information in the next chapter.

SUMMARY

The very factors that give rise to market failure also cause hierarchical failure. Information asymmetry and team production externalities create possibilities for undetected shirking in firms and make it generally impossible for managers to create incentives that completely realign individual self-interest and organizational efficiency. Managers cannot afford to pay risk-averse employees the output-tied bonuses that would eliminate any incentive for moral hazard. Nor can they afford to pay interdependent team members the output-tied profit shares that would eliminate incentives for all members to shirk at one another's expense. All of this leaves managers and employees in a hierarchical version of a social dilemma. Forcing risk-averse employees to accept risky bonuses tied to profits is expensive for managers and unpleasant for employees.

The mutual shirking in team production is also inefficient. Holmstrom's solution – a residual-generating joint forcing contract – would eliminate the individual incentives for shirking but would in fact create incentives for the owners of the residual to sabotage the efficient scheme.

Another problem with the joint forcing contract is that implementation requires the superior to have information that may not be available. That is, before the manager can decide what level of effort to force from the employees in pursuance of a company project, it is necessary to know something about the labor cost functions and potential benefits of the project. This information is generally private knowledge held by subordinates in the firm.

Thus, in order to implement the joint forcing contract that Holmstrom envisions, it is necessary to elicit private cost and benefit information from the subordinates themselves. Can an incentive system be designed that will achieve this? Information asymmetries of this kind are a fundamental rationale for the existence of hierarchy. The next chapter will argue that, ironically, information asymmetries are also the fundamental obstacle to the efficient operation of a hierarchy.

7

Hidden information in hierarchies
The logical limits of mechanism design

WITH THOMAS HAMMOND

> These results show that the difficulty is due not to our lack of inventiveness, but to a fundamental conflict among such mechanism attributes as the optimality of equilibria, incentive-compatibility of the rules, and the requirements of informational decentralization. Concessions must be made in at least one of these directions.
>
> Hurwicz (1973:24)

Chapter 6 focused on the problem of hidden action. Even when a manager knows what actions she wants from a group of subordinates, she can be hindered in her efforts to elicit those actions by an inability to sort out those efforts from the confounding effects of unknown random variables and of other team members' actions.

Holmstrom's solution to the problem of hidden action within teams is to impose a forcing contract – one that requires the desired team outcome and punishes every team member severely for any team member's shirking. While Holmstrom's joint forcing contract may be a theoretical solution to the problem of hidden action, it runs aground on the even more fundamental problem of hidden information. The primary problem is that managers require information in order to decide what outcomes they want to elicit from the forcing contract – and that information is generally hidden from them. Would it be profitable to adopt a new product line? What level of profits should be expected from each division? The answers to these and similar questions depend on information that is best known (or only known) to the subordinates themselves. Superiors require information from subordinates in order to set goals and expectations for those subordinates.

Are there ways to elicit this hidden information from the relevant subordinates? In general, subordinates will have every reason to use this information strategically in order to get favorable compensation for the production of the new product, if adopted. Theoretically, it is possible to overcome this strategic misrepresentation of hidden information by an "efficient" incentive system – just as it is theoretically possible to overcome the hidden action problem by an efficient incentive system.

However, two related problems limit any ideal solution to the hidden information problem. First, the mechanisms that enable firms to elicit hidden information from subordinates require substantial incentive payments to the subordinates. From the standpoint of the profit-maximizing owners and managers of a firm, it may be simply too costly to use mechanisms that elicit hidden information. The profit-maximizing motivation of the chief executive officer (CEO) may be at odds with an efficient solution to the problem.

Second, an efficient solution to the problem of hidden information may be inconsistent with an efficient solution to the problem of hidden action, as economists Jeffrey Miller and Peter Murrell have shown. When a manager (contrary to self-interest) imposes an incentive system to obtain information from subordinates, she has already deprived herself of the tools necessary to use that information effectively (Miller and Murrell 1981).

The ironies in the story of hierarchy are thus compounded. While hierarchy was initially justified as a means of solving market failures due to information asymmetries, hierarchy itself seems vulnerable to the same information asymmetries. The strategic misrepresentation of hidden information is itself the most profound obstacle to effective hierarchical performance.

THE STRATEGIC USE OF HIDDEN INFORMATION

A member of a hierarchy may fail to reveal fully and accurately the information available to him because the misrepresentation of private information may cause the hierarchy to make decisions that he finds preferable. The strategic misrepresentation of effort cost functions in the piece-rate model of Chapter 5 is just one example.

Misrepresentation in voting

The problem of misrepresentation in voting is simply a manifestation of a quite general and powerful result in social choice theory: that any social choice rule creates incentives for misrepresentation. For instance, suppose three voters are using majority rule to vote on a bill or a substitute amendment, with the winner of that vote being voted up or down against a status quo. The preferences of the three voters are as in Table 7.1. Clearly, a majority of people (players 2 and 3) prefer the amendment to the original bill. Players 1 and 2 would then support the amendment against the status quo. However, this would be the outcome only if the players accurately revealed the (hidden) information about their own preferences. Player 3 has every

Table 7.1. *Misrepresentation in voting: a typical example*

Choice	Player 1	Player 2	Player 3
First	Original bill	Substitute amendment	Status quo
Second	Substitute amendment	Status quo	Substitute amendment
Third	Status quo	Original bill	Original bill

Vote	Agenda
First	Original bill vs. substitute amendment
Second	[Winner of first vote] vs. status quo (no bill)

reason to misrepresent her own preferences. By voting for her last choice in the first vote, she can guarantee that the original bill beats the substitute amendment. Her reason for doing so is that the original bill would then lose to the status quo in the final vote. Thus, she would get her first choice by misrepresenting her second and third choices.

Is there any voting rule that is immune to this kind of misrepresentation? In other words, is there any way of combining individual preferences that gives every player a dominant strategy to tell the truth about information that is essentially private? Two theorists (Gibbard 1973; Satterthwaite 1975) independently proved that every social decision rule that relies on the input of more than one actor is manipulable. Although the theorem has been used heavily in voting theory, the result is equally meaningful for hierarchies. In any hierarchy in which the CEO relies on any second party for advice or action, the party relied on will find that he can sometimes do better by misrepresenting private information about his own beliefs or preferences.

Misrepresentation in bureaucracy

The Vietnam War offered a striking example of the strategic use of information in hierarchies. The Defense Intelligence Agency repeatedly misrepresented information in attempts to influence decision makers and the public. During the period from 1964 until early 1967, the U.S. military wanted to build up troop strength, and the Defense Intelligence Agency found it politically appropriate to emphasize and exaggerate the extent to which North Vietnamese troops were infiltrating and recruiting in South Vietnam. After that time, the military wanted to prove to Secretary Robert McNamara and others that it was winning. "Then the paramount interest became to show the enemy's reduced capability to recruit and a slowdown in infiltration due to our bombing. The tone and emphasis of reports from the field changed radically, and so did those put out by DIA" (Halperin

1974: 102). Bureaucratic officials throughout the military bureaucracy found it expedient to first exaggerate, then minimize, the North Vietnamese threat in an attempt to influence the political decisions concerning the war.

Misrepresentation in firms

This phenomenon has been abundantly studied in government hierarchies, but the same principles and behaviors apply to private firms. Just as the generals in Vietnam used body counts to influence Robert McNamara, as secretary of defense, the plant managers at Ford used false production statistics to influence their boss Robert McNamara ten years earlier.

One production manager, for instance, secretly shortened the wooden sticks that separated one auto frame from another on the assembly line in order to produce an extra number of cars (called the "kitty") that could be kept secret from Detroit (Halberstam 1986: 219). The purpose of the "kitty" was production smoothing – a secret reserve of autos made it possible to avoid punishment for failing to keep up with impossible quotas under difficult conditions. Moreover, maximum production possibilities during good times had to be kept hidden from Detroit. Just as a factory worker does not want his boss to know exactly how many units he can produce when he works his hardest, the plant manager did not want Detroit to know exactly how many cars he could produce when conditions were best. The plant manager knew that if maximum production possibilities were known, they would become the required norm.

One production manager who came to be trusted by plant managers found that their inner world "was filled with secrets, and the name of the game was Screw Detroit" (Halberstam 1986: 218). The same thing could be said of the lower-level employees of many large private firms. At Sears, buyers were long granted the autonomy to make their own decisions about which products to buy, at what price, and in what quantities – and to report the details to no one. By the time the crisis hit in the midseventies, the central office felt it essential to have access to that information, but "demands for documentation were often circumvented. The buyers envisaged the privacy of their numbers as one of the last remnants of their former latitude. After the numbers would go the power" (Katz 1987: 123). In hierarchies, keeping the power that goes with expertise inevitably requires the occasional misrepresentation of private information.

When subordinates are forced to submit planning figures, they normally do so with an eye not toward accuracy, but toward looking good in the future. When Phil Purcell came to Sears as vice-president of planning, he sent out surveys and planning documents to store managers, hoping to get hard data about expected sales and profits. He found instead that "a store manager would usually pick a 3-percent sales rise out of his hat, and then exceed the estimate by two digits for the fun of it" and in order to look good

141

at bonus time (Katz 1987: 82). The self-supplied reports turned out to be useless for planning or for any other purpose, except the self-seeking manipulation of the store manager's own image.

ELICITING HIDDEN INFORMATION
FROM SUBORDINATES

The problem of eliciting hidden information in order to make efficient decisions is common to both governments and firms.

Hidden valuation of public goods

The government has the ability to write a "forcing contract" with its citizens. That is, it can overcome the incentives for free riding on the provision of public goods – a dam, for example – simply by coercing tax payments, sanctioned by possible foreclosure of property, garnishment of wages, or imprisonment. But these powerful sanctions are worth little if the government cannot ascertain whether the dam is worthwhile. Would a dam cost more than its potential benefits? Some people may want to have motorboats on the lake produced by the dam, but other citizens may hate motorboats and prefer to canoe on the natural stream that would be destroyed by the dam. It would be helpful to find out whether the net evaluation of the dam by the citizens exceeds the cost of construction. But the evaluation of public goods is private information.

With accurate information about every citizen's positive or negative valuation of the dam, combined with an accurate assessment of the costs of construction, it would be possible to make an accurate decision about whether the dam was efficient. It would also be equitable to impose the construction costs on the people who were going to benefit most from the dam. But if the taxes for the construction of the dam were in any way linked to the message provided by a citizen about his evaluation of the dam, there would be a systematic reason for each citizen to undervalue the dam. If citizens' taxes went up with their reported valuation of the public goods supplied to them, each citizen would underreport his or her valuation in an effort to shift the burden of taxation to others.

If, however, the taxes were not linked to citizens' disclosure of information, those in favor of the dam would have every incentive to exaggerate the benefits wildly, while those opposed would have every reason to exaggerate the costs. Of course, this form of behavior is widespread in public policy making. People who favor a new weapons system (such as Star Wars) unblushingly claim that it will singlehandedly end war as well as unemployment in every congressional district with a subcontractor. People who oppose the same project predict military disaster and economic ruin.

Hidden information in hierarchies

Thus, while government coercion in the form of taxation can overcome the tendency for free riding in the voluntary provision of contributions for public goods, coercive taxation does nothing to solve the more fundamental problem of retrieving hidden information. As citizens we depend on our government to spend tax money efficiently, but no one of us has any reason to tell the truth about the value of governmental projects.

Hidden cost and benefit information in teams

Exactly analogous arguments are true for a firm. The central headquarters of a corporation may have the authority to decide whether to undertake a new product line or to purchase a centralized computing facility. But it will need to know the effects on all its various divisions before it can make a wise decision.

Just as a government official is dependent on accurate information from citizens in order to make efficient decisions, so a firm's top management is dependent on information from the division managers:

> If the center or agent responsible for choosing the quantity of this service/resource for the firm does not know (with sufficient precision) the value of the resources to the divisions, then it must obtain this information from the divisions themselves. Thus, it is essential for optimal decisions that the divisions report accurately or "honestly" to the center and a nontrivial question is what incentives they have to do so. (Groves 1985: 95)

As an example, consider two team members, Anne and Bill, who can by their joint efforts produce something that will generate $100 in revenue. Whether they should undertake to produce the good depends on the costs they bear in the production process. There is no assumption that their individual costs are equal, but one could easily see that each of them would have to receive a revenue in excess of individual costs for each to regard it as worthwhile participating in the process. This could easily result in strategic exaggerations of their individual costs in order to obtain the largest possible share of the $100 in revenue.

For instance, both might privately regard the minimum compensation they would accept as $45. However, Anne might claim that her costs (including both economic costs and the psychic cost of her effort) would require a minimum of $60 of compensation to make it worthwhile for her to participate. Bill would then have to demand no more than $40 in compensation, or else the two of them would have to pass up the opportunity to make $100. If both exaggerated their individual costs, they could easily fool one another into passing up an opportunity that would in fact be worthwhile.

This problem is analogous to the problem discussed by Holmstrom. There, team members' individual cost functions were known, and revenue

143

shares were to be allocated in order to encourage the members to take costly hidden actions. Here, we are assuming that the actions taken by Anne and Bill may well be observable, if they commit themselves to undertaking the production process. However, the problem is to allocate the revenue shares beforehand in order to induce the revelation of hidden information needed to make an efficient decision.

Not only is the current problem analogous to the Holmstrom problem, but there is also an analogous result. Just as Holmstrom demonstrated that there is no budget-balancing revenue-sharing rule that will induce team members to take efficient levels of action in Nash equilibrium, Groves (1985) and others have demonstrated that there is no budget-balancing revenue-sharing rule that will induce team members to reveal private information. In order to assess the significance of this, it is important first to understand how a revenue-sharing rule could induce Anne and Bill to tell the truth about their costs.

Solutions: the simple incentive-compatible mechanism

The solution that has been proposed is a decision rule that eliminates the incentive for team members or citizens to lie about their evaluation of a public good (Groves 1973; Groves and Ledyard 1977). Tideman and Tullock (1976) called such decision rules "demand revealing mechanisms." They are also known as "incentive-compatible mechanisms" (Groves and Loeb 1975, 1979). With these rules, the government would allocate taxes in such a way that individuals would realize that it would be to their own advantage to tell the truth. Similarly, firms could allocate revenues in such a way as to induce truthful cost-revelation messages from employees.

Imagine that Anne and Bill work for a CEO who is trying to create a set of incentives that give them every reason to reveal their costs accurately. With that information, the firm can decide whether to sign a contract committing Anne and Bill to produce the special product that will generate $100 in revenue. Both subordinates are specialists whose expertise is required for the job; the CEO does not have any idea how much costly effort will be required by each subordinate, nor does either subordinate know this about the other. The CEO does not know whether the two have private effort cost functions that would allow them to be compensated for the required effort and still leave the CEO with some profit from the $100 in revenue.

Again, one method would be to split the $100 in proportion to the costliness of Anne and Bill's individual efforts. This would be fair, if true effort costs could be determined, because it would grant higher compensation to the subordinate whose production effort was more costly. Each subordinate, however, would then have reason to exaggerate his or her own costs in order to justify a higher reward. The two could very easily exaggerate their own costs to such an extent that the CEO would be convinced the contract was unprofitable for the firm – even if the individual effort costs involved were in fact a small proportion of the $100. The same problem would apply if the compensation were based on the number of hours each subordinate spent on the process – each would have reason to engage in the kind of systematic shirking observed in time-based employment.

The obvious alternative to linking compensation and reported costs is to divorce them; for instance, the CEO could simply state a fixed compensation for each employees, so that the exaggeration of costs would not result in larger compensation. However, this would also result in an incentive to lie. For example, if Anne were told she would get $40 for her share of the $100, she might have an incentive either to exaggerate or to understate her true effort costs. If her effort costs were less than $40, she would have every reason to minimize the effort costs – sending in a cost message of $0, for instance – in order to make sure that the CEO signed the contract. If her effort costs were slightly more than $40, she would have every incentive to exaggerate her effort costs in order to convince the CEO not to sign the contract. In either case, the CEO would not have the kind of information from Anne and Bill that would allow him to make an efficient decision.

There are schemes that induce subordinates to reveal costs accurately. One such scheme, denoted as incentive-compatible scheme 1, is summarized in Figure 7.1. In order to guarantee efficiency, the CEO should announce that the contract will be undertaken only if the sum of the cost messages from Anne and Bill $(C_a + C_b)$ is less than the revenue to be generated:

$$C_a + C_b < \$100.$$

Another way of stating this efficiency condition is that the central office will undertake the project if Anne's stated costs are less than the difference between the total revenue and Bill's stated costs:

$$C_a < \$100 - C_b.$$

Now suppose the central office stipulates, as a second rule, that Anne's *compensation* will equal $100 - C_b$ if the project is undertaken. Then Anne will want the contract signed whenever it is efficient to sign it: when her private cost (C_a) is less than her payment ($100 - C_b$). Whenever her private cost is greater than $100 - C_b$, the project will be inefficient, and she herself will want the project to be stopped.

By making Anne's payment equal to the difference between the revenue generated by the project and Bill's statement of costs, the firm has created a perfect fit between Anne's self-interest and the requirements of

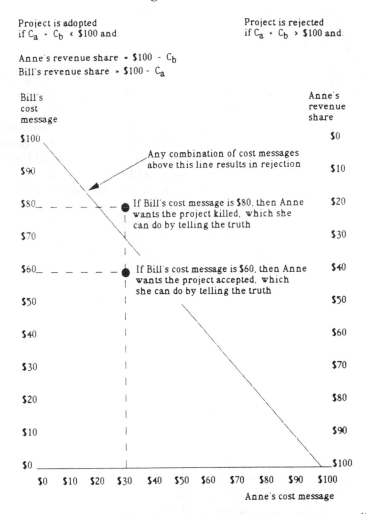

Figure 7.1. Incentive-compatible scheme 1. Assume $30 is Anne's true cost figure; a message of $30 is thus Anne's dominant strategy.

organizational efficiency. Anne can get efficient contracts signed by telling the truth (resulting in a positive net benefit for herself) and she can kill inefficient projects by telling the truth (thereby preventing a negative net benefit for herself).

For example, suppose Anne's true anticipated costs are $30. Anne's payment will depend on Bill's cost message; her compensation will be greater than $30 if Bill's cost message is less than $70, or it will be less than $30 if Bill's cost message is greater than $70. In either case, telling the truth is optimal for her.

Hidden information in hierarchies

In the first case, suppose Bill's cost message is less than $70 (say, $65), resulting in a cash payment to Anne of $100 − $65 = $35. This is greater than her $30 effort cost, so she wants the contract to be signed. Telling the truth will get the CEO to sign the contract, because $65 + $30 < $100. Anne cannot make the project any more likely, or her payment any greater, by understating the costs to herself. Exaggerating the expected cost (by reporting effort costs of, say, $40) would result in the desirable project being killed (because a cost message of $65 from Bill and $40 from Anne totals more than the expected revenue of $100). Thus, telling the truth is beneficial and lying potentially harmful.

In the second case, suppose Bill's cost message is greater than $70 (say, $75). Now Anne's compensation is $100 − $75 = $25, and Anne would like the project killed because her payment is less than her true $30 effort cost. Telling the truth would accomplish that end, because $75 + $30 > $100. Exaggerating her costs would not make the project any less likely than would telling the truth, nor would it increase her compensation. Understating her costs (by reporting C_a = $20) would only result in the undesirable project being approved (because $75 + $20 < $100).

Since it is assumed that Bill and Anne submit their cost messages separately, Anne does not know whether Bill's cost message will result in a payment to her of less than or more than her true costs of $30. In one case, understating the truth would hurt. But in either case, telling the truth would be beneficial.

Note that this incentive to tell the truth remains whether or not Bill is honest, because the CEO's decision and Anne's self-interest depend on Bill's report in exactly the same way. But if Bill's revenue share is set equal to $100 minus Anne's cost message, Bill will also have an incentive to tell the truth. Thus, the CEO can now be confident that both messages he receives will in fact be accurate depictions of Anne's and Bill's costs for the jointly produced project.

As far as Anne and Bill are concerned, then, the imposition of an incentive-compatible rule creates an Invisible Hand game: Each has a dominant strategy to tell the truth, enabling the CEO to acquire the information necessary to make efficient decisions. But here is the sticking point: Does the CEO have any reason to use incentive-compatible scheme 1? Or is there another mechanism that would make the CEO better off?

Perverse incentives for the CEO

The only problem with scheme 1 is that the CEO will be forced to pay Anne and Bill *more* than the contract generates in revenue. As far as the CEO is concerned, getting the truth is more costly than it is worth. For instance, if Anne's true (and reported) costs for the project are $30 and Bill's are $65, Anne's payment will be $100 − $65 = $35 and Bill's payment will be

147

$100 - \$30 = \$70$. The CEO will have to make incentive payments of $105 with only $100 of revenue.

In general, the total incentive payments to Anne and Bill will equal

$$\$100 - C_a + \$100 - C_b = \$200 - (C_a + C_b).$$

But this sum is less than the revenue *whenever* the project is efficient (i.e., whenever $C_a + C_b < \$100$). In fact, the smaller the effort costs for the two subordinates, the more efficient the project and the *greater* will be the deficit for the CEO. In order to get the truth with the incentive-compatible scheme, the CEO must run a deficit on all efficient projects.

A stake in inefficiency

The situation, then, is much like that for the hidden action problem described in Chapter 6. Holmstrom demonstrated that there is an efficient incentive system (the joint forcing contract) that can induce team members to make efficient levels of hidden effort; however, the employer will have every reason to choose an inefficient incentive system that increases his profits. Similarly, the literature on incentive compatibility shows that there is an efficient incentive system that can induce team members to reveal hidden information about themselves; however, the employer will have every reason to choose an inefficient incentive system that increases his profits.

What incentive scheme could the CEO use to keep from always running a deficit? He could simply lie to the employees about the revenues generated by the contract, a subject about which he presumably has expert (i.e., hidden) information.[1] This would result in a different incentive scheme, one that was less efficient, but less costly for the CEO. Suppose, for instance, the CEO announces that the contract will generate $90 rather than $100. This would result in a revised decision rule for the firm: The project will be adopted if and only if $C_a + C_b < \$90$. The compensation payments for Anne and Bill would then be fixed at $\$90 - C_i$.

With this misstated cost figure and altered decision rule, some efficient projects (with cost totals between $90 and $100) would be killed. But for combinations of employee cost messages totaling less than $90, the central office would have to absorb less loss than if it told the truth, and might make a profit. For instance, if Anne's true effort costs were $30 and Bill's $55, Anne's incentive payment would be $\$90 - \$55 = \$35$ and Bill's incentive payment would be $\$90 - \$30 = \$60$. Total incentive payments would equal $95 for a project that would bring the firm $100. The small lie by the CEO would stop some efficient projects from being undertaken but produce a possibility of profits instead of an inevitable loss for the CEO.

---

[1] Remember that in the case of Du Pont's profit-based incentive scheme, many employees were convinced that the management could play secret accounting games to avoid having to pay bonuses (*Wall Street Journal* 1988).

Given the advantages to the CEO of a small lie, is there any reason for him to stop with a $10 understatement of the revenues of the project? Obviously not. Assuming that the central office is willing to trade off the probability of killing off somewhat efficient (but deficit-generating) projects in exchange for smaller deficits and larger profits, the CEO has an "optimal lie" that depends on his subjective estimation of the distribution of cost messages.

If the CEO simply lies about the expected revenue of a project (but otherwise keeps the basic form of incentive-compatible scheme 1), it does not spoil the incentive for the subordinates to tell the truth. Suppose Anne knows that her incentive payment is $90 $-$ C_b and that the decision rule is to accept the project if the sum of the reported costs is less than $90. She will still have every incentive to report the truth. Thus, exaggerating costs results in a different mechanism that still supplies accurate information to the center, but sacrifices efficiency in organizational decision making to the CEO's self-interest.

The irony is clear: A mechanism that would enable the center to obtain the information it needs to make efficient decisions has been found. However, the implementation of this mechanism would require the CEO himself to withstand a constant temptation to lie and make inefficient decisions. Indeed, if any firm were to announce its intentions to implement fairly and neutrally an incentive-compatible mechanism as a way of allocating its capital investments among divisions, the divisions would have to regard that as a noncredible commitment. A concern for firm profits, net of incentive payments to subordinates, is inconsistent with the neutral implementation of incentive-compatible mechanisms.

Is there any mechanism that gives subordinates an incentive to tell the truth, without creating an incentive for superiors to lie and make inefficient decisions? Unfortunately, there is not; the next section shows that *every* mechanism that induces subordinates to tell the truth creates perverse incentives for superiors.

THE INCONSISTENCY OF PARETO EFFICIENCY AND PROFIT MAXIMIZATION

In his discussion of incentive problems in firms, Radner correctly emphasizes the distinction between organizational efficiency and firm profits. Firm profit maximization regards the payments to members of the team other than owners as costs. "For the owner, any compensation to the division managers is a cost of doing business, and this compensation is to be subtracted from the enterprise output. In this case 'efficiency' is measured by the expected net profit of the enterprise" (Radner 1987, 16). This is in contrast to Pareto efficiency, in which the well-being of the team as a whole is regarded. "With this approach, one would want to take account of each manager's expected utility, which would reflect the direct utility or disutility to him of his own actions, as well as his compensation" (17).

The literature on incentive compatibility, though concerned with Pareto efficiency, has failed to recognize that incentive compatibility is inconsistent with profit maximization. This is because of the constant (generally implicit) assumption that the central official who imposes an incentive-compatible scheme and collates the resulting citizen valuation messages is an altruist, interested in nothing but making efficient decisions for society.

This assumption, which differs markedly from the rest of the assumptions made in economics, is so ingrained in the literature on incentive compatibility that it is rarely mentioned explicitly. An exception is the following statement of Green and Laffont (1979): "We consider a central decision-maker whose action is selected from among a given set of alternatives. He is benevolent and, ideally, if the full description of the economic system were known to him, he would select according to some rule from among the Pareto optima" (vii). This assumption is suspicious in the case of government officials and completely untenable in the case of decentralized business firms. There are alternative incentive schemes producing results *outside* the Pareto optima that provide the central official with more profit.

The rest of this chapter argues that, if firms act in a profit-maximizing way, they must implement incentive schemes that reward some employees for lying. Providing sufficient rewards for perfect truth telling would be too costly in terms of profit. The omnipresence of strategic misrepresentation in firms is not thereby an accident or a passing flaw in organizational design; it is a structural inevitability in profit-maximizing firms.

One solution proposed by Groves and Loeb (1975, 1979) is a special form of incentive-compatible mechanism that is guaranteed to result in efficient decision making and to produce a profit for the firm, after the payment of inducements to subordinates. We will call this the "modified incentive-compatible mechanism." The next section provides an example of such a mechanism and demonstrates that it, too, creates perverse incentives for the CEO.

The modified incentive-compatible mechanism

In order to guarantee that the center will not run a deficit, it is essential to create a revenue allocation rule that is certain to leave a profit for the center if the project is adopted. To do this, it is necessary to put "caps" on the incentive payments to subordinates. This results in a modified incentive-compatible mechanism, denoted by incentive-compatible scheme 2 (Figure 7.2).

For instance, assume once again that the CEO is considering whether to sign a contract that will bring in $100 of revenue. The CEO wants to find an incentive system that will simultaneously cause Anne and Bill to tell the

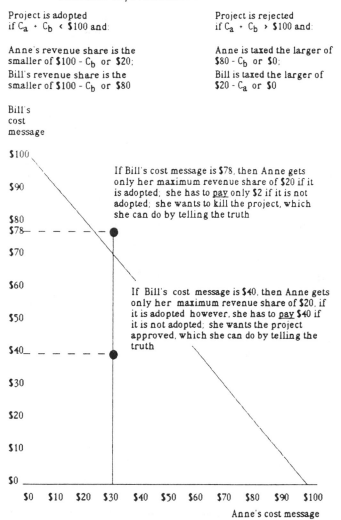

Figure 7.2. Incentive-compatible scheme 2. Assume $30 is Anne's true cost figure; a message of $30 is thus Anne's dominant strategy.

truth about the effort costs involved in the subsequent fulfillment of the contract and that will result in the contract being signed if and only if the costs to Anne and Bill are less than $100. In addition, the CEO wants an incentive system that will leave himself a profit after making incentive payments to Anne and Bill.

The basic allocation of that revenue to Anne and Bill will depend on one another's cost messages, as before. Anne's basic incentive payment will equal $100 less Bill's cost message, and vice versa. However, to ensure that the CEO does not pay out more than $100 in incentive payments, the

151

incentive payments will receive "caps" that sum to $100. For instance, Anne's maximum incentive payment may be $20 while Bill's is $80. (How these maximum payments are determined falls outside the model and would presumably be the subject of a great deal of political action independently of the decision regarding the project; but the incentive system will "work" as long as they sum to $100.)

This maximum incentive payment could very easily destroy the incentive compatibility of the mechanism. Anne, facing a maximum payment of $20 if the project is adopted, would have an incentive to overstate her expected costs if they are more than $20, in order to kill the project. For instance, if Anne's expected costs are $30, and Bill's are $40, then a truthful message from Anne would result in the project being adopted, yielding Anne only the maximum incentive payment of $20. The project, although efficient, would result in an incentive payment of $10 *less* than her true costs. She would then be better off lying about her costs, giving a cost message of, for example, $70, which would kill the project. The cap on her earnings could destroy the incentive compatibility of the system.

In order to counter this problem it is necessary to destroy Anne's incentive to lie when her expected costs are more than her maximum payment. Her cap goes into effect whenever Bill's message is less than $80. So the solution is to charge Anne a *tax* in those circumstances if the project is *not* adopted. This constitutes a tax for depriving the firm of an efficient project by exaggerating her costs. This can be implemented by charging Anne a tax of $0 or $80 − C_b, whichever is greater, if the project is *not* adopted. This tax for an unsuccessful project is effective whenever Bill's message is less than $80, which is precisely when the cap on Anne's revenue share is binding. The threat of a tax being imposed when a project is not adopted serves to counter Anne's incentive to lie. This is illustrated in Figure 7.2.

Suppose that Anne's true costs are $30. When Bill's statement of costs is $40, a truthful message will result in the project being adopted, and Anne will get only her maximum payment of $20. However, if she exaggerates and gets the project killed, she will have to pay a tax of $80 − $40 = $40. Thus, she will be even worse off lying than telling the truth. The modified incentive-compatibility mechanism maintains every reason to tell the truth, even when the maximum payments are not sufficient to cover the true costs. Thus, with this scheme, incentive compatibility is maintained, and at the same time the center is guaranteed that it will not have to run a deficit.

Problems with the modified incentive-compatible scheme

Despite its advantages, the profit-guaranteeing incentive-compatible mechanism has two critical problems. The first is that the system can guarantee a profit for the center only by imposing losses on the subordinates. The subordinates have to pay money for projects that are not adopted, and one division or the other could easily run a deficit even if the project were efficient and were adopted. For instance, if Anne's costs are $30 and Bill's are $60, Anne's payment will be her maximum of $20 and Bill's payment will be $70. The center's profit of $10 will be achieved by forcing Anne to operate at a loss. A cap on incentive payments is necessary to guarantee that the center runs a profit, but it destroys any reason for subordinates to remain in the organization. This problem is known as a "violation of individual rationality"; that is, rational employees will prefer to stay at home rather than work for a firm that will impose losses on them. It seems unreasonable to use a mechanism that gets subordinates to tell the truth by taxing them so much that they would rather not play the game at all.

The second problem is that the scheme still leaves incentives for the CEO to lie and make inefficient decisions. Although the CEO is guaranteed not to run at a loss, that is not the same thing as profit maximization. Just as with the original incentive-compatible scheme, the CEO can make a larger profit by lying about the revenue generated and allowing inefficient decisions to be made.

For instance, suppose the CEO announced that the revenues from the proposed contract would equal $90 instead of $100. He would then state that the project would be adopted if the sum of the cost messages from Bill and Anne summed to $90 or less. He could then set lower payment caps for Anne and Bill at $15 and $75, summing to $90. If Anne's true costs were $30 and Bill's $55, Anne would receive her maximum payment of $15 and Bill would receive a payment of $60. This would result in total incentive payments of $75 and a profit for the CEO of $25, instead of a profit of $10 if the CEO were to reveal the revenue accurately.

The inefficiency caused by the CEO's misrepresentation of revenues is clear – those efficient projects costing Bill and Anne between $90 and $100 would be disapproved. For all projects that were approved, however, the center would get a *larger* profit minus incentive payments by misrevealing revenues. And the center would be generating profits for itself in those situations in which the minimum tax for unapproved projects applied.

Budget balancing again

With the simple incentive-compatibility mechanism, the employees were provided incentive payments that induced them to tell the truth, but the CEO ran a deficit. With the modified incentive-compatible mechanism the CEO was guaranteed a profit, but the employees were left running a loss. With both, the CEO could increase profits (at the expense of efficient decision making) by misrepresenting his own private information. Is there no mechanism that satisfies incentive compatibility for subordinates and guarantees efficient decision making by the superior?

The only incentive-compatible mechanisms are those that do not balance the internal budget of the firm; that is, payments made to subordinates to tell the truth cannot balance the revenue generated by their efforts. What Holmstrom demonstrated with regard to hidden action Groves demonstrates with regard to hidden information: This budget-balancing requirement is inconsistent with the creation of incentives for efficient Nash equilibria. As Groves (1985) writes:

> Either the full cost feature, incentive compatibility, or optimality of decisions must be sacrificed. If making optimal decisions is the main task of the procedure and managers are trusted to follow the incentives defined by the firm, then it appears that full cost allocation schemes are inappropriate for these purposes, regardless of how useful they might be for purposes other than making optimal decisions. (96)

The existence of an inevitable residual has been regarded as simply a technical problem in much of the literature on incentive compatibility (Tideman 1985). However, it is clear that the inevitable residual is a telltale for conflict in the organization. The use of an efficient incentive-compatible mechanism leaves the residual unmaximized and the owner thus has a stake in inefficiency. Otherwise, the selection of an efficient incentive-compatible scheme would leave the N team members and the owner in an $N + 1$ budget-balanced, efficient Nash equilibrium, contrary to the theorem of Groves (1985).

THE MANAGERIAL DILEMMA: SELF-COMMITMENT

The point is clear: Since wages for subordinates are costs for the owner of residual profits, profit maximization by the center is an obstacle to the efficient resolution of both the hidden information and hidden action problem. The desire of owners to maximize revenues less payoffs for team members constantly tempts them to choose incentive schemes that encourage strategic misrepresentation and inefficient production behaviors by subordinates.

It is compelling that both the analysis of hidden action in the preceding chapter and the analysis of hidden information in this chapter end up at the same point. There do exist incentive mechanisms that can induce efficient levels of effort (Holmstrom's joint forcing contract) or accurate revelation of information (Groves–Loeb mechanisms), but they all violate budget balancing. Furthermore, because they violate budget balancing, they provide a temptation for those who own shares in the residual profits to choose inefficient incentive schemes in order to increase the size of the residual. In short, efficient incentives for subordinates require self-denial by superiors. The need for credible commitment by employers not to undertake actions that subvert efficient outcomes for short-term profits is not peculiar to piece rates, but is quite general.

Thus, the results with regard to hidden actions in teams and hidden information in decentralized organizations seem to be parallel. The only mechanisms that induce subordinates to act appropriately, and to reveal information appropriately, in equilibrium are those that do not balance the budget. These mechanisms can be engineered to guarantee a profit for someone. But whoever that someone is will have an incentive to intervene in the managerial process to limit the efficiency of the mechanism in order to increase the size of the inevitable residual. Profit maximization and efficiency are at odds in the firm.

The central dilemma in a hierarchy is thus how to constrain the self-interest of those with a stake in the inevitable residual generated by an efficient incentive system. The superior in the organization has the means to reconcile conflicts of interest among subordinates, so that team members will find it in their interest not to shirk and not to provide misinformation about future strategic decisions by the organization. However, maintaining this state of efficiency requires a degree of self-denial by the center. There will be a set of managerial alternatives available to the owner that will decrease the overall size of the pie, while increasing the owner's share of that pie. When the owner gives in to the temptation to choose these short-term profit-maximizing alternatives, it touches off a string of corresponding self-interested actions by other members of the hierarchy that result in a globally less efficient equilibrium.

From this perspective, organizational efficiency requires that the manager be a philosopher-king who can be content with an efficient kingdom even though his court is less regal than those of more acquisitive neighboring lords. An attempt by the king to squeeze the last surplus out of the kingdom for his own use will induce his subjects to hide their gold rather than invest it and to shirk rather than work productively to produce revenue that the king will only take away. While this conclusion will be jarring to modern organization economists, I find striking confirmation of it in modern economic history and in the practical literature on organization management.

"Tying the King's Hands"

North (1981) argues that the profit-maximizing motives of political leaders has been the primary obstacle to the development of institutionalized incentives supporting economic efficiency:

From the redistributive societies of ancient Egyptian dynasties through the slavery system of the Greek and Roman world to the medieval manor, there was persistent tension between the ownership structure which maximized rents to the ruler (and his group) and an efficient system that reduced transaction costs and encouraged economic growth. (25)

155

The tension is exactly what emerges from the analysis of incentive-compatible mechanisms in this chapter.

North and Weingast (1989) illustrate this general argument via an analysis of Renaissance societies. The actions of monarchs in reneging on loans and other contracts systematically created incentives that led to fewer savings and less investment. Economic growth in Great Britain was dependent on restraining the king from taking these self-interested actions.

In "Tying the King's Hands," Root (1989) makes a similar argument regarding the monarchs of France's Old Regime:

> Because the king claimed full discretion, he had less real power. Claiming to be above the law in fiscal matters made it more difficult for the king to find partners for trade. Creditors took into account the king's reputation for repudiating debts and therefore demanded higher interest rates than otherwise would have been needed to elicit loans. (259)

The solution lay in finding a credible commitment to property rights that would provide incentives for the kind of investment and economic activity that would lead to economic growth.

For the king, as for the manager in the rest of this book, the problem is how to commit oneself credibly to efficient mechanisms.

Constraining the manager

The classics of organizational management seem to provide an intuitive grasp of this tension. Chester Barnard (1938) claimed that "Organizations endure . . . in proportion to the breadth of the morality by which they are governed" (282). Unbridled acquisitiveness by managers leads to inefficiency, instability, and chaos in the firm. Like kings, managers may find that a reputation for opportunism discourages subordinates from taking the actions needed for economic growth. Like them, managers may find it useful in the long run to acquiesce to institutions that tie their hands.

The piece-rate incentive systems studied in Chapter 5 illustrate the same tension. A piece-rate incentive provides rewards for hard work and effort. However, it also provides information about the effort cost function, which a CEO can use against employees. Armed with full information about employee effort cost functions, an employer can approximate a forcing contract – manipulating piece rates in such a way as to induce maximal effort at minimal compensation for employees. The employee gold-bricking described in Chapter 5 is based on employees' assumption that employers will violate this trust. If employees could trust their superiors to restrain themselves from the profit-maximizing use of the information provided by piece rates, both sides could be better off. The success of the

Lincoln Electric Company can be attributed to a set of norms and institutions that credibly constrain management from self-interested manipulation of piece rates.

Indeed, economists themselves are becoming increasingly aware that "trustworthiness" on the part of managers seems to be a necessary element of an effective incentive system. In their study of "compensation and incentives," Baker, Jensen, and Murphy (1988) note "empirical evidence that is inconsistent with our traditional economic theories." They point out that subjective measures of performance are generally unsuitable in modern organizations because of our inability to specify and measure precisely the behaviors desired from subordinates; misspecification clearly leads to inappropriate behaviors. They point out that, although subjective performance evaluations have potential advantages as a basis for compensation, these advantages are generally overlooked because of a lack of trust. "The lack of trust between employees and supervisors and their distaste for conflict lead organizations to avoid pay-for-performance systems based on subjective performance evaluation" (Baker, Jensen, and Murphy 1988: 599). Employees recognize the primary theoretical result of this chapter — that superiors frequently face self-interested incentives that are at odds with their own best interests.

In many ways, then, managers and kings face similar political problems: how to commit themselves to actions contrary to self-interest. A firm will be better off if it can guarantee its subordinates a secure "property right" in a given incentive plan and a right to control certain aspects of their work environment and work pace — just as the Renaissance societies were better off once merchants had secure property rights. Security in these property rights can give employees reason to make investments of time, energy, and social relationships that produce economic growth. The major threat to employee property rights is the dictatorial power of the ruler to appropriate all the rents generated by subordinates — the kind of appropriation proposed by the economic literature on "optimal forcing contracts." The problem, for the firm as for the British economy, is how to constrain the self-interested depredations of the ruler in order to motivate the actions necessary for economic growth.

CONCLUSION

How can managers resist the temptation to select inefficient incentive schemes? The rest of the book examines various solutions to this problem. One of them is the market mechanism. While the hierarchy has been regarded in this book as an autonomous entity created because of market failure and insulated from market forces, clearly there is a market for managers. Perhaps the market setting in which managers are recruited and rewarded will provide incentives – aside from the incentives obtained by the internal distribution of the surplus generated by team production processes – that "correct" the temptation to cheat by managers. If this is the case, markets will "correct" hierarchical failures by allowing managers to commit themselves to actions that would not otherwise be in their self-interest.

8

Hierarchical failures and market solutions
Can competition create efficient incentives for hierarchy?

> It is commonly thought that a widely held corporation that is not being run in the interests of its shareholders will be vulnerable to a takeover bid. . . . [But] shareholders can free ride on the raider's improvement of the corporation, thereby seriously limiting the raider's profit.
>
> Grossman and Hart (1980: 42)

The first chapter established that markets can break down due to team production externalities, market power, and information asymmetry. These failures provide the theoretical justification for hierarchy. The analysis so far, however, has established only that hierarchy has the capacity to work ideally *in the absence* of team production externalities, market power, and information asymmetry. The same factors that promote market failure promote hierarchical failure.

As long as information about employee types is hidden, it is impossible for managers to say exactly what behaviors they expect from subordinates. Therefore, it is impossible to write the kind of joint forcing contract suggested by Holmstrom. Subordinates are left in a state of ambiguity that affords them the opportunity to shirk strategically, hiding behind a veil of ignorance about which team member, or which external shock, is responsible for unsatisfactory observed outcomes.

Hierarchical superiors are not just the victims of team production externalities and information asymmetries. Hierarchy, by its very nature, gives each hierarchical superior monopsony powers as "buyer" of team efforts. In piece-rate organizations, the incentive to lower piece rates to take advantage of this position is at odds with efficiency. In general, Holmstrom demonstrated, employers who share in the revenues produced by joint efforts must have reason to take inefficient actions. Hierarchy provides the motive and opportunity for exploiting the market power that accompanies the top position in a hierarchy. We are left with a notion of hierarchical failure that

159

is completely analogous to that of market failure: The pursuit of individual self-interest by the purchasers and suppliers of team production efforts results in outcomes that are Pareto inefficient.

EFFICIENCY AND MARKETS

At first, the notion of hierarchical failure seems to fly in the face of the efficiency hypothesis of organizational economics: "Except when there are perversities associated with the funding process, or when strategically situated members of an organization are unable to participate in the prospective gains, unrealized efficiency opportunities always offer an incentive to reorganize" (Williamson and Ouchi 1981: 355). While this statement is true, it begs the question "reorganize to what?" The impossibility results of Arrow, Sen, Holmstrom, and others suggest that the result of every possible reorganization will itself be flawed. The incentive to reorganize does not resolve the logical inconsistencies that limit any possible institutional design.

Relative efficiency vs. ideal efficiency

As offered by Williamson, Jensen, and others, the appropriate response to the impossibility of fully efficient hierarchical designs is to rely on an argument of *relative* efficiency. From this perspective, the results of Chapter 7 verge on irrelevancy; from a common-sense perspective, it is simply to be expected that the benchmark of ideal efficiency can never be attained in a hierarchy.

This position is most clearly defended by Jensen and Meckling (1976):

> The reduced value of the firm caused by the manager's consumption of perquisites . . . is "non-optimal" or inefficient only in comparison to a world in which we could obtain compliance of the agent to the principal's wishes at zero cost. . . . But these costs (monitoring and bonding costs and "residual loss") are an unavoidable result of the agency relationship. (327–8)

Agency costs are therefore just costs to be considered in a maximizing problem, just like the costs of raw materials or land. This suggests that the notion of "efficiency" be modified to refer to those outcomes which are the best that can be achieved given the structure of costs available. Thus, to say that hierarchy does not eliminate the losses due to opportunistic behavior is the same as saying that hierarchy does not reduce the cost of materials to zero. An efficient outcome is simply one that maximizes surpluses, given the inevitable cost of materials and the equally inevitable losses due to opportunistic behavior. A certain hierarchical arrangement can reasonably be called "efficient" when it reduces those costs to a minimum, although there will inevitably be some such losses in any regime. Hierarchy is "efficient" when it is the best that self-interested individuals can do under any feasible arrangement.

Hierarchical failures and market solutions

This is a reasonable and defensible position; Williamson and Ouchi are therefore not claiming that there is an institutional arrangement that eliminates social dilemmas, but that there are forces that lead individuals to find those social arrangements that keep the losses to a minimum.

Market forces and relative efficiency

Later in this chapter, I will return to the reasonableness of this definition, but for now I would like to ask, What are the forces that, according to organizational economists, keep efficiency losses to a minimum? These forces, ironically, are not internal to the hierarchy. They are market forces: "The primary theoretical 'engine' driving agency theory is not capital market failure but, rather, capital market efficiency" (Barney and Ouchi 1986: 210). As Dann and DeAngelo (1983) write:

An important premise of corporate finance theory is that markets discipline managers to maximize all stockholders' wealth. Competitive forces in two markets, the market for corporate control and the market for managerial labor services, are widely viewed as providing complementary enforcement of the stockholder wealth maximization rule. (275)

To the extent that this argument is true, the implications for organizational behavior are enormous. The "maximization of stockholder wealth" entails the making of a great many decisions by a manager – decisions involving not just product choice and marketing strategy, but the motivation and training of subordinates and managerial style. If markets "discipline managers to maximize all stockholders' wealth," then all of these decisions must be made with the single goal in mind. It means that one good answer to the question "Why does this manager take the action she does?" is: "Because it is the efficient action to take, and a less efficient action would result in a threat from an alternative management team."

Furthermore, the supposition that financial markets discipline managers in the interest of shareholders would seem to entail the parallel supposition that similar principal–agency problems are solved all the way down the firm's long hierarchy. It does very little good for the capital market to discipline the CEO of a firm if the CEO is unable to transfer that discipline down the hierarchy. Market discipline is effective only if it is binding on the entire hierarchy.

In such a case, the incentive problems of hierarchy studied in the preceding three chapters would be irrelevant; even though hierarchies have logical limits on their efficiency, markets coerce CEOs, who effectively coerce subordinates all the way down the line, in the name of shareholder wealth maximization. Financial economics may supply us with little substantive information about the incentive systems that CEOs install to work this magic, but that can be supplied by simple empirical observation: Whatever

161

managerial practices we see in place in the real world are by definition the most efficient. Since any deviation from efficiency would result in an opportunity for efficiency gain by an alternative management team, we can be satisfied that the failure to observe a takeover attempt is sufficient evidence that the existing practices of management are efficient.

It is worth noting that, in such an instance, markets would serve as a credible commitment mechanism for resolving the tension between undisciplined managerial self-interest and organizational efficiency. When employees ask of a manager, "Why should we believe that you are not going to cheat us?" the credible answer is: "Because if I were not committed to organizational efficiency more than my own self-interest, the value of the stock would go down, a raider might come and take over my job, and I could never get another job." According to this perspective, it is the threat of competitors for top management positions that is the external force keeping managers credible. And if this threat constrains managers from opportunistically pursuing self-interest, the biggest obstacle to the design and implementation of efficient incentive systems is overcome.

The biggest corporate buyout ever

The buyout of RJR Nabisco in December 1988 illustrates many of the issues surrounding the market as a potential device for disciplining managers. RJR Nabisco was headed by a management team under F. Ross Johnson. The team was represented on the board of directors, and many of the board members were friendly to it. In late 1988, Johnson and his team announced their intention to take this publicly traded corporation private by means of a leveraged buyout, or LBO, in which they would borrow sufficient funds to purchase all the company's publicly traded stock. Their initial bid was $75 a share, worth a total of $17 billion to the shareholders of the company (Burrough and Helyar 1990: 190–1).

Other management teams felt that this was significantly below the true value of the company. In particular, the firm of Kohlberg Kravis Roberts (KKR) responded with its own bid of $90 a share (Burrough and Helyar 1990: 199–230). This initiated a bidding war in which the RJR Nabisco management team ultimately bid $112 a share, while the KKR final offer was $109 a share.

The board of directors ultimately accepted the KKR offer, despite the fact that it was smaller. The reasons they did so are significant. The RJR directors wanted to keep the firm intact, whereas it was clear that the RJR management team was intent on splitting it up. Furthermore, the RJR directors felt that the KKR offer was more equitable for the shareholders because it distributed 25 percent of the equity in the future company to shareholders, rather than 15 percent with Johnson's offer. The KKR offer consisted of more equity backing the huge debts that would result from the buyout of the firm. The directors were also concerned about employees; while Johnson was clearly planning to fire a good many employees, KKR was committed to saving jobs and providing severance benefits. One director said, "Employees are assets, and any manager who doesn't see that is a fool. We could see Johnson didn't" (*Wall Street Journal* 1988b).

The directors perceived the current management team to be not only insensitive to workers, but also greedy and sloppy:

Not only were directors irate over [Johnson's] handling of the buy-out, but also their review of the company's operations during the bidding process left them appalled. Management was spending huge sums on lodgings in Palm Springs, Calif., on security measures for Mr. Johnson, on a fleet of corporate jets so large that some directors dubbed it the "RJR Air Force." Although the directors had benefited from this lavish style, they hadn't known the total extent and cost of it. That belated realization helped convince them that KKR could run the company better than Mr. Johnson, and without stripping it down to just the tobacco operations. Directors believed that KKR could save millions just by excising Mr. Johnson's excesses. (*Wall Street Journal* 1988b)

Thus, the bidding war between management teams allowed the directors, representing the shareholders and employees, to make comparisons on a variety of dimensions. The crucial factor seemed to be the willingness of the winning team to resist the opportunistic temptation to divert the firm's surplus to excess salaries and managerial perquisites, at the expense of the employees and shareholders.

Indeed, Johnson's management team was frequently compared against that of KKR in the press in the aftermath of the bidding war. The losing bidder, Johnson, not only would earn more than $25 million from his shares of the stock, but would also continue to get his salary and bonuses, totaling approximately $1.7 million a year, through 1991. His record-breaking golden parachute was worth a total of $53.8 million (*Business Week* 1989a).

The news media were also concerned about the performance of the stock under Johnson's management. The stock had been selling on Wall Street for much less than the original offer of $75, yet Johnson himself was ultimately willing to pay $112. If the assets were potentially worth that much, why hadn't Johnson been able to make the assets of the firm live up to their potential as manager? Why would he behave differently as owner of a privately held firm than he had as manager of the publicly held firm?

The RJR Nabisco buyout demonstrates the possibility that market competition can supplement the internal incentives of hierarchy, and do so to the benefit of some of the actors. The shareholders of RJR Nabisco benefited by huge windfalls in the value of their stock; in effect, the competition between potential management teams forced Ross Johnson to reveal a more accurate valuation of the firm ($25 billion) than his original offer of $17 billion. The shareholders were thus guaranteed a larger share of the surplus generated by the assets than they would have received if the company had remained in the hands of managers who spent millions on executive airplanes and other perquisites. Furthermore, the employees benefited by getting a new management team that was, in the opinion of the directors, more concerned about protecting their rights and morale than Johnson's team had been.

Clearly, market competition is potentially of great value as a shaper and constrainer of managerial behavior. But the RJR case also raises several questions: Why had the value of RJR Nabisco assets been allowed to drop so far below their potential value for so long? How rigorous is the disciplining effect of the market? Do directors always act in the best interests of shareholders and employees when a firm goes up for auction?

Another question is raised by the ultimate outcome – a publicly traded firm was taken private. The huge gap between ownership and control that characterizes the modern publicly held firm was erased. The new owner-managers of the firm, being in debt for billions of dollars, will have a huge incentive to manage the firm efficiently. What does this say about the publicly held firm? Is it possible for the shareholders in a publicly held firm to constrain the actions of their managers? Or is the lesson of the RJR Nabisco case that the separation of ownership and control is an insuperable obstacle to efficient management?

MANAGERS AS AGENTS OF STOCKHOLDERS

The central questions raised by the RJR Nabisco case have to do with the separation of ownership and control. This separation creates yet another principal–agent relationship in the hierarchical firm, one potentially fraught with all the problems of shirking and misrepresentation that plague other such relationships. These problems are magnified because the stockholders are a large and diffuse group, and therefore limited in their ability to direct management (Berle and Means 1932). Why should ownership and control be separated in the modern firm?

The theoretical advantage of separating
ownership and control

In an argument referred to in Chapter 6, Bengt Holmstrom demonstrated that balancing the budget of revenues generated and incentives expended among the members of a firm would necessarily result in inefficiency. He argued that one way to alleviate this problem was to create an external "depository" for the residual generated by the actions of the members of the firm – the owners. "The enforcement problem can be overcome only by bringing in a principal (or a party) who will assume the residual of the non-budget balancing sharing rules" (Holmstrom 1982: 327). Ideally, the owners should be completely separated from the management of the firm, so that none of their actions can affect the size of the residual – otherwise, their interest in the residual would cause them to take opportunistic actions that would hurt the efficiency of the firm as a whole while increasing the size of the residual. "Note that it is important that the principal not provide any (unobservable) productive inputs or else a free-rider problem remains" (328).

Holmstrom noted that this prescription bears a striking resemblance to the reality of the modern corporation. The partnership, Holmstrom notes, is essentially a budget-balancing scheme in which all the revenues generated by the partnership are distributed among the partners; this scheme necessarily results in strong incentives for free riding among the partners. In a capitalistic firm, however, shareholders who supply the capital for the firm also hold the ownership rights for the residual profits generated after the employees, managers, bondholders, and other stakeholders are paid off. The shareholders are normally a large, diffuse, and ever-changing group. They know little about the management of the firm and have even less ability to affect individually the behavior of anyone in the firm. Consequently, they satisfy the conditions of Holmstrom's ideal residual owner – having no ability to interfere opportunistically in the efficient operation of the firm. This allows the managers to operate under a non-budget-balancing incentive scheme in which free riding is discouraged. Furthermore, if shareholders *could* effectively monitor and discipline managers, the Holmstrom problem would pop up again: They would undoubtedly exercise their disciplining power in the interest of maximizing the size of the residual rather than in the interest of organizational efficiency. This would destroy what Holmstrom describes as the theoretical advantage of separating ownership from control for the purpose of using the owners as a "sponge" for the efficient (not maximal) residual.

However, the separation of ownership and managerial control raises a host of derivative problems. If the management is, in most cases, not coextensive with the owners of the firm, what does motivate the managers? If the managers are motivated by a share in the residual generated by the firm, they will have the same incentives discussed in the preceding two chapters to take inefficient actions in order to increase their shares. Is it possible to write managerial contracts that create a stake in efficiency? Why should managers be motivated to improve the efficiency of the firm?

Incentives for managerial shirking

In fact, the separation of ownership and control may solve the problem of opportunistic intervention by owners *without* solving the problem of motivating the managers. As Michael Jensen has pointed out, managers have a strong incentive to engage in inefficient opportunistic behavior of their own. Once efficient levels of inputs are selected and purchased, managers have no reason to hand the resulting residual profits over to the shareholders in the form of dividends:

Conflicts of interest between shareholders and managers over payout policies are especially severe when the organization generates substantial free cash flow. The problem is how to motivate managers to disgorge the cash rather than investing it at below the cost of capital or wasting it on organizational inefficiencies. (Jensen 1986: 323)

Managers find it unattractive to pay out dividends to shareholders for several reasons:

Payouts to shareholders reduce the resources under managers' control, thereby reducing managers' power, and making it more likely they will incur the monitoring of the capital markets which occurs when the firm must obtain new capital. . . . Managers have incentives to cause their firms to grow beyond the optimal size. Growth increases the managers' power by increasing the resources under their control. It is also associated with the increases in managers' compensation, because changes in compensation are positively related to the growth in sales. (323)

According to this analysis, self-interested managers may make managerial decisions that increase the size of the firm beyond the efficient level, that divert resources to managerial perquisites and salaries, and that make the job of managing the firm easier rather than more efficient.

Shareholders, of course, have the power to remove managers who are using the firm's resources for excessive managerial salaries, company planes, or inefficient growth. However, exercising this power would require the resolution of a (normally) huge collective action problem. Organizing such a disciplining action, in the form of a fight for control of the board, would be very costly, and the benefits would go to all of the shareholders, whether or not they helped pay the costs of the disciplining action. Consequently, shareholders normally free-ride on one another to avoid any such costly action, satisfying themselves with occasional attendance and voicing of complaints at annual meetings.

Furthermore, it normally requires a large amount of information to establish whether a particular management team is diverting free resources from the most efficient ends. Monitoring the performance of managers is another costly public good, and again shareholders have every reason to free-ride on one another.

Shareholders may choose to sue managers in court for larger dividends, as the Dodge brothers sued Henry Ford early in his career. Ford was especially open about his disinterest in shareholder profits, and the Dodge brothers were successful. Normally, however, the courts are closed off to unhappy shareholders because of the "business judgment rule." This rule is a principle propounded in the U.S. court system declaring that the judgment of managers may not be challenged in court; usually managers are liable only for gross violations of their fiduciary responsibilities.

Hierarchical failures and market solutions

The legal ability of shareholders to control managers is further limited by the fact that many large firms have received their corporate charters from the state of Delaware, which successfully competes for the legal location of many large firms by offering a legal system that is very friendly to the rights of management.

With or without a Delaware charter, the board of directors is charged with the responsibility of monitoring the management in the interests of shareholders. However, the board is normally selected by a nominating committee of directors, which is itself controlled by management. The board is often thought of more as an arm of management than as a legislative representative of the mass of shareholders.

Managerial compensation

The size of executive salaries has become a major issue in the press in recent years. A cover story in *Business Week* (1989a) asked, "Is the Boss Getting Paid Too Much?" The chairman and president of Walt Disney were the two most highly paid executives in the country, earning more than $40 million and $30 million respectively in 1988. In this and many other cases, the high pay resulted in part from new incentive plans that link executive pay with firm performance. However, as *Business Week* noted, many other executives were paid very well despite their firms' poor performance. *Business Week* singled out Lee Iacocca as someone whose $41 million in pay over three years was way out of proportion to the mediocre performance of Chrysler. When E. F. Hutton was found to be involved in illegal check overdrafting, the board responded by increasing the CEO's salary by 23 percent to $1.2 million and gave him 12,000 shares of stock. The CEO, Robert Fomon, was quoted as saying, "No chief executive can be held accountable for any single thing that happens in a corporation" (*New York Times* 1986).

Several economists have recently demonstrated that compensation practices for managers and employees constitute striking anomalies from economic theory (Baker, Jensen, and Murphy 1988; Stiglitz 1987). These anomalies raise serious doubts about the general ability of markets to provide the necessary external discipline to resolve internal hierarchical failure. Economic theory would predict that pay-for-performance compensation could radically improve the efficiency of hierarchical performance. However, most firms have very weak or nonexistent links between performance and pay. Instead, firms traditionally rely on opportunities for promotion to motivate performance; real increases in economic incentives come not from merit pay in a given job, but from promotion to a higher rank. But this is itself problematic for efficiency. The main problem is that "the best performer at one level in the hierarchy is not the best candidate for the job one level up – the best salesman is rarely the best manager, for example, and the

167

best scholar is rarely the best dean" (Baker, Jensen, and Murphy 1988: 602). But if promotions are made on the basis of something other than the best performance (e.g., if promotion is based on suitability for a higher job), then the incentive for the people in a lower job to perform in their current jobs diminishes markedly.

Given the unacceptability of incentive systems based on promotions, why don't firms attempt to motivate employees by means of merit incentive systems? The main drawback seems to be the inability of firms to induce supervisors to give accurate performance evaluations. In organizations that attempt to link pay with performance, supervisors almost universally hand out good to excellent performance evaluations. They do not want to risk the animosity of their subordinates by giving low evaluations.

From an economic perspective, of course, this explanation is not adequate. It does not matter if managers feel uncomfortable giving low performance evaluations; if efficiency requires it, those firms whose supervisors undertake the unpleasant task will outperform those who do not, and competition should eventually weed out the less efficient organizations. Top-level managers who allow this kind of laxity should be either replaced or disciplined by the capital and managerial markets. Thus, the question is still why the market allows managers to ignore the efficiency benefits of pay-for-performance incentives.

Executive compensation

Informally at least, the management controls the process of appointment to the board of directors and may well control the composition of the compensation committee that sets managers' salaries. Salaries and other managerial perquisites are a telltale aspect of firm policy, further evidence of the weakness of market disciplining forces on hierarchical failure.

We know that, at least at the top levels, greater emphasis is placed on pay-for-performance contracts, linking executive bonuses to stock price, for example. Once again, however, the evidence suggests that the linkage is not nearly as strong as normative economic theory would recommend. "On average, each $1,000 change in shareholder wealth corresponds to an increase in this year's and next year's salary and bonus of only two cents" (Baker, Jensen, and Murphy 1988: 611). If the managers themselves own a great deal of the company's stock, they might have sufficient incentive to act in shareholders' interests. But the evidence suggests that managers who own little stock have no stronger incentive contract than managers who own much stock.

If performance does not determine management compensation, what does? Empirical evidence documents that executive compensation varies closely with firm size. A firm that is 10 percent larger than another will pay its executives, on average, 3 percent more (Baker, Jensen, and Murphy 1988: 609). This is not just cross-sectional data; as firms increase in size, they pay their executives more. Knowing this, managers could develop a bias in favor of inefficient growth. "This could explain some of the vast amount of inefficient expenditures of corporate resources on diversification programs that have created large conglomerate organizations over the last 20 years" (609).

How can we explain not only the size of managerial compensation, but the lack of incentive for efficiency and the specific incentive for inefficient growth? Baker, Jensen, and Murphy point out that boards of directors and CEOs are imperfect agents of shareholders and that imperfect agents will create imperfect incentives for subordinates farther down the hierarchy. "The absence of pay-for-performance compensation systems for managers implies that managers have few incentives to structure and enforce value-maximizing contracts with subordinates" (614). Loss of control in the first agency relationship – between shareholders and boards of directors – is passed on and amplified down the hierarchy.

Assuming that managers do have "slack" to divert organizational resources from profit-maximizing uses, how do they use them? One obvious way is to provide excess salaries and perquisites for themselves, as already noted. But as Baker, Jensen, and Murphy (1988) point out, organizational slack can also be used to make the management process itself less costly. This can be done, for instance, by the implementation of a more lax promotion and reward system rather than a tough pay-for-performance system:

Consider, for example, a division manager deciding whether or not to terminate a popular but nonproductive employee. The personal costs borne by a manager making an unpopular termination decision are high and include personal discomfort with the task, chastisement by other employees and peers, the loss of important friendships, and the possibility of being sued for illegal discharge. Firing the unproductive employee will increase divisional profits, but this increased profitability will only benefit the manager to the extent that his or her compensation is tied to divisional performance. (614)

The same argument can be made for avoiding tough pay-for-performance systems. One of the most frequent uses of organizational slack is to ease the social stress caused by constant hierarchical pressure to meet tough performance standards.

Baker, Jensen, and Murphy point out that the widespread use of egalitarian incentive systems, divorced from individual performance, poses a dilemma for economics. If there is some reason that these incentive systems are in fact more efficient, normal organizational economics cannot explain why. If, however, these incentive systems are not the most efficient, economics cannot explain why markets do not discipline organizational hierarchies to eliminate them.

Managerial dilemmas

Given the considerable constraints on shareholder action, what can a shareholder do who is unimpressed with the performance of management? On an individual basis, the answer seems to be simply: Sell. When enough people are willing to sell and few others are willing to buy, the price of the stock goes down. Thus, the price of the stock becomes an indication not only of the shareholders' evaluation of a firm's assets, but also of the shareholders' evaluation of the management's capabilities.

But the price of stock acts as something other than an indicator of shareholder satisfaction. When the price of stock becomes depressed due to a lack of confidence in managerial ability, it is easier for a different management team to buy enough stock to take over control of the firm. Competition in the capital market can create a threat to current managers – a threat that should give managers an incentive to serve shareholder interests. Thus, the possibility of a takeover is a valuable disciplining device for those at the top of a hierarchy. As Michael Jensen points out, the "Pac-Man defense" used by Martin Marietta in response to Bendix's takeover attempt resulted in a race by each company to acquire the other's shares. This "makes it clear that the crucial issue is not whether the two companies will merge but which managers will be in control" (Jensen 1984: 110).

The interesting thing about competition is that it forces self-interested individuals to take actions that benefit a passive third party. Competition between two gas stations forces each to lower prices, benefiting totally passive consumers. Similarly, Jensen argues, competition for corporate control forces managers to take actions in the interests of largely passive shareholders. "Although managers are self-interested, the environment in which they operate gives them relatively little leeway to feather their nests at shareholders' expense" (Jensen 1984: 110). In summary, it has become virtually an article of faith in the field of finance that the "agency costs" incurred by the inability of shareholders to control managers can be (and are) controlled by an active and competitive market for capital and for corporate control.

The best empirical evidence on takeovers suggests that they act as a disciplining device. This is demonstrated by the fact that the value of stock of the target company increases systematically. Furthermore, the value of the stock of the takeover firm does not decrease (Jensen and Ruback 1983). Shareholders benefit from the fact that managers who have not been maximizing the value of the firm's assets are displaced.

One of the common results of takeovers is the fragmentation of the firm – the selling off of assets and divisions to other firms. This suggests that previous managers were pursuing a strategy of increasing their own pay and status by increasing the size of the firm beyond efficient levels – as with the breakup of the huge oil conglomerates that were created by oil profits in the seventies (Jensen 1984).

Hierarchical failures and market solutions

A takeover of one firm disciplines managers at other firms by example. The wave of takeovers in the eighties convinced many managers to return larger proportions of profits to shareholders in the form of dividends than they were accustomed to doing (*New York Times* 1989). There is little doubt, then, that competition in the capital market serves as an external corrective for managerial shirking – a corrective that is felt not just by top managers but throughout the hierarchy.

LIMITS ON THE MARKET AS A DISCIPLINING DEVICE FOR HIERARCHY

Although takeovers provide a device for disciplining managers, it is not necessarily a *perfect* device. If it were, agency costs would go to zero. There seems to be no evidence that this is the case, and no reason to think it should be. As Jensen and Meckling (1976) have noted, agency costs are an inevitable cost of doing business. Jensen and Meckling believe that capital markets drive those agency costs as low as they can be, but "low" is a relative term. The unanswered question is how much "slack" remains in the system. Unfortunately, evidence suggests that a great deal of slack remains – that takeovers provide only broad constraints on the profit-diverting activities of managers.

Limits on the market disciplining of hierarchies

The source of this slack has been traced to the presence of social dilemmas in the takeover market. That is, self-interested behavior on the part of all the participants – shareholders, raiders, managers – can lead to inefficiency in the capital market.

Assume for the moment that the current management of a firm is slothful and that the shareholders are unhappy. A more efficient management team feels that it could increase the value of the firm's shares; it offers to buy enough shares to take over the hierarchy and reform the firm. The shareholders have to calculate whether it would be better to sell the shares or to keep them. If the shareholders are convinced that the new management could do a better job than the old management, they would do well to keep the shares rather than sell them, even at increased prices. In fact, if they could anticipate how much better the new management would do, they would individually refuse to accept any tender offer that was less than the value of the stock under the new management. But if the raider were forced to pay that high a price, it would no longer be worth his while to make the tender offer – he would have to give away all the anticipated efficiency gains from his own improved management in order to demonstrate his improved management skills.

Thus, for the good of the company, it would be better if each individual shareholder sold his or her shares to better managers; but individually, each shareholder would have an incentive to "free-ride" on other shareholders' actions and on the raider's improved management. The net result of all this free riding would be that the efficient manager might have less incentive to engage in the disciplining activity by threatening a takeover.

Grossman and Hart (1980) summarize the problem in their article on free riding in the takeover market:

> If a shareholder thinks that the raid will succeed and that the raider will improve the firm, he will not tender his shares, but will instead retain them, because he anticipates a profit from their price appreciation. As a result, a takeover bid may not be profitable even though current management is not acting in the interest of shareholders. Hence, even in a corporation, the public good is a public good. (43)

And even inside the corporation, a market failure is a market failure.

This means that corporate mismanagement has to be extreme if the expensive corrective of a takeover attempt is to be worthwhile. T. Boone Pickens indicates that, as a leading raider, he is fully aware of the costliness of this form of disciplining activity. He noted that 800,000 stockholders had made a combined $14 billion as a result of his company's six attempted takeovers. Mesa had made less than 5 percent of that gain "and we did all the work and took all the heat" (*St. Louis Post Dispatch* 1987). If corporate raiders get only 5 percent of the benefits of their costly efforts, the corporate mismanagement would have to be about twenty times worse than it would otherwise have to be in order to motivate a takeover attempt. The fact that other actors get 95 percent of the benefits of Pickens's raiding activities limits the incentive for Pickens to undertake this means of disciplining except in the case of the most extreme inefficiencies.

Theory of managerial market failure

Just as externalities in the capital market can create capital market failure, so market power can create inefficiencies in the market for managerial talent. While a truly competitive market may force the disclosure of hidden information about managers, the market for managers is not perfectly competitive, especially at higher levels. Some managers can differentiate themselves from other managers by reason of their expertise in the specialized operations of a given firm, the technology of a particular industry, or their proven ability to motivate subordinates. This "product differentiation" results in what is known as "monopolistic competition," in which competition in a market for homogeneous goods is replaced by much more constrained competition among buyers and sellers for goods (in this case, managers) that are not substitutes for one another. The net result is that managers who might not otherwise be able to extract monopolistic "rents" from the supply of their labor and expertise are able to do so. The interaction of this factor with information asymmetries is obvious.

Empirical evidence on the limits of market discipline

The practical importance of the theoretical arguments about free riding in the capital market and monopolistic competition in the managerial market is that managers may be able to demonstrate a significant amount of shirking, corruption, and ineffective management without having to worry about takeover attempts. Is this theoretical possibility supported by evidence from financial markets? There is a wide range of data from the capital markets suggesting that managers systematically take actions that are contrary to the interests of shareholders.

Supermajority amendments. If takeovers are an effective disciplining device, one of the most striking ways in which managers reveal a strong tendency to shirk is by trying to use their corporate and political influence to limit takeover activity. A case in point is the use of supermajority amendments, which require the approval of two-thirds to nine-tenths of the voting power for a merger or takeover. Given the limited ability of shareholders to organize such a political coalition, and the increased cost to a raider who is trying to get control of a firm, these amendments provide effective protection for current management.

A study by Jarrell and Poulsen (1987) demonstrated that shareholders react negatively to supermajority amendments. These amendments cause on average a 3 percent reduction in stock price. Because they are harmful to the interests of stockholders, managers have to exert great effort to pass them, even with the extensive use of managed, proxy voting. Institutional investors, who are more capable of opposing managers on these amendments, are generally opposed to their use. Jarrell and Poulsen show that firms that pass them have fewer institutional investors. They also have a relatively high proportion of holdings by insiders; insiders are less likely to object to supermajority amendments because they are normally passed with a provision that they will go into effect only if management triggers the supermajority voting requirement.

Standstill agreements. One means for managers to insulate themselves from the disciplining force of takeovers is an agreement with a substantial stockholder that would limit the stockholder's ownership to a certain proportion of shares. It offers some special treatment of the large block shareholder in return for this promise. By this strategy, "incumbent management removes a credible threat of control transfer and thereby obtains job protection at the expense of non-participating stockholders" (Dann and DeAngelo 1983: 299). Dann and DeAngelo have demonstrated that such agreements have significantly negative effects on the returns to nonparticipating stockholders. This result, the authors argue, offers support for the "managerial entrenchment hypothesis," according to which managers are willing and able to protect their jobs and their benefits at the expense of shareholders (300).

Greenmail. Another technique by which target managers can defend their position and insulate themselves from the disciplining action of takeovers is to repurchase the raider's stock at a premium. This is known as "greenmail"; it amounts to using the company's money to bribe raiders not to discipline the managers. In their review of the literature, Jensen and Ruback (1983) find that greenmail results in significantly negative stock returns.

Poison pills: Delaware corporation law. "Poison pills" is the name given to shareholder rights that are triggered by particular events such as takeover attempts. They may include the right to sell shares to the target firm at very attractive prices, for example. The creation of poison pills may also harm shareholders, to the benefit of managers, by making the cost of a takeover impossibly high.

A very large number of firms have their corporate charters through the state of Delaware. One of the advantages of these charters, as already mentioned, is that Delaware has a highly developed, probusiness corporate law. Therefore, it was significant that the Delaware Supreme Court ruled in *Moran v. Household International* (1985) that poison pills can be implemented without a majority vote among shareholders. In fact, Ryngaert (1989) found that important court decisions upholding poison pill provisions have negative effects on stock prices and that most court decisions rejecting poison pill provisions in favor of a raider have a positive effect on stock prices.

Despite the fact that Delaware law was already the most promanagement law in the United States, management teams of major firms lobbied hard for new Delaware legislation to secure the ability to defend themselves against takeovers. By late 1987, twenty-seven other states had enacted explicit antitakeover legislation, and in the words of one Delaware state official, "The feeling was out there that the corporations would start leaving the state" (personal communication 1988). Since 17 percent of the state's revenues come from incorporation fees and taxes, this was regarded by Delaware's predominantly rural legislators as a serious threat. As a result, the Delaware Bar Association drew up proposed legislation that would allow management to veto a hostile takeover for three years even though a majority of up to 85 percent of the shareholders agree to the takeover.

The debate before the state legislature was interesting. Speaking for the legislation were managers from General Mills, General Motors, and Du Pont, all of whom argued that the legislation was good for shareholders. Speaking against the legislation were various representatives of shareholder organizations, who argued that the legislation was actually intended to protect managers. Also opposed was SEC commissioner Joseph A. Grundfest and various economists, including Kenneth Koford of the University of Delaware. Koford (1988) argued that the legislation could introduce major inefficiencies into the corporate market.

The passage of the legislation, over the opposition of economists, the SEC, and shareholder groups, allowed managers to enact powerful poison pills for their firms. Nearly 250 companies adopted poison pills in 1988, bringing the total up to 786, including almost half the firms in the Fortune 500.

Theoretically, of course, the shareholders could sue their directors if they felt their legal rights as shareholders were being violated. However, in Delaware the "business judgment rule" has been used to stop shareholders from accepting quite lucrative tender offers. This was the case in the attempted takeover of Time, Inc., in the summer of 1989. Paramount Communications, Inc., made a bid of $200 a share for Time. Shareholders were enthusiastic, since the price was far above the market price for the stock. Time's management, however, sued to block the takeover attempt on the grounds that it had a long-term strategic plan that involved the purchase of Warner Communications, for $14 billion. The managers were upheld in the Delaware Chancery Court, which wrote:

The financial vitality of the corporation and the value of the company's shares is in the hands of the directors and managers of the firm. The corporation law does not operate on the theory that directors, in exercising their powers to manage the firm, are obligated to follow the wishes of a majority of shares. In fact, the directors, not shareholders, are charged with the duty to manage the firm. (*Wall Street Journal* 1989b)

The managers' decisions to pursue their own long-term business strategy thus took precedence over an outstanding offer; this decision left Time's shareholders with a price per share of only $143.

The politics of corporate governance

It has been claimed that agency theorists "proceed as if the monitoring of the market for corporate control were a constant, always ready to protect shareholders from 'opportunistic' managers" (see Davis and Stout 1990: 23). However, a recent study shows that the degree of takeover activity and the characteristics of target firms have not been constant over the past fifteen years (20–4).

The large takeovers of the eighties were aided by innovations in financing such as junk bonds, which allowed small bidders to buy targets on the strength of the sale value of the pieces of the acquired firm. They also received a boost from the political climate of the Reagan administration, in which a takeover could be undertaken with little worry about antitrust enforcement. Together, these made possible successful takeovers of Fortune 500 firms that had previously been virtually immune from such a threat.

The counterattack by management may well have limited the potential for future hostile takeovers. The number has declined rapidly since 1988 as a result, in part, of management's legislative successes in Delaware and elsewhere. Furthermore, unlike target firms in the early eighties, more recent target firms have not been associated with cash flow. As Davis and Stout (1990) conclude:

Contrary to the claims of agency theorists, the market for corporate control operates with a light touch and plays at best a limited "disciplinary" role. Moreover, the extent to which it provides any discipline at all, as well as the grounds for this discipline, are contingent on institutional factors that vary over time. (23)

While the period of rapid and large takeovers coerced managers to reorganize, improve performance, and return extra dividends to shareholders, the evidence summarized in this chapter suggests that managers have fought back. They have elaborated a new and effective array of political and organizational weapons insulating themselves from the threat of takeovers. In the words of law professor Victor Brudney (1985), "Management's discretion remains significant in terms of its power to divert assets to itself, and more than trivial in terms of its power to refrain from maximizing shareholder wealth" (1443–4).

SUMMARY

It is clear that competition in the capital and managerial markets can serve as a device for disciplining managers. Otherwise, current managers of large corporations would not be trying so actively to limit that competition through legislation, regulation, and court action. However, the disciplining potential of markets is not perfect. The ability of managers to obtain favorable state legislation, protecting themselves from the threat of takeovers, is strong evidence of this fact. Further evidence of managerial entrenchment exists in the anomalies of executive compensation, which cannot be explained in terms of current economic theory without sacrificing the assumption of effective disciplining forces in the marketplace.

Is it reasonable to question the notion of "relative efficiency," and with it Williamson and Ouchi's (1981) "efficiency hypothesis"? I would argue that it is. While market forces make for partial efficiency, there is no reason to suppose that there are no more publicly held firms like RJR Nabisco whose value could be greatly increased by a reduction in agency costs. The costs of transacting a hostile takeover of a firm with an entrenched and inefficient management are enormous, and the raiders who are the instruments of this disciplining force reap only a small fraction of the benefits of their actions. In many firms, in many industries, the losses due to the opportunistic be-

176

havior of individuals at all levels of a hierarchy are likely to be substantial. For this reason, it is still reasonable to picture hierarchies as settings for social dilemmas. Are we to say that the inefficient Nash equilibrium in a social dilemma is really efficient just because the participants have not yet figured out a way to garner the gains from cooperation? I think not.

Why insist that hierarchies are settings for social dilemmas? It is because the behavioral implications of a group of people faced with a suboptimal outcome are quite different from those of a group who have reached the efficient limits of their joint effort. If hierarchies are governed by the invisible hand, managers need neither expect nor demand deviations from self-interested behavior. We can understand organizational behavior simply as the result of self-interested responses to efficient contracts – contracts that are themselves the self-interested responses of self-interested managers to all-determinative market-driven incentives.

If, however, the net result of self-interested responses to imperfect contracts is some degree – *any* degree – of inefficiency, there will be efficiency gains to be realized by those managers who seek the benefits of a co-operative solution to a social dilemma – by means outside of incentive design and market discipline. Indeed, markets themselves may reward those managers who find ways to elicit nonopportunistic, cooperative solutions. Managers' attempts may go beyond normal economics – they may use psychological and political means to induce self-interested individuals to cooperate.

In a hierarchy, the notion of "relative efficiency" may lead to the incorrect conclusion that, once one has found an institutional arrangement that minimizes losses due to opportunistic behavior, one has reached an efficient outcome. The rest of this book intends to document the viability of strategies that transcend the "relative efficiency" that can be achieved by writing the best possible incentive contracts for self-interested actors. Cooperation will be defined as occurring when individuals in a social dilemma select alternatives that are *not* rewarded by the formal incentive system but that result in Pareto-efficient outcomes. Cooperation will offer efficiency gains that short-term hierarchical incentives cannot promise. In the limit, indeed, cooperation will reestablish ideal efficiency as a benchmark for organizations that can never achieve it otherwise. The last three chapters in this book will examine the managerial possibilities for cooperation in hierarchy.

PART THREE

Cooperation and Leadership

In 1974, when the U.S. automobile industry was just beginning to sense the end of business as usual, the Volvo company was building a new plant in Kalmar, Sweden. It was a final assembly plant, with a capacity of thirty thousand cars per year per shift. And yet it was not an assembly line plant. In a break from the tradition established by Henry Ford, the production process was developed to accommodate cooperative work teams. In the Kalmar plant, each auto chassis is placed on an electrically driven carrier and is moved from work area to work area. Each area is "owned" by a work team of fifteen to twenty people, who complete a major subassembly – the steering gear or electrical system, for example (Katz and Kahn 1978: 729–30).

How does the hierarchy monitor, control, and reward the individuals in the thirty work teams? For the most part, it does not monitor, control, or reward the individuals at all. Those jobs have been delegated to the work teams themselves. The team decides its own allocation of manpower to tasks, determines its own pace and rest schedules, and inspects its own work. The firm's compensation is based on team, rather than individual, production. Group-based compensation should theoretically create an incentive for individuals in the team to shirk; but the firm allows the team to deal with that problem as it sees fit. The team monitors itself and motivates itself. It can decide that one of its own members should transfer out. The team designates its own leader, who is confirmed by the firm; but the leader has no formal authority over any other team member.

The Kalmar plant is successful. There is less downtime at Kalmar than at Volvo's more traditional assembly line plant, fewer white-collar workers, less turnover and absence. Direct assembly times are the same as those at the assembly line plant. Employee morale is very high.

Cooperation and leadership

The success of the Kalmar plant would seem to be a challenge to organizational economics. The innovations were instigated not by a takeover attempt in Sweden's capital market, but by a cooperative effort between unions and management in response to labor dissatisfaction in the late sixties. Contrary to the story told by Alchian and Demsetz, the primary mechanism for employee motivation has nothing to do with individualized incentive contracts based on closely monitored individual performance; on the contrary, individuals are carefully agglomerated into those interdependent teams that, according to Alchian and Demsetz, induce team shirking. Contrary to Holmstrom, no attempt is made to induce maximal team effort by means of forcing contracts. Private information is not induced from stubborn subordinates by means of an incentive-compatible mechanism. The problems of hidden action and hidden information are seemingly handled by accepted norms of freely shared information and high commitment.

The theme of the last three chapters of this book is that organizational changes like the one at Kalmar are comprehensible not so much in terms of neoclassical economics as in terms of the new repeated game theory, property rights theory, and political economy.

The basic insight derives from the folk theorem of repeated game theory. As is discussed in Chapter 9, this theorem demonstrates that under certain conditions rational individuals in long-term, interactive groups like the Kalmar work teams can achieve cooperative solutions to social dilemmas. Indeed, the Kalmar experiment is founded on the presumption that this is so; and many aspects of its management can be understood only in terms of eliciting long-term cooperation rather than of managing short-term self-interest.

Unfortunately, the folk theorem also demonstrates that there are an infinite number of equilibria in a repeated social dilemma game. Some equilibria are more efficient than others, and the distribution of benefits across equilibria can vary enormously. As a result, a major problem is understanding which particular (more or less cooperative) outcome is achieved at a particular time. The achievement of a particular equilibrium outcome is a coordination problem of enormous proportions. Chapter 10 argues that the solution to this coordination problem requires the construction of mutually reinforcing psychological expectations among all the players involved. This provides a game-theoretic interpretation of concepts such as norms and organizational culture that are normally regarded as being squarely in the behavioral, rather than the economic, tradition of analysis.

Chapter 11 provides a discussion of the means by which organizational leaders in hierarchies address the coordination problem indicated by the folk theorem. It is rational for employees to use cooperative strategies in a repeated social dilemma only if they are convinced that the other players, and especially hierarchical superiors, are themselves committed to the appropriate cooperative plays. This means that hierarchical leaders hoping to focus organizational expectations on a cooperative long-term equilibrium must find a way to commit themselves credibly to the appropriate behaviors. Central to this signaling problem is the appropriate dispersion of political and property rights within the organization. The design of a system of political representation, and the commitment to a system of property rights for employees, can solve coordination problems within hierarchies and provide much more efficient solutions to the inevitable social dilemmas within hierarchies.

9

The possibilities of cooperation
Repeated vertical dilemmas

> This is the fundamental message of the theory of repeated games of
> complete information; that cooperation may be explained by the fact
> that the "games people play" – i.e., the multiperson decision situations
> in which they are involved – are not one-time affairs but are repeated
> over and over.
>
> Aumann (1981: 13)

For managers of business firms, the evidence described in Chapter 8 offers
only cold comfort. It suggests that there are, to greater and lesser extents in
different industries, competitive pressures on managers to achieve the greatest levels of efficiency they can. Markets may "discipline" managers who
fail to achieve efficiency; but the literature on capital markets does not tell
managers anything about how to elicit greater efficiency in the hierarchies
they manage.

From the standpoint of evolutionary economics, academics can maintain
that those organizations that are not driven into bankruptcy are probably
managed in a "better" way than those that are; managers who are not replaced by takeovers are presumably more able than those who are. Individual managers, however, would like to know what characterizes those more
efficient firms, so that their firms can be among the "survivors" in the evolutionary competition. Are the survivors those firms that delegate decision
making according to certain social choice rules? If so, which rules? Are the
survivors those firms that adopt certain forms of incentive systems? If so,
which incentive systems? The literature on efficient markets is silent on this
subject.

The message of the Holmstrom theorem is that any incentive scheme will
leave some member of a team reason to "shirk" in ways that cannot be efficiently discovered and sanctioned; if not the employees, then the residual
owner will have such an incentive. For that reason, the more efficient or-

ganizations may well be those in which managers convince or inspire employees not to engage in this opportunistic shirking even when it is in their short-term interest to do so. In other words, if managers can convince employees to cooperate, their firms will have an edge over those firms that have resigned themselves to the world of second best — the world of agency costs generated by opportunistic behavior by subordinates.

If it is possible to elicit cooperative behavior from subordinates, then (theoretically) the "inevitable" agency costs associated with loss of control and imperfect contracting can shrink to zero. The manager's task will then be more than defining, monitoring, and enforcing pecuniary incentive systems — it will be to exhibit whatever behaviors induce cooperativeness from subordinates. The rest of this book is concerned with this second aspect of managerial performance. With an examination of the possibilities for cooperation that emerge with an analysis of repeated game theory, the sharp distinctions between organizational economics and organizational behavior will begin to soften. The rational economic manager will be concerned with the same issues of interpersonal communication, trust, and loyalty that have been the traditional concerns of organizational behaviorists.

REPEATED GAMES

The managerial imperative to elicit non-self-interested, cooperative behavior will seem nonsensical to economists in the neoclassical tradition. Yet the necessity of inspiring cooperation has been a strong theme in the literature on organizational management for many years. Chester Barnard's classic *Functions of the Executive* (1938) claimed that organizations were essentially cooperative groups of individuals and regarded the executive's primary job as the facilitation of this cooperation. At the center of this definition of the manager's task is the inspiration of "sacrifice," not the manipulation of self-interest:

[The organization's] abilities will not be put forth, will not even be developed, without that sense of responsibility which makes the sacrifices involved a matter of course, and which elicits the initial faith in cooperation. . . . Organizations endure, however, in proportion to the breadth of morality by which they are governed. This is only to say that foresight, long purposes, high ideals, are the basis for the persistence of cooperation. (282)

The contrast with neoclassical economics is clear. Neoclassical economics is based firmly on the notion that social scientific prediction is equivalent to deducing equilibrium outcomes reached by self-interested actors. After all, if individuals could be convinced to ignore their own self-interest, the market failures that supposedly motivate hierarchy would not be a problem: Monopolists would not inefficiently raise prices, used-car dealers would not exploit information asymmetries, citizens would voluntarily contribute

183

Cooperation and leadership

Table 9.1. *One-period team Prisoners' Dilemma game*

	Player II's choices	
Player I's choices	Work	Shirk
Work	$2, $2	$0, $3
Shirk	$3, $0	$1, $1

Note: Underlined payoffs are player I's.

toward public goods. Barnard offers the view that organizations are the vehicles for cooperative response to such collective challenges.

Are these two views incompatible? Is it possible to reconcile Barnard's view of organizations as vehicles for cooperative sacrifice with economics' view of individuals as self-interested rational maximizers? Perhaps the most striking development in political economy in the past ten years has been the burgeoning of interest in social norms of cooperation and commitment among economic actors. In the process, a bridge between economics and behavioral sciences has been designed. At the same time, the limits of organizations as incentive-setting devices have been transcended, with the possibility that the most effective organizations are, as Barnard suggests, vehicles for cooperative collective action.

The evolution of cooperation

In 1984, Robert Axelrod published his seminal work, *Evolution of Cooperation*. Axelrod argues that in repeated plays of Prisoners' Dilemma games, players can achieve the benefits of the Pareto-optimal outcome by playing a strategy of "tit-for-tat." A tit-for-tat multiperiod strategy is defined as playing the cooperative (dominated) alternative in the first play of the game and thereafter mimicking the other player's previous choice. Thus, if an opponent fails to cooperate in period 3, his tit-for-tat partner will fail to cooperate in period 4.

Is such a strategy the "right" strategy for a rational individual playing a repeated Prisoners' Dilemma game? To answer this question, imagine that two members of a team production process are playing a Prisoners' Dilemma game, as in Table 9.1. Let us assume that, after the first period, there is a probability equal to w that the game will be repeated. Every subsequent period has the same probability of being followed by yet another period. Thus, the game is potentially infinitely repeating, but the probability that the game will last through at least k periods is w^{k-1}.

Thus, if both players play their dominant strategies against one another, each of them will certainly earn $1 in the first period, and each will have a

184

Table 9.2. *Generalized payoffs in a repeated Prisoners' Dilemma game*

Player I's choices	Player II's choices	
	Tit-for-tat	Always shirk
Tit-for-tat	$2/(1 - w)$, $2/(1 - w)$	$-1 + 1(1 - w)$, $2 + 1/(1 - w)$
Always shirk	$2 + 1/(1 - w)$, $-1 + 1/(1 - w)$	$1/(1 - w)$, $1/(1 - w)$

Note: Underlined payoffs are player I's; w is the probability of continuing to the next period.

w probability of earning another dollar in the second period, a w^2 probability of earning another dollar in the third period, and so on. Thus, if each one chooses to defect in every period against the other, the expected sum of each player's earnings is

$$EV(\text{all defect}) = 1 + w + w^2 + \cdots .$$

This infinite sum is known to equal $1/(1 - w)$. The other payoffs for the repeated version of the team Prisoners' Dilemma game are shown in Table 9.2. Does either player have a dominant strategy in the repeated game? If one's opponent always shirks, one's best strategy is always to shirk, because $1/(1 - w)$ is always greater than $-1 + 1/(1 - w)$.

However, if one's opponent is playing tit-for-tat, it is *not* always best to shirk. The expected payoff from playing tit-for-tat against tit-for-tat equals $2/(1 - w)$, which is greater than the expected payoff from always playing shirk against tit-for-tat whenever w is greater than ½. Thus, in a game that is likely to be repeated enough times, it is better to cooperate if one's opponent is cooperating.

This is illustrated in Tables 9.3 and 9.4, which show the payoffs from playing the team shirking game in Table 9.1 with repetition probabilities equal to ⅓ and ¾, respectively. Table 9.3 shows that when there is a low value of continuing the game, each member of the group has a dominant strategy always to defect in the repeated game. Even if one's opponent is going to play tit-for-tat, the best strategy is still to defect in the first and later periods of the game. The possibility of getting $3 by defecting in the first period swamps the unlikely possibility of getting a future stream of $2 payoffs as a reward for mutual cooperation.

However, all of this changes with a high enough value of continuing the game. (The critical value of "high enough" depends on the payoffs in the original Prisoners' Dilemma game.) When $w = ¾$, for example, player I is better off playing a tit-for-tat strategy against her opponent if (and only if) her opponent will do likewise. Because each cooperates as long as the other does, each will get $2 in each period, as long as the game lasts. The sum of

Table 9.3. *Shirking as a dominant strategy when* w *is small*

Player I's choices	Player II's choices	
	Tit-for-tat	Always shirk
Tit-for-tat	$3, 3	$0.50, 3.50
Always shirk	$3.50, 0.50	$1.50, 1.50

Note: Underlined payoffs are player I's. Assume $w = \frac{1}{3}$.

this infinite series is $2/(1 - w)$; when $w = \frac{3}{4}$, the players can expect the game to last long enough to gain $8 from cooperating with one another. This expectation is large enough to overcome the short-term gain from defecting in the first period.

Even when $w = \frac{3}{4}$, however, tit-for-tat is not best against every other strategy. If player I knows that player II is going to play "all defect," then cooperating in the first period is pointless. In other words, player I has no dominant strategy. Her rationally best choice depends on what her opponent decides to do. For that reason, stable cooperation in a team shirking game requires that the members of the group have high subjective probabilities that others are playing tit-for-tat – playing cooperatively as long as others do. We will denote this latter belief state by the term "trust." "Trust" does not imply the belief on one member that other members of the group will always cooperate regardless of one's own play. Rather, it implies the belief that other members are currently cooperating and will do so as long as it appears that everyone else will.

Implications for cooperation in work groups

This game-theoretic analysis has three immediate implications for small work groups that stack up very well against fifty years of behavioral research. The first is that cooperation is most likely to occur in very long run organizations. In short-run relationships, the long-run gains from mutual cooperation do not balance the short-run incentive to cheat in a social dilemma.

The second implication is that work groups will engage in activities that create a shared confidence in one another's cooperativeness. People do not have a dominant strategy to cooperate; rather, cooperation is rational only when each player has a great deal of confidence that others are cooperating. Cooperation can unwind very quickly; if I think that you want to cooperate, but I also think that you don't know that I want to cooperate, then I may not cooperate because I am afraid that your uncertainty about my be-

Table 9.4. *Multiplicity of Nash equilibria when* w *is large*

	Player II's choices	
Player I's choices	Tit-for-tat	Always shirk
Tit-for-tat	$8, 8	$3, 6
Always shirk	$6, 3	$4, 4

Note: Underlined payoffs are player I's. Assume $w = \frac{3}{4}$.

havior will cause you to back off from cooperating. In other words, we must share what game theorists call "common knowledge" that each of us is planning to cooperate, that each of us knows the other plans to cooperate, that each of us knows the other knows that each of us plans to cooperate, and so on to the *n*th degree (Schofield 1985: 218).

The third implication is that reciprocity will be a strong norm in successful small work groups. It is worth repeating that cooperation in a repeated game need not be based on mutual altruism; it is based on the shared knowledge that each of us can punish the other (by future noncooperation) if either of us fails to cooperate in this period.

Repeated N-Prisoners' Dilemma games

These three implications are even stronger in an *N*-Person repeated game. In order to keep anyone from free riding, the best operationalization of tit-for-tat in an *N*-person game is for one player to cooperate in period *k* if and only if all other players cooperated in the previous period. However, this creates a real coordination problem, since any slip-up by one player would cause all to defect, and no one person would have any reason to initiate cooperation again.

For this reason, cooperation in a repeated *n*-prisoners' dilemma is very tenuous indeed. Any one person's defection could result in a total collapse of cooperation by everyone. Indeed, in experimental settings in which individuals cannot punish another's defection by any means other than their own defection, this collapse is exactly what is observed. In experiments with ten subjects, slightly more than half of the subjects will cooperate initially, but this level decreases rapidly in subsequent periods. Each individual knows that it is rational for him- or herself and others to punish past defectors by their own defection; defection inevitably snowballs.

Groups that manage to maintain cooperative outcomes over time must therefore have other means of punishing and correcting defectors. The literature on horizontal cooperation in small work groups provides examples of the resourcefulness with which groups invent means of punishment.

187

Cooperation and leadership

HORIZONTAL COOPERATION

Beginning with the famous Hawthorne experiments, the ability of small groups to create social norms enforcing stable and effective (although not necessarily perfect) cooperation has been repeatedly demonstrated. The study of the bank wiring observation room at the Hawthorne Works of Western Electric Company illustrates the role of social interaction in team production settings (Roethlisberger and Dickson 1939: 379–550). In the bank wiring room were two inspectors, nine wiremen, and three solderers. Their task was to connect wires to banks of terminals used in central office telephone switching systems. A wireman would work on two pieces of equipment at a time, moving back and forth from one to another. A solderer could solder the connections made by three wiremen. The two inspectors split the work done by the three soldering groups.

The incentive system: an induced social dilemma

The fourteen men in the room were paid on a group piecework basis. For each piece of equipment shipped out, the department received a fixed sum of money, and the fourteen men were paid out of the pool of money thus generated. The pool of money was first split by paying each person his base wage rate times the number of hours he worked. The surplus was split in proportion to these wages.

As Homans (1950) notes in his perceptive analysis of the bank wiring room, this method of payment generated a social dilemma:

His hourly wage rate remaining constant, a man could increase his earnings only if the output of the department as a whole increased. A rise in his own output, unless that of others rose in the same measure, would hardly show at all in his pay envelope. A fall in his output, if that of others did not fall, would also hardly affect him. (59)

Thus, making the standard assumption that individual effort is costly, each person had a strong incentive to free-ride. His own costly effort had only a tiny impact on his wages. If these fourteen people were like those in similar groups in experimental laboratories, their level of effort would show a rapid decline.

But this was not the case. The level of effort in the shop was high and stable. Nor was it a function of the observation itself – effort levels were the same as they had been before the workers were moved to the observation room for close scrutiny. (The "Hawthorne effect" – increased effort due to special attention – gets its name from a different part of the study.) The output was two major pieces of equipment per day, with virtually no variation. This was regarded as high and "wholly satisfactory" by the company, the foreman, and the men themselves. How did this group of fourteen

188

men manage to solve the team production dilemma facing them in such a stable and effective way?

Enforcement of productivity norms

The management had addressed the free-rider problem facing the work group through a special feature of the incentive system, through the work rules imposed on the men, and through hierarchical monitoring. However, none of these hierarchical procedures for generating stable contributions was sufficient to ensure, nor perhaps even contributed to the outcome.

The feature of the incentive system that was intended to motivate individual contributions was the linkage between individual reported output and hourly wage rate. Management examined the reported output of individuals in determining the wage rate. In the long run, then, a person could increase his share of the pool of wages generated for the room by increasing his reported output.

However, this aspect of the incentive system was almost completely negated by social norms dictating roughly equal reported output. The two pieces of equipment per day averaged out to 825 connections an hour by each of the wiremen. Those who worked above this norm suffered some degree of social ostracism. They were given nicknames such as "Speed King" and verbally chastised. They were also likely to be the butt of a game known as "binging," in which one person hit another as hard as possible on the upper arm, to which the other nominally had the right to respond by hitting back. If a large number of people chose to play the binging game with the same norm violator, this amounted to a significant negative sanction:

Oberleitner: Why don't you quit work? Let's see, this is your thirty-fifth row today. What are you going to do with them all?
Krupa: What do you care? It's to your advantage if I work, isn't it?
Oberleitner: Yeah, but the way you're working you'll get stuck with them.
Krupa: Don't worry about that. I'll take care of it. You're getting paid by the sets I turn out. That's all you should worry about.
Oberleitner: If you don't quit work I'll bing you.

Oberleitner then struck Krupa and chased him around the room. Krupa decided he was finished for the day and went to help other wiremen (Roethlisberger and Dickson 1939: 422–3).

These were the most obvious outward manifestations of the decrease in status and social belonging that accompanied a violation of the norms. The four people who met or exceeded this norm were Krupa, Capek, Mueller, and Taylor. (The fictitious names are supplied by Homans [1950].) Krupa, Capek, and Mueller were also the three most unpopular men in the room. Taylor was highly popular, but managed his productivity without violating the norms. While he was the only person in the room who consistently met

189

the 825 prescribed connections per hour, he also consistently reported making fewer connections than he actually did! Because he underreported his output, his productivity could not be regarded as a greedy attempt to get a larger share of the fixed revenue generated by the two pieces of equipment produced per day; instead, his efforts could be interpreted only as pure contribution to the public good.

Krupa, who sought unsuccessfully to be a leader in the room, also reported lower output than he actually produced. Only Capek and Mueller openly defied the production-limiting norms by producing and reporting a higher level of output; they were also openly contemptuous of the less productive workers and were unhappy at work. Mueller, nick-named "Cyclone" for his output record, talked very little, and was no one's friend. Capek constantly sought a transfer to a different job in the plant.

While the punishment of noncooperators is clearly understandable in light of the social dilemma they faced, why should the high-level producers be punished? One reason was the possibility of layoffs or wage cuts if productivity increased too much. Oberleitner insisted that the extra effort by Krupa and others endangered the jobs of others: "Now just suppose the fellows in that room could increase their output to 7,000 [connections]. I think some of them can. That would mean less work for others. . . . Somebody could be laid off" (Roethlisberger and Dickson 1939: 419). Thus, overproduction was as much a sign of noncooperation as was underproduction. The only kind of overproduction that was not socially harmful was that of Taylor and Krupa since they consistently failed to claim credit for their above-average contributions.

There were other people in the room who produced less than the norm. They were tolerated with greater equanimity because their nonproductivity was not at such a level that it threatened the prescribed two unit per day goal; most important, their nonproductivity was not perceived as "greediness." Instead, they constituted a closely knit "clique" in the "back of the room" who were accepted as being slightly less productive than the clique in the "front of the room," had slightly less status, but were otherwise members in good standing in the workplace.

The social standing of the low-productivity group was demonstrated by the fact that two members, Green and Hasulak, consistently overreported their efforts. Green, who had the highest score on a standard IQ test, never got above 600 connections per hour, but reported a higher number. He was well liked, however, and his overreporting was allowed, evidently in the spirit of an egalitarian norm.

Social interactions not directly related to work

Other forms of social interaction among the employees included gambling, games, afterwork activities, and sharing of candy and other items from the commissary. These social activities served two closely related and vital purposes. First, they provided a social "selective incentive" for those who contributed at or near the prescribed level of effort. Equally important, however, they provided a means by which the members of the social cliques could demonstrate to one another in a continuous way their trustworthiness and capacity to cooperate.

The group purchase of candy illustrates both of these features. Occasionally someone would solicit money for candy, which would be purchased and shared among the contributors. This action created some "common knowledge" – the members of the room (with the exception of Mueller and Capek) trusted one another with money – and it served as a model for the cooperative collective action in which they were all engaged as part of their official activities. The symbolic value of this demonstration was underlined dramatically on one occasion when members of the back-room clique asked the unpopular Krupa (nicknamed the "Speed King") to contribute to the purchase of some candy, but then refused to give him his share after it was purchased. Social standing in the group was clearly conditional on abiding by group norms; those who did could trust one another to cooperate in ways that those outside the group could not.

Reciprocity and egalitarianism

The candy incident illustrates both aspects of reciprocity simultaneously: punishment of defectors and rewarding of cooperators. Indeed, reciprocity was built deeply into the group's code of behavior.

Reciprocity could also be seen in the work patterns in the shop. The firm explicitly forbade the employees to help one another or for wiremen to switch jobs with solderers for occasional relief from boredom. However, this prohibition was countermanded by informal norms. There was exchange of work between the wiremen and the solderers, and wiremen would help one another to achieve the stated goal of two units per day. This kind of help may or may not have had a direct positive effect on group productivity. As Donovan reported:

It's a funny thing, I'll be working along and be behind and I'll feel all fagged out. Then somebody comes over and starts in wiring on my equipment with me, and you know I perk up to beat the band. I don't know; it just seems to put new life in you, no matter if he only helps you for a couple of levels. (Roethlisberger and Dickson 1939: 506)

Whether or not it contributed to overall efficiency, this reciprocation of assistance served as a social reinforcement of the lesson of reciprocity. As Donovan said, "It seems like if a fellow is loafing and gets behind, nobody will help him out, but if he is making an honest effort he will be helped" (504). Thus, Taylor, who was the steadiest and most popular worker in the

191

room, received more help than anyone else. Helping others became a way of demonstrating personal appreciation and social standing rather than a means of raising the technical efficiency in the room.

The reciprocity that supported and sanctioned group cooperation implied a strong concern for equity, defined as a minimization of differences in the treatment of members of the same work group. Once again, this norm was solidified by being applied across the range of social interactions available to the group, not just the shop work. Thus, members of the group were not allowed to "put on airs" by appearing to be better educated or better dressed than other members. Such a distinction might presume to indicate that the person was sufficiently exalted as to justify an unequal contribution to the cooperative work effort. Indeed, any attempts by group members to seek such a socially distinct status were regarded by other members as almost as dangerous as free riding itself – and were sanctioned in the same spirit of tit-for-tat. Nor was the equity norm at the Hawthorne plant unusual. Indeed, the emergence of an equity norm is the most striking and frequently noted social norm in small-work-group settings.

Ineffectiveness of hierarchy

The formal hierarchy played a very small role in the group's maintenance of effort levels. The people at the top of the organization no doubt had little idea of the extent to which their rules and prohibitions, though intended for the greater efficiency of the work group, were ignored in reality. If asked to explain the successful performance in the bank wiring room, upper management would undoubtedly have mentioned the incentive system, work rules such as those prohibiting mutual assistance, and close supervision. In fact, none of these formalisms was observed in reality, and informal norms were specifically hostile to them.

A supervisor over the fourteen men supposedly enforced firm rules. For instance, the supervisor was supposed to take an actual count of the connections completed each day by each of the men. In fact, the supervisor allowed the individuals to report their own output and was perfectly aware that on any given day the reported output might not bear much relation to the actual output:

To enforce the rules would have required his standing over the men all day, and by so doing he would have sacrificed all hope of establishing good relations with them. He would have lost even that minimum of influence that he needed if he was to do any kind of a job at all. Under these circumstances he chose to side with the group and wink at much that was going on. (Homans 1950: 63)

The inspectors, too, were in something of a hierarchical relationship with the rest of the workers, because they had to monitor and check their work. This put the inspectors in a delicate position similar to that of the supervi-

192

sor. One inspector, Mazmanian, did not acknowledge the superiority of the informal work norms. Unlike the other workers, he had had some college education. He did not take part in the social activities in the room, and "he tended to pose as a man of superior knowledge, who knew big words" (Homans 1950: 75). In return, the men made fun of him and misadjusted his testing equipment. Mazmanian "returned the favor by finding their work unsatisfactory" (74). He went to the Personnel Division and formally charged that the men were undermining his work. The Personnel Division asked the supervisor about these charges; the supervisor, true to his loyalties, denied that the men had been obstructive. The other inspector, Allen, let the men in the group know that Mazmanian had "squealed." They were furious and refused to cooperate with Mazmanian at all, who had to be transferred out of the room.

The cost effectiveness of informal cooperation

Despite the group's high levels of performance, there was still some activity that was not directly productive. The two pieces of equipment per day were produced with time left over for games, conversation, and relaxation. The men tended to work quite hard in the morning, until it was clear that the two units would be produced, and then to ease off. What would have happened if the management had attempted to crack down in an attempt to get the group to produce, say, 2.4 pieces of equipment? They might have replaced the current supervisor with one who was committed to enforcing the rules and measuring output himself. The supervisor could have forbidden horseplay such as "binging" and gambling, and could have made an honest effort to report individual output objectively. What would have been the effect of such an experiment in hierarchical control?

The effects would most likely have been negative. It is clear that the gambling, games, and social interaction constituted a vital part of the means by which the men reinforced one another's expectations of cooperative play in their team production dilemma. The cooperation that enables them to produce two units every day, while stable, was nevertheless fragile; without any means of reinforcing that expectation, the motivation for each individual to work as hard as he did would have been decreased.

The status quo, based on the clear goal of two pieces of equipment per day, was no doubt arbitrary. It was clearly a technical possibility to increase production to 2.2 units. However, the mutual understanding would have been disrupted by such an ambitious goal. Each individual would have been thrown into doubt: Does the new regime mean that each person is to produce exactly 20 percent more than before? Or are the slackers expected to increase their output to that of the previously scorned rate busters? Should the faster workers help the slower workers? An overall increase in expected output would require that the entire network of mutually reinforced expectations be recalibrated at another level, without the benefit of ample free time to engage in the social interactions that both reinforced individual contributions and bolstered shared perceptions of trustworthiness.

At the same time that the informal network of cooperation was attacked, a more hierarchical system of control would have to be implemented. But there is no reason to suspect that such a control system would be more successful than numerous other piece-rate or other incentive systems in other organizations. A rational actor, such as Taylor, under the existing laissez-faire regime had every incentive not only to work hard himself but to support a system of norms that encouraged hard work from the others in the room. Under a system of reinforced hierarchical control, that same rational actor would have every incentive to find means to shirk where possible. Support for a more active hierarchy would be irrational because such a system, after establishing that producing 2.2 units was feasible, would be perfectly capable of lowering piece rates to the point that the higher level of output was generated with the same aggregate labor rates. Taylor, and the other men in the room, would have every reason to subvert to the degree possible any extension of hierarchical monitoring and control into the work room, especially if they valued workplace autonomy or social interaction. It is easy to imagine that the informal network in the bank wiring room, which was basically tolerant of the (laissez-faire) hierarchical superstructure, would have quickly become a mechanism for quiet obstruction or outright rebellion.

Rationality and cooperation

The task facing the men in the bank wiring room was just the sort of interdependent team production problem that Alchian and Demsetz describe in their explanation of hierarchy. The production of two pieces of wired and soldered equipment required the combined and synergistic efforts of individuals in a way that was difficult to monitor and reward. Yet the activities of the supervisor were not those that would have been prescribed by Alchian and Demsetz. Instead of closely monitoring each individual's behavior, the supervisor largely let the individuals self-report their output. Instead of writing and enforcing a performance-based contract based on individual output, the hierarchy created a contract that provided incentives for each man to shirk. Yet the output was stable and high.

Were the individuals in the bank wiring room rational? From the perspective of a one-period game, any one of them would have had an incentive to free-ride on the others; yet the fact that they were in a repeated, complex game allowed them to create a set of social incentives that reinforced high levels of effort. There were individuals who clearly would have preferred not to work as hard as they did; however, they faced a wide range of sanctions that allowed a norm of reciprocity to be enforced, without the collapse of all effort in the room. Group norms made cooperation rational and resulted in high levels of output.

What does this say about the proper role of supervisors in a hierarchy? Should they simply hope that small-group norms of reciprocity and cooperation spontaneously emerge, or can they play a more active role?

COOPERATION IN A VERTICAL DILEMMA

In earlier chapters, it was argued that hierarchies are constrained by a vertical dilemma in which self-interested behavior by subordinates and superiors leads them to mutually unsatisfactory outcomes. The first example of the vertical dilemma was provided by the piece-rate system. Employers set monopsony prices given their best information about employee effort cost functions; and employees, fearing that accurate information about their effort cost functions will result in lower piece rates, engage in strategic misrepresentation in order to keep rates as high as possible. The equilibrium result is inefficient: Employee piece rates are too low to achieve optimal levels of effort.

What might a tit-for-tat cooperative solution to the piece-rate dilemma be like? Employers would agree not to lower piece rates simply to keep aggregate payroll to a minimum, as long as employees agreed to provide high levels of effort. Employees would agree to reveal effort cost functions accurately as long as employers did not use that information against them. Just as in the repeated horizontal dilemma, such an outcome would be an equilibrium if and only if each side perceived a long-term relationship; a short-term perspective would cause each side to take the short-term gain from defection over the long-run benefits of mutual cooperation. And as in the analysis of the horizontal dilemma, cooperation would be rational only in the context of mutual confidence in the other side's intentions.

The isolated instances in which managers use the piece-rate incentive system without initiating strategic effort bargaining by subordinates seem to support the game-theoretic analysis. At Lincoln Electric, employees were convinced that the management had made a firm commitment not to adjust piece-rates downward, even in the face of employee earnings that were much higher than those offered by nearby employers. Management was convinced that a violation of that commitment would lead to a tit-for-tat retaliation by employees. Employees responded in kind with high levels of effort and voluntary provision of technological information that enhanced productivity.

Furthermore, management specifically increased the likelihood of cooperation by making long-term commitments to employees in the form of security against layoffs. Employees knew that promotion occurred almost entirely from within, making lifelong careers in the firm possible. In terms of repeated game theory, these policies created the perception of a high

195

probability of repeated play (w), which made the long-term benefits of co-operation loom large by comparison with the short-term gains from defection.

From a game-theoretic point of view, once again, the most salient fact about this repeated vertical dilemma game is that neither side has a dominant strategy to play cooperatively. For that reason, a necessary condition for cooperation is the mutually compatible expectations of the players: Unless each side expects that cooperation will be reciprocated, neither side will have any reason to cooperate itself. At Lincoln Electric, "common knowledge" was created by management and employees in their joint intentions to cooperate. This was done by management's symbolic gestures of unity in which they denied themselves privileges such as executive dining rooms and executive parking spaces. It was also accomplished through regularized institutions of joint decision making that involved employee representation and involvement. These policies reduced the asymmetries between management's and employees' information regarding the other side's intentions and degree of commitment to cooperation.

Obstacles to vertical cooperation

Vertical cooperation would seem to be much more difficult to develop than horizontal cooperation. In the horizontal work group, reciprocal cooperation is easily operationalized via a norm of equal treatment – members are expected to regard themselves as roughly equal, provide roughly equal contributions to the team production process, and receive roughly equal compensation and chances for promotion. Furthermore, the members of a face-to-face work group are in a position to monitor one another's contributions in a way that gives them confidence that the "bargain" is being fulfilled in a roughly equal way.

However, in all but the smallest and most informal hierarchies, the supervisor–subordinate relationship is based on an asymmetry that makes it difficult to operationalize the norm of reciprocal cooperation. The supervisor gets more pay, and this is likely to arouse jealousy and a lack of trust. The supervisor has greater guarantees of job security. The supervisor's contributions to the organization are different from those of the subordinate, making it hard to judge who is providing greater effort. This makes it hard for each side to monitor the other's actions. The superior distrusts the subordinate's levels of effort; the subordinate distrusts the superior's decisions regarding work conditions and compensation.

A successful hierarchy, therefore, consists of actors who find numerous convincing ways to demonstrate their continued commitment to cooperation. This coincides dramatically with one traditional definition of managerial responsibility in firms, which insists that the central role of leadership is much more than simply monitoring and rewarding subordinate efforts.

196

The possibilities of cooperation

Chester Barnard (1938) placed willingness to cooperate at the center of his elaborate scheme. He stated that cooperation was difficult to achieve because of the conflict between individual motives and common purpose:

The inculcation of belief in the real existence of a common purpose is an essential executive function. It explains much education and so-called morale work in political, industrial, and religious organizations that is so often otherwise inexplicable. (87)

Indeed, in many successful firms, a great deal of organizational resources are used to inculcate the belief in a common purpose and a willingness to make sacrifices for that purpose. The substance of this "morale work" is primarily the following: "We are all in this together, and if you will cooperate, everyone else will respond in kind." In other words, the purpose of this rather expensive educational effort is to create the expectation among the multiple players in a large firm that cooperative behavior will be met in kind – and that it will not all unravel.

Hewlett-Packard provides a fascinating example. This firm has a policy of vertical cooperation between managers and employees. Founder Bill Hewlett describes this cooperative philosophy as the"HP way":

[The HP way consists of] the policies and actions that flow from the belief that men and women want to do a good job, a creative job, and that if they are provided with the proper environment they will do so. It is the tradition of treating every individual with consideration and respect and recognizing personal achievement. This sounds almost trite, but Dave and I honestly believe in this philosophy. (Peters and Waterman 1982: 244)

The reality of cooperation is suggested by the open lab stock policy, which not only allows engineers access to all equipment, but encourages them to take it home for personal use. According to this philosophy, innovation will be forthcoming only through an open exchange of information and ideas that would be limited by a locked equipment room door. However, the open door symbolizes and demonstrates management's trust in the cooperativeness of the employees. The commitment to cooperation is also demonstrated by flexible work hours and a lack of time clocks. Hewlett reports, "This is meant to be an expression of trust and confidence in people" (244).

The elimination of time clocks and locks on equipment room doors is a way of building a shared expectation among all the players that cooperation will most likely be reciprocated between employees and management. Like the cooperative purchase of candy by the men in the bank wiring room, the elimination of time clocks and door locks has created a shared "common knowledge" in the ability of the players to reach cooperative outcomes. Without this shared perception, employees (and managers) would find it tempting to engage in short-term maximizing behavior that was inimical to long-term efficiency.

Another condition for the achievement of cooperative equilibria in a repeated game is the mutual expectation that the relationship will go on long enough to justify the investment in cooperation. This was achieved at Hewlett-Packard by an early decision by the two founders not to be a "hire and fire company," but one in which employees would have the security of employment commitment. In the 1980 recession, this policy was tested severely, but everyone in the organization took a 10 percent cut in pay and worked 10 percent fewer hours so that no one would be fired (Peters and Waterman 1982: 244). This confirmed everyone's subjective belief that the relationship was long-lasting and that employee efforts were not going to be exploited for short-term gain by Hewlett-Packard.

SUMMARY

The message of the Holmstrom theorem is that there is no way to make an organization of diverse individuals into a machine. Managers should look at their organizations as being composed of individuals with diverse interests who will occasionally find themselves in conflict. Information asymmetries (in the form of monitoring limitations) and production externalities (in the form of high levels of synergy among subordinates) make it impossible for managers to realize the full efficiency potential of team production processes through the manipulation of short-term economic incentives alone. Managers need to inspire among their employees a willingness to cooperate and trust one another by setting an example of concern and trustworthiness themselves.

Cooperation in a repeated social dilemma can be sustained by rational actors as long as the probability of continuation from one period to the next is sufficiently high and as long as all the actors involved have mutually consistent expectations about the others' intentions to reciprocate. To the extent that incentives fall short of guaranteeing efficient outcomes, the manager's job must include the creation of both these conditions.

10

The indeterminacy of cooperation
Conventions, culture, and commitment

> Corporate culture . . . accomplishes just what the principle should – it gives hierarchical inferiors an idea ex ante how the organization will "react" to circumstances as they arise – in a very strong sense, it gives identity to the organization.
>
> Kreps (1984)

Barnard (1938) argues that encouraging cooperation is a central role of management; however, he does not claim that cooperation is inevitable:

> It is readily believed that organized effort is normally successful, that failure of organization is abnormal. This illusion from some points of view is even useful. . . . But in fact, successful cooperation in or by formal organizations is the abnormal, not the normal, condition. . . . most cooperation fails in the attempt, or dies in infancy, or is short-lived. . . . Failure to cooperate, failure of cooperation, failure of organization, disorganization, disintegration . . . are characteristic facts of human history. This is hardly disputable. (4–5)

But why shouldn't the evolution of cooperation be inevitable? As long as the relationship is guaranteed to be long term, and the participants have a shared expectation of reciprocated cooperation, then cooperation should be sustainable as a long-run equilibrium by rational, self-interested players.

Unfortunately, even when the conditions for cooperation are fulfilled, cooperation is not a unique, determinate outcome of long-term social interaction. The folk theorem proves that, in any repeated Prisoners' Dilemma game, there are an infinite number of outcomes that are sustainable as long-run equilibria by rational, self-interested actors. Achieving any one of these equilibria requires the solution of an immense coordination problem. Solving this problem is a difficult task, requiring social and political skills that are normally associated more with the politician than with the technocratic manager.

199

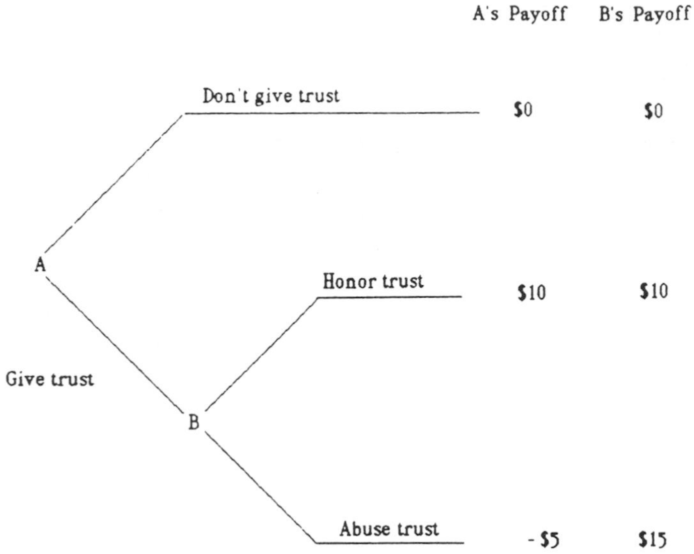

A's Payoff   B's Payoff

Figure 10.1. The trust/honor game. (From Kreps 1990.)

THE FOLK THEOREM

A multiplicity of outcomes is sustainable in repeated games – cooperation is not the only outcome that can be reached by rational individuals. This fact is best illustrated in an organizational context by a game devised by Kreps in his important paper "Corporate Culture and Economic Theory" (Figure 10.1). In this game, player B faces the temptation of abusing the trust placed in her by player A. Knowing this, player A will choose not to place trust in player B. But this results in both doing worse (zero each) than if both players did what was irrational.

As Kreps observes, one solution to this problem would be to write a contract that would effectively change the incentives. Under the contract, B could promise to submit to a large (larger than $10) penalty for abusing the trust. A potential problem would be the transactions costs associated with drawing up the contract and hiring a credible enforcer. These transactions costs would eat into the potential gain from escaping the prisoners' dilemma and could make it not worthwhile to write the contract.

An alternative solution is available if the game is repeated. For instance, Kreps imagines a scenario in which at each round there is a 10 percent chance that the round will be the last. Then, player A could announce a strategy of placing trust in player B until such time as player B abused the trust. Player B would then have the possible incentive of multiple future rounds of gaining $10 to balance against the $5 incentive to violate the trust in a given period. This would make it viable for player B to honor the trust, simply from a self-interested perspective. This is an equilibrium outcome in the repeated game, in that each player's strategy is best given the other player's strategy.

Kreps notes that this outcome is only one of an infinite number of possible outcomes that can be achieved as equilibrium outcomes in repeated games of this sort. There are other strategy pairs for which each person's strategy is best given the other person's strategy. For instance, player B could announce that he will violate player A's trust one time out of three. If A ever retaliates by choosing not to trust B in any given period, player B will retaliate massively by violating A's trust on *every* subsequent opportunity. Given this announced strategy, player A's best choice is still to trust player B at every opportunity, as long as B does not violate the trust more than one-third of the time. To do otherwise would sacrifice the considerable gain to be realized from even having player B prove trustworthy two-thirds of the time.

This equilibrium outcome is more favorable to player B than one in which he honors the trust every time. The problem is that game theory does not give any basis for choosing between these and a large number of other possible equilibrium outcomes — some favoring A, some favoring B, some efficient, some inefficient. Once the game is played as a repeated game, the folk theorem says that "we can sustain as a noncooperative equilibrium payoff any feasible vector of expected payoffs for players that are sufficiently above the worst that others can inflict upon them" (Kreps 1984: 14).

This means that anything from mutually cooperative, to mutually noncooperative, to one-sided exploitative outcomes can be sustained by rational actors playing the same repeated game. There are at least two significant implications: (1) We cannot predict what will happen in repeated social interactions using game theory alone, and (2) in any given organizational setting, cooperation is not inevitable.

SOCIAL CONVENTIONS

The evidence from organizational behavior is that there are indeed a wide range of ways in which rational individuals can react to the repeated social dilemmas that occur in hierarchies, even in hierarchies that are addressing similar tasks with similar structures of economic incentives. In some manufacturing organizations, a piece-rate incentive system results in shirking, misrepresentation, low productivity, and low profits (Whyte 1955). In other organizations, such as Lincoln Electric, the same piece-rate incentive system results in high motivation, group norms that support high levels of effort, rapid technological advancement, and large profits. The differences seem to be largely the result of differing expectations and beliefs. In productive piece-rate systems, employees are convinced that managers will not respond to high wage levels by cutting piece rates; and at the same time, managers are convinced that employees will not respond to generous incentive plans and the delegation of authority by shirking and abusing the trust. The range of stable outcomes across organizations with similar technologies, organizational structures, and incentive systems is evocative of the multiplicity of equilibria predicted by the folk theorem.

This embarrassing richness of possible outcomes has led numerous game theorists to embark on a program of "equilibrium refinement" – trying to narrow down the wide range of possible predictions in repeated games by defining concepts of equilibrium that are narrower than the Nash equilibrium (Harsanyi and Selten 1988). In other words, the assumption is that reality cannot be as varied as the Nash equilibrium conception allows. The approach in this chapter is quite different. I assume that the range of possible equilibria in repeated games does in fact occur, depending on the various beliefs and expectations of the participants. The focus of this chapter is on the widely differing sets of mutually consistent expectations observed in organizations and on the role that political leadership plays in this process.

Coordination and conventions

The Battle of the Sexes game is a paradigm for games in which there are numerous possible Nash equilibria. In these games, the principal problem is to coordinate expectations so that one of the many efficient Nash equilibria is reached; this is known as the coordination problem.

David Lewis noted some years ago that a social convention is a useful solution to the problem of coordination created by a Battle of the Sexes game. Lewis's (1969) simplest definition of a convention is as follows:

A regularity R in the behavior of members of a population P when they are agents in a recurrent situation S is a *convention* if and only if, in any instance of S among members of P, (1) everyone conforms to R; (2) everyone expects everyone else to conform to R; (3) everyone prefers to conform to R on condition that the others do, since S is a coordination problem and uniform conformity to R is a proper coordination equilibrium in S. (42)

Social conventions allow groups to focus on one possible equilibrium instead of another. Their usefulness has been recognized by many theorists (Lewis 1969; Hardin 1982; Calvert 1987; Leibenstein 1982, 1987; Hechter 1987). One outstanding example of this is the convention known as "gift exchange" – which seems to play a central role in a wide variety of settings, including hierarchical firms.

The "gift exchange" convention in hierarchies

Anthropologists have known for some time that entire economies can be motivated by conventions of gift exchange. In simple hunter-gatherer societies, individuals who do well on a given hunt give gifts to others in the society, in confident expectation of receiving a comparable gift at a future time (Sahlins 1972). These exchanges may be viewed as repeated games in which all players are better off; the folk theorem suggests that the exchanges are perfectly rational, as long as everyone in the society expects the norm to apply to everyone and expects that nonsharing would lead to reciprocated selfishness by everyone else. Not only is gift exchange rational, it is also efficient. Societies with such a norm do better than hunter-gatherer groups in which successful hunters glut themselves and unsuccessful hunters starve.

The more advanced "potlatch" societies are based on more elaborate gift exchange rituals. The leading figures mobilize their families' energies toward the accumulation of large amounts of wealth, which are periodically given away in ceremonial demonstrations to reluctant recipients as a way of achieving status. The sullen recipients leave the ceremonies determined to regain status by accumulating large amounts of wealth to give away themselves (Harris 1974: 97).[1] Once again, ambitious individuals in societies in which this convention exists do well to abide by it. And the efficient risk-spreading effects of the convention are clear as well.

Economist George Akerlof (1982) argues that similar kinds of gift exchange conventions can be sustained – with similar efficient effects – within hierarchies. Akerlof made this claim after reading the description of a small group of women posting customer cash payments for a utility company (Homans 1954). These employees consistently posted an average of about 15 percent more than the minimum work requirement for the company. This level was achieved despite the fact that a failure to achieve the minimum resulted in only a mild reprimand and exceeding the work requirement resulted in no wage differential or improved promotional opportunities. At the same time, all of the employees (both those who exceeded the average and those below the average) were paid more than what it would have taken to replace them.

Akerlof argues that relationships within the utility company are governed by gift exchange conventions. He views the workers as giving a "gift" of effort that goes beyond what is called for given the incentive system and the limited ability of the supervisors to monitor individual effort. In return, workers receive the gifts of higher-than-market-clearing wages, a degree of autonomy, and flexible application of work rules. This gift exchange leaves both sides better off than they would be if the firm refused to pay more than the market-clearing wage and the employees refused to work at more than minimum standards. The gift exchange is just what would be necessary to escape a vertical dilemma between superiors and subordinates.

[1] Akerlof (1982) notes the etymological similarity between the words for "gift" and "poison" in several languages, since receiving a gift carries the burden of responding in kind.

Cooperation and leadership

Akerlof points out that the existence and persistence of gift exchange conventions explain a long-standing problem in labor economics. The problem is involuntary unemployment of the sort that would not occur in a normal neoclassical market, in which demand and supply equilibrate. While the neoclassical implications regarding market clearing seem to apply to virtually every market in the U.S. economy, they consistently do not apply to the labor market, where the supply of labor is consistently in excess of demand. As Akerlof argues, the tendency of many firms to pay employees more than the market-clearing equilibrium wage rate in order to elicit voluntary and nonmonitorable employee effort in return would result in a stable excess supply. Firms would prefer to hire fewer employees at the higher wage, and more employees would prefer to work than could find work at that wage.

Is the mutual exchange of gifts described by Akerlof irrational? Not according to the folk theorem. The mutual exchange of gifts, leaving both parties better off, is quite rational, *as long as each party expects that the other party's continued participation is conditional on its own contribution.* No more altruism is necessary in the exchange of gifts than in the highly competitive, status-oriented gift exchange economies of the Pacific coast Indians.

If the exchange of gifts is rational, is it inevitable? Certainly not. The maintenance of a gift exchange convention is only one of the stable Nash equilibria that can be maintained in a repeated game, given the right set of expectations and beliefs. Without the clear expectation of each party that all other parties know their roles and intend to comply, the exchange of gifts could unravel. In fact, gift exchange conventions do unravel in response to urbanization and commercialization, as participants begin to doubt that their gifts will be reciprocated.

Similarly, the literature on organization behavior is filled with examples, both of sustained levels of mutual commitment to a gift exchange convention and of organizations in which such conventions never develop or fall apart. That is why the traditional literature on organizational behavior has emphasized the centrality of individual perceptions and beliefs and of social conventions. The fundamental impact of the folk theorem is to integrate this concern with belief and social norms into repeated game theory and economics.

Second-order norms

It may be objected that one of the two "parties" in the Akerlof gift exchange model is in fact composed of multiple actors – the employees. The employer's "gift" of higher-than-market wages is a public good for the employees. Each employee will therefore have an incentive to free-ride on other employees, hoping that their high levels of effort will be sufficient to keep the employer reciprocating with high wages.

This is true, but the group-pressure work norms described in Chapter 9 are just as surely a sustainable Nash equilibrium for the work group as are the gift exchange conventions described by Akerlof. It is rational for the individual employee to comply with informal work group norms, as long as the employee expects that other employees will enforce the group norms. For instance, the individuals in the Hawthorne Works bank wiring room (discussed in Chapter 9) were not behaving irrationally when they maintained consistent and generally high levels of effort, despite the laxity of formal supervision. On the contrary, they knew that shirking on their part would lead to a number of unpleasant consequences: the other group members would fail to reciprocate "helping" and "job switching," they would fail to cooperate on group purchases of candy or games, and they would undoubtedly experience painful group sanctions in the form of binging, snubbing, and exclusion.

But why should the other employees at the plant enforce group norms? This enforcement would most likely be costly: If one employee in a small work group were shirking, the employee who undertook to sanction that shirking (by binging, snubbing, scolding, or whatever) would be likely to pay the social costs of antagonism from the sanctioned group member. If enforcement of group norms were costly to the enforcer, there would be a second-order collective action problem: Each employee would be better off if other employees undertook the costly sanctioning, but no one would be willing to undertake the sanctioning him- or herself (Oliver 1980; Yamagishi 1986).

Heckathorn (1989) answers this question by discussing three kinds of cooperation. "Private cooperation" exists when individuals cooperate in the first-order collective action problem but do not themselves contribute to the enforcement of group cooperation norms. "Hypocritical cooperation" is the reverse, in which individuals enforce norms of cooperation on other individuals without themselves complying with those norms. "Full cooperation" is cooperation on both the first- and second-order cooperation problem. Heckathorn examines the relative attractiveness of these strategies (along with complete noncooperation) and argues that second-order norms are more robust than first-order norms. That is, it is often rational for people to support norms of cooperation and chastise noncooperators *even when they themselves are likely to cheat.*

He also demonstrates that "hypocritical cooperation can potentially serve as a bridge spanning the chasm from collective inaction to full cooperation" (Heckathorn 1989: 28). That is, individuals may begin to support and enforce norms of cooperation even before they themselves decide to cooperate. But if a sufficient number of people begin to enforce second-order norms, more and more individuals will choose to cooperate rather than face the sanctions of the (potentially hypocritical) norm enforcers. Heckathorn gives as examples the frequently brutal and corrupt law enforcement in the old American West, which nevertheless had the effect of strengthening order in the society.

An account of rationality in convention-governed games

One important implication of the notion of second-order norms is that the account of rational behavior in organizations takes on an entirely new content. In the market institution, rational behavior consists of individual maximizing behavior. The market liberates the individual to undertake simple maximizing behavior by the fact that he or she is, like everyone else, a price taker. Being a price taker means that no one person has to worry about the effects of his or her own behavior on anyone else. Rational behavior in the competitive market is atomistic behavior.

In convention-governed coordination games, by contrast, everyone has to anticipate the behavior of everyone else, and the effect of one's own behavior on the expectations of others. In a repeated Prisoners' Dilemma game, people must worry about the effect of their own deviations from social norms on others' behavior; the tit-for-tat strategy is based on the notion that one's opponent can be rationally constrained by the knowledge that self-interested behavior will lead one to reciprocate in kind. In repeated games, rationality requires just this kind of calculation about the effects of one's behavior on the subsequent behavior of others. If one member of a small work group starts to shirk and stops supporting antishirking work norms, what will be the effect on the behavior of others? What will be the effect of that deviation on the viability of the norms, and on the effects of erosion of those norms? "Rational choice" in such a setting may move an employee to make a "gift" of costly effort – even in the absence of a punishment mechanism – simply because the ultimate effects of deviation from the norm may be large, uncertain, and negative.

HIERARCHICAL CULTURE: MUTUALLY REINFORCING EXPECTATIONS

This leads us to ask if there is anything left to the frequently heard distinction between economics and sociology: "Economics is about how individuals make choices, and sociology is about how individuals have no choices to make." The gap between economics and sociology has certainly shrunk dramatically as economists have learned to accept the possibility that individual choices in coordination games are rationally constrained by social conventions and norms. However, individuals in social settings constrained by social norms still have important choices to make. The choices they

The indeterminacy of cooperation

make help to determine the expectations that others have about how the game is to be played and help to shape and alter the conventions that govern the outcome of coordination games.

Basically, the viability of a convention is dependent on the mutually reinforcing expectations of a set of players regarding how all other players will behave. The term "corporate culture" denotes these mutually reinforcing expectations in a firm. A "cooperative" corporate culture is one in which each player expects all others to cooperate and to enforce the norm of cooperation. A "noncooperative" corporate culture would entail the opposite sets of expectations. In the context of the repeated game between superiors and subordinates, for example, Kreps (1984) defines "corporate culture" in part as "the means by which a principle [of group decision making] is communicated to hierarchical inferiors. . . . It says 'how things are done, and how they are meant to be done' in the organization" (5).

Different organizations in the same industry might have quite different cultures. Indeed, the same individual might behave very differently in two different organizations as a result of differing sets of expectations within the organizations. A notorious shirker in one piece-rate firm (like Ray Starkey in Whyte 1955) might well find it rational to work very hard in a company like Lincoln Electric, where informal work norms support high levels of effort and where managers can be counted on not to lower piece rates whenever total salary inches above industry averages.

Unraveling of expectations: the rigidity cycle

The folk theorem suggests that the beliefs of the various players about the likely responses of other players are all-important: It is this psychological network of mutually reinforcing expectations that makes one perfectly feasible outcome (e.g., cooperation) occur instead of another perfectly feasible outcome (e.g., noncooperation).

This suggests a certain fragility in cooperative equilibria. While it is rational for an employee to cooperate under the perception that others are cooperating and that one's own noncooperation would be sanctioned and/or reciprocated, a relatively few examples of nonsanctioned noncooperation could change these expectations drastically. Even in a company like Lincoln Electric, a few key decisions by management might cause an "unwinding" of the mutually consistent expectations that support high levels of effort and high wages.

There is an entire literature in organizational behavior on "sociological dysfunctions" that illustrates that cooperation is not inevitable and can in fact disintegrate under the impact of changing perceptions and norms. A classic example is Gouldner's (1954) work on the bureaucratic "rigidity cycle." Gouldner studied the operations at an Indiana gypsum mine and factory in a rural region with very modest status differences and close family and friendship networks. The conventional management style at the gypsum plant was informal, egalitarian, and lax. The plant manager and personnel manager were on first-name terms with the employees and dressed in work clothes as they did. The personnel manager had never finished high school, hated paper work in general and impersonal rules in particular. "He regarded everything that happened as the exception to the rule" (62). He preferred to hire established members of the rural community, and especially friends or relatives of current employees. The policy was to let work groups get the job done with as little hierarchical interference and as few fixed rules as possible. People were given a second and third chance before being fired. People who were injured on the job would get "fair compensation" and would then be given light duty in the "sample room," a place where work was done sitting down.

Workers were allowed to take gypsum board home for personal use, and even dynamite for fishing! At the same time, employees were highly motivated. Work in the mine was especially dangerous and difficult, but the mine supervisors regarded the miners as very highly self-motivated and industrious. As one supervisor said, "I think they should be given the chance to show initiative. Here in the mine we give the man a job to do and he does it without being watched. . . . The men have to do a job themselves. They're not controlled" (Gouldner 1954: 139). During an emergency, the miners were willing to put in extra hours. One mine mechanic said proudly, "Last week, when they had the cave-in, I worked seventeen hours straight. But that was an emergency, and everybody helps out then" (141). Thus, while the managers were seen as being informal and lenient, the employees saw themselves as reciprocating in kind. The gift exchange convention in the plant consisted of company leniency and employee autonomy in return for employee effort and commitment.

The norm of reciprocity was strong in the plant. In fact, Gouldner specifically documents that workers would have been uncomfortable if the managers had allowed themselves to be taken advantage of. "Leniency is not merely forbearance but consists, also, of positive Company actions which conform with sentiments shared by workers" (54).

When the old plant manager died, he was replaced by Vincent Peele. One of Peele's first acts was to fire an employee named MacIntosh who had worked at the plant for twelve years, for taking dynamite home. Everyone regarded MacIntosh's actions as being within the bounds of custom at the plant, and MacIntosh himself demanded arbitration hearings in the hopes of getting his job back. During the hearings Peele announced that lax enforcement of company rules was a thing of the past; "he would no longer allow foremen to honor them, and . . . henceforth, foreman–worker relationships were to be bound by the formal regulations of the Company" (60–1). He made it clear that he was using MacIntosh as an example.

Shortly thereafter, the old personnel director was demoted. The new personnel director, named Digger, wore business slacks and a checkered sport coat, which the other employees regarded as an attempt to create a status differential between himself and them. He had been to college, and he obviously enjoyed paper work. He did not recognize that rules could have exceptions. He liked to hire people with a competitive attitude, and preferably not relatives of current employees.

Peele and Digger together began an attack on the old lax and informal style of management. They initiated a new system of weekly and daily reports from foremen and building supervisors. Whereas the men had previously been allowed to roam around the factory chatting with friends and relatives during work breaks, new rules banned talking, horseplay, and freedom of movement. Disciplinary measures were formalized. The no-absenteeism rule, which had not previously been enforced, was now enforced vigorously. Men were forced to check in and out at fixed times. The sample room was no longer used for rehabilitating injured workers – they were simply sent home. Rather than rely on informal work groups to enforce high levels of effort, the new plant manager attempted to enforce high levels of effort directly through hierarchical supervision and explicit rules.

The effect of hierarchy and the imposition of rules was to weaken the mechanism – informal work group norms – that had previously been responsible for productivity. The conventional exchange of company leniency for voluntary effort was ended. The emphasis on hierarchical direction violated the norms of informality and egalitarianism. The workers hated the new management for thinking it was better than they were.

Instead of feeling responsible for getting the job done on their own, the workers began to look for ways to do as little as they could get away with. Conveniently, the rules imposed by the new managers clearly specified minimal effort levels, and the workers were determined to follow the rules to the letter. As one foreman said, "If I catch a man goofing off, I tell him in an a,b,c way exactly what he has to do, and I watch him like a hawk 'til he's done it" (Gouldner 1954: 159). But at the same time, one worker said, "If the foreman doesn't work well with us, we don't give him as good work as we can. . . . I just don't care, I let things slide" (160). The employees perceived themselves as engaging in tit-for-tat, reciprocating minimal effort for a reduction in their autonomy.

Gouldner saw this as a clear unraveling of the voluntary exchange of cooperation between employees and supervisors. He called it the "cycle of increasing rigidity." Hierarchy reduces worker motivation, and the imposition of clearly defined rules induces employees to do no more than the minimum specified by those rules. This is never sufficient for the firm, especially when conditions are changing rapidly. This confirms managers' assumptions that employees are lazy and not to be trusted. Managers then respond with more coercive hierarchy and more carefully spelled out rules. This increases employee unwillingness to be flexible or volunteer special efforts when needed, which leads to further managerial use of hierarchy and rules.

The new management's rules about punching in at the time clock are a good example. Peele did not allow workers to punch in early in order to accumulate some overtime. Two employees responded:

Well, if that's the way he wants it, that's the way he wants it. But I'll be damned if I put in any overtime when things get rough and they'd like us to.

O.K., I'll punch in just so, and I'll punch out on the nose. But you know you can lead a horse to water and you can lead him away, but it's awful hard to tell how much water he drinks while he's at it. (Gouldner 1954: 175)

The new expectations and conventions at the plant were just as rational and sustainable as the previous ones. But this vicious cycle of increasing bureaucratic rigidity was clearly not as efficient as one in which managers give employees some leeway and employees respond with high morale and cooperation. The trick is maintaining this outcome as the expected outcome over repeated plays of the Prisoners' Dilemma game. And "trick" is the right word. There is no magic incentive-system formula in which mutual cooperation always emerges as the unique Nash equilibrium behavior. While this outcome is in the set of feasible outcomes in repeated play, it is only one of a large set of feasible outcomes.

HIGH-INVOLVEMENT MANAGEMENT

In both the classic Hawthorne bank wiring room study and the early part of Gouldner's case study of the gypsum plant, groups of individuals evidently maintained high informal work group norms of productivity as equilibrium outcomes in repeated team production settings. Without the benefit of highly coercive hierarchical sanctions or strong links between individual performance and pay, the groups established expected levels of productivity, sanctioned shirkers, and got the job done.

Were these situations flukes? The evidence of the past decade indicates that similar situations exist in a wide number of settings – in fact, they have been described as the wave of the future in U.S. industry (Walton 1985; Lawler 1986).

Early experiments in cooperative work teams

After World War II, the British coal industry initiated a program of technical modernization. The program did not initially lead to the improvements in productivity that were expected. Research undertaken to find out why revealed that productivity varied. It was in fact highest among a group of workers who had spontaneously established cooperative work teams.

210

The indeterminacy of cooperation

These work teams, like the informal work group in the Hawthorne bank wiring room, were characterized by informal norms of work trading and mutual assistance, supported by informally enforced norms of cooperation and effort (Trist and Bamforth 1951).

The research detailing these results was highly influential in Europe. Experiments were conducted in Scandinavia on delegating authority to semi-autonomous work groups or work teams (Lawler 1986: 102), and Volvo built the Kalmar auto plant based on a work team technology. In the United States, two companies began to experiment with work teams. General Electric created more than a hundred highly interactive work teams in its factories. Procter & Gamble, after early successful results with self-managed work teams, began in 1970 to build an entirely new manufacturing organization around plants designed for self-managed work teams.

The high-involvement strategy

These early efforts were picked up by the Cummins Engine plant at Jamestown, New York, and the General Foods plant at Topeka, Kansas. By this time, a common management strategy was emerging. The "high-involvement" firms, as they were called, reduced the levels of hierarchy in the firm. This increased the span of control of managers and made close monitoring of work group behavior much more costly, or nearly impossible, for any given midlevel manager. Managers were in effect forced to delegate authority to work teams.

Obviously, under these conditions worker performance could not be dictated from above. Rather, management had to count on the development of strong norms of cooperation and effort within the work groups. How were these strong norms encouraged? Work teams were in effect given new "property rights": First, they were guaranteed a great deal of control over performance standards. Second, they were given strong guarantees of employment security, so that they would not be putting themselves out of work by increasing production. Third, workers were generally guaranteed opportunities for training, retraining, and promotion. Fourth, compensation schemes were changed so that work groups were given "equity" in the firm through profit-sharing plans or stock ownership plans. Short-term compensation was generally based on work group, rather than individual, productivity; this guaranteed that employees had a stake in monitoring one another's behavior and in maintaining high work group norms. Fifth, individuals were given more challenging tasks with wider scope, a process known as job enlargement. Sixth, employees were guaranteed participation in high-level plant decision making and were provided previously secret information in order to make their participation meaningful.

By 1985, Walton predicted in the *Harvard Business Review* that this trend was in fact accelerating and becoming a "revolution." It seems that

Cooperation and leadership

Walton's prediction has been borne out in succeeding years. In 1985 General Electric, Champion International, and LTV Steel started to use participative work teams. In 1986 Caterpillar, and in 1987 Boeing and A. O. Smith, followed suit.

The A. O. Smith story is illustrative. This firm manufactures auto and truck frames. Individuals historically were paid with piecework contracts, and attempts to maximize output resulted in very low quality. In 1981, 20 percent of the frames produced on the Ford Ranger line had to be immediately repaired before they could be shipped. At this time, management and workers alike worried about a shutdown as a result of competition from high-quality competitors in Japan and elsewhere.

That year the company, without the support of the union, initiated a program of "quality circles," in which employees shared ideas for product improvement. However, in 1984, when General Motors began to reduce its purchases of car frames from A. O. Smith, the seven unions agreed to form joint problem-solving committees. Traditional hostility between employees and management began to wane. New contracts were negotiated in 1987, the year that 1,300 workers were laid off. In the contract negotiations, both sides agreed to eliminate the piecework contracts that had been in existence for fifty years. But management did not ask to freeze earnings – an action that unions interpreted as a sign of good faith.

At the same time, the company and union agreed to set up work teams of five to seven members who would rotate from job to job. The team members would elect their own leaders who would take over management functions including production scheduling, granting overtime, ordering maintenance, stopping the line to maintain quality, even revising engineered work standards. A large number of supervisorial positions were eliminated. A profit-sharing plan was instituted. Defects on the Ranger dropped to 3 percent from 20 percent, and the productivity growth rate doubled (*Business Week* 1989c: 66).

A 1989 *Business Week* cover article entitled "The Payoff from Teamwork" claimed:

Companies that only a few years ago disdained participation are rushing to set up so-called self-managing work teams, the most advanced state of EI [employee involvement]. The team concept is spreading rapidly in industries such as autos, aerospace, electrical equipment, electronics, food processing, paper, steel, and even financial services. (1989d: 57)

Economics and high-involvement management

Given the enthusiasm for high-involvement work teams in recent years, would game theory caution us about the limitations of this model? It is worth remembering that, in the absence of a significant degree of team interdependence, there may be no advantage to be gained from high-involvement management. When tasks are separable, it may be perfectly possible for managers to program, monitor, and reward employees by means of a traditional style of hierarchical management. Holmstrom's impossibility result about moral hazard in teams assumed interdependent team effort. With independent tasks, it would be perfectly possible to create a budget-balancing division of revenue that induced an efficient Nash equilibrium within the team.

Why, then, has high involvement been growing in popularity in the past two decades? If the degree of complexity and interdependence in technology is increasing, then management based on hierarchical monitoring and control will be less and less efficient at the margins. There is good reason to believe that the confounding team interdependencies assumed in Holmstrom's theorem are increasing over time:

Instead of simple stand-alone jobs that an individual can do alone, many jobs now involve the operation of complex machines, continuous process plants, or the delivery of services that require the integrated work of many individuals. The type of work that exists in the United States today, therefore, is less amenable to individual measurement and to the specification of a normal level of individual production. Instead, performance can only be measured reliably and validly when a group of workers or even an entire plant is viewed. (Lawler 1987: 74)

Furthermore, the degree of information asymmetries has no doubt increased. With the replacement of unskilled jobs by a combination of machines and computers, the workforce is increasingly composed of individuals who are highly specialized in complex tasks. The efficiency losses may be minor if the degree of information asymmetry and interdependence is also minor. However, as subordinate behavior becomes more and more cloaked in the obscurity of specialized information and synergistic complexity, the efficiency losses from trying to achieve heavy-handed control may become much more severe. At some point, it will become cheaper to attempt the voluntary, long-term cooperation that is the principal reason for high-commitment management.

Repeated game theory and management

While the economics of informal asymmetry and team production may provide insight into the increasing inefficiency of control-oriented management strategies, repeated game theory may provide insight into the characteristics of self-managed work teams. If one were trying to induce a cooperative outcome to a repeated social dilemma, one would follow several lessons from repeated game theory – all of which are closely related to the reported characteristics of the "new wave" of management strategies.

First of all, one would be careful to "lengthen the shadow of the future," in the words of Robert Axelrod (1984). Cooperation is not a maintainable outcome if the game is not going to last for a very long period.

Self-managed work teams are careful to provide guarantees of long-term participation in the organization, and in the work group itself. If they did not, employees would have no incentive to make the costly investment in the enforcement and maintenance of social norms supporting high levels of individual effort.

Furthermore, the folk theorem implies that cooperation is not a dominant strategy, even in a very long run repeated social dilemma. As a result, it is essential to develop the appropriate expectations and conventions that allow for the emergence of an efficient Nash equilibrium. Clearly, firms that have successfully implemented high-performance self-managed work groups have invested a great deal of time and effort in creating the appropriate expectations. Implementation is often accompanied by prolonged socialization and training periods in which the values of cooperation and trust are ingrained. "Sensitivity training" sessions may be part of team-building exercises in which cooperative efforts are explicitly undertaken in order to reinforce team members' expectations that each can rely on others to contribute to cooperative outcomes.

Finally, as a way of reinforcing the importance of work group norms, incentive systems must be based on group output. If a firm is relying on informal work group conventions rather than hierarchical compliance to motivate effort, it certainly makes sense to base compensation on informal work group output. This, once again, provides an incentive for work group members to undertake the costly effort of sanctioning cooperative work norms.

SUMMARY

As information asymmetries and team interdependence increase, there is a greater possibility that self-interested employees will shirk and misrepresent private information. Agency costs are large under any feasible incentive system. It becomes essential to find something other than hierarchical monitoring to motivate subordinates.

The origins of hierarchy lie in market failure. Yet rational goal-oriented behavior will be different in hierarchies than in markets because "success" in hierarchies often consists of establishing mutually enforcing expectations about when cooperation and teamwork are appropriate and how they are to be reciprocated and rewarded in the long run. For this reason, managers who can induce norms of cooperation and trust among employees will realize more of the gains from team production than managers who rely on formal incentive systems only. While cooperation in a repeated social dilemma is sustainable by rational actors as a Nash equilibrium, so are a variety of noncooperative or exploitative outcomes. Repeated play makes cooperation in a team possible, but not inevitable.

The indeterminacy of cooperation

As a result, a successful manager, recognizing the goal-oriented "rationality" of subordinates, will adopt strategies that induce employees to depart from the narrow self-interest maximization that constitutes a sufficient definition of rationality in markets. She will demonstrate trustworthiness in the hope of training subordinates to be trustworthy themselves; she will recognize and encourage a multiplicity of goals, including group acceptance and professional self-actualization, recognizing in these the building blocks of cooperation. She will train herself and subordinates to be aware of both the dangers of short-sightedness that are inherent in every hierarchy and the possibilities of escaping those dangers through the rational evolution of cooperation in the ongoing plays of the hierarchical dilemma.

11

The political economy of hierarchy
Commitment, leadership, and property rights

> A critical factor surrounding the rules governing economic exchange is the degree to which the political regime or sovereign is committed to or bound by these rules. Rules that are readily revised by the sovereign differ significantly in their implications for performance than do exactly the same rules when not subject to revision. The more likely property rights are to be altered by the sovereign for his own benefit, the lower the expected returns from investment and the lower in turn the incentive to invest. A necessary condition for economic growth is that the sovereign or government, beyond establishing the relevant set of rights, establish a credible commitment to them.
>
> North and Weingast (1989: 1)

Firms such as Volvo have developed an organizational style based on self-managed teams. Volvo's success, and the challenge from Japan, began to have an impact on U.S. auto companies by the late seventies and early eighties. Ford Motor Company, without the capital for the high-tech renovations of General Motors, by 1982 initiated a similar program of cultural change encouraging productivity, cooperation, and teamwork. By 1986 Ford had started to outearn General Motors, despite the fact that the latter had just embarked on a much-heralded capitalization program. General Motors responded by hiring William Scherkenbach, one of Ford's experts in cultural change. Mr. Scherkenbach was quoted as saying, "At Ford, the sense of community and teamwork is a lot more obvious than it is here" (*Wall Street Journal* 1989a). Union leaders were convinced that the subsequent corporate dialogue about "the General Motors family" and teamwork was merely cosmetic, but even cynics were impressed that the leadership was convinced that something was wrong with the corporate culture.

The developments at Ford and elsewhere are based on the implications of the folk theorem. Members of small teams can transcend the built-in limi-

216

tations of hierarchical control by developing norms of reciprocated cooperation and effort. With a healthy system of work norms, management may delegate many traditional managerial functions to work teams, including the allocation of tasks, monitoring, and motivation. In fact, the work group has responsibility for much of what the new organizational economics has defined as the role of the manager in a hierarchy.

This raises an obvious question: Why have a manager at all? Put another way, the question is even more striking: Why have hierarchy? The economic explanation developed at the beginning of this book is that hierarchy is an inevitable and efficient response to market failure caused by team production externalities. But if small teams can cooperate in the production of what amount to public goods (as suggested in Taylor's 1982 defense of anarchy), then perhaps we should consider what it is that hierarchy offers as an organizational form. The theme of this chapter is that hierarchy does have a great deal to offer, but that a political-economic interpretation gives hierarchical leadership a far different set of responsibilities than that traditionally defined for it by the new organizational economics. From this perspective, the advantage of hierarchy over markets is that it can be a means for creating common knowledge and cooperative work norms.

While economists since Alchian and Demsetz have defined the manager's role as the specialized monitoring and motivation of members of a team production process, the literature on cooperation in repeated social dilemmas offers quite a different picture of the appropriate behavior for hierarchical leaders. An understanding of the difficulties of implementing a cooperative hierarchical culture is based on a consistent recognition of the message of the folk theorem: Cooperation is possible, but not inevitable. The successful implementation of a high-commitment work system is not an accident, and it is not inevitable.

The role of the hierarchical leader is to give closure where repeated game theory offers none. It is to shape expectations among subordinates about cooperation among employees, and between employees and their hierarchical superiors. This is done through a set of activities that have traditionally been in the realm of politics rather than economics: communication, exhortation, symbolic position taking. Most important perhaps, the leader has a central role in committing the organization to what is in effect the "constitution" of the hierarchy – the allocation of generally accepted responsibilities, rules of the game, and property rights that provide the long-run incentives for investment in the firm.

The cooperative organizational culture is in effect a form of contract between supervisors and subordinates. As we shall see, it is a form of contract that provides strong ex post incentives for reneging by hierarchical superiors. If subordinates anticipate self-interested reneging by superiors, they have every incentive to engage in actions that will ruin the effectiveness

217

of the managerial strategy. Once again, it is therefore essential that hier-archical superiors find ways to commit themselves credibly to a coopera-tive culture. This commitment is necessary to sustain the more efficient cooperative outcome that will solve the repeated social dilemmas within the hierarchy. This chapter argues that creating this credible commit-ment is a highly political, even personal, process – a process of political leadership.

MANAGERIAL TEMPTATIONS

In a repeated social dilemma, cooperative play is always in some sense ten-tative. Individuals in such a game never have a dominant strategy to coop-erate. At best, they can try to maintain a contingent reciprocation: "I will cooperate if you will."

The short-term incentive to cheat is ever present. For instance, imagine the benefits to an employer in a piece-rate organization who can encourage employees to commit themselves to high levels of effort, and to monitor and sanction one another through work group activities, and then cut piece rates and lay off a large number of employees to keep profits high. Profits, in the short run, would be very high indeed from the savings on midlevel supervisors and monitoring procedures, the high levels of productivity, and the cutting of labor costs at the right time.

This temptation is exacerbated by the need for many high-level managers to develop good short-term profit figures for their own career purposes. While we may think of the game between subordinates and superior as in-finitely repeated, in reality any one individual in a key executive position will have private information about his or her own career plans – a move to a key position in a different organization, for example, or retirement. Short-term defection just before such a move would definitely be rational, resulting in large short-term profits just before the negative consequences of defection manifested.

Even when they are not anticipating a major career change, managers face constant temptations to hedge decisions toward greater short-term profits, especially if (as is necessarily the case) they are aware of key deci-sion variables that cannot be directly observed by subordinates. In the Du Pont example discussed in Chapter 6, workers were suspicious that man-agers would deprive them of their profit-sharing bonus by unknown ac-counting stratagems – a very real possibility. Unless managers could find a way to credibly commit themselves not to undertake such actions, the ra-tional suspicions of Du Pont employees would subvert the very aims of the profit-sharing plan.

Indeed, employee suspicions are a major obstacle to successful implemen-tation of worker-participation, cooperative styles of management. This is just another way of restating the commitment problem.

218

The political economy of hierarchy

Rational suspicions

Although the leadership of United Auto Workers (UAW) has supported co-operation with management, other union stalwarts have articulated precisely the suspicions that arise from management's difficulty in making credible commitments. These union officials have argued that the so-called cooperative managerial style is only a temporary ploy to increase employee effort, lacking any long-term commitment to share the surplus profits generated by that greater effort. Furthermore, if cooperative management leads to a weakening or elimination of union representation in a plant, then management will be free to renege on other promises without the threat of union retaliation.

In the Cyprus minerals copper mine in Miami, Arizona, management used wage concessions and "transactional analysis" sessions to improve labor–management relations and woo workers away from unions, despite fifty years of bitter hostilities in the plant. Employees found themselves being treated like adults; their recommendations brought about technical improvements in the plants, and they were given more flexibility in getting their jobs done. but union dissidents regarded this simply as a self-serving ruse to destroy the union, which "won't serve the workers' best interest in the long run" (*Wall Street Journal* 1989c).

These suspicions were the focus of debate at a UAW showdown on the policy of cooperation with management, or "jointness" as it is called in the auto industry. The debate took place at the triennial convention of the UAW in Anaheim, California, in June 1989. Two dissident leaders, Jerry Tucker and Donny Douglas, charged that the jointness program in the auto industry was merely a way for management to obtain a speedup and union concessions, while destroying the union's capacity to respond to future managerial abuse. One UAW local president said, "The company has a hidden agenda to erode the collective bargaining system, to lessen resistance to changes that are more favorable to the company than they are to the employees" (*Business Week* 1989e: 61).

Dissidents point to several instances that seemed to demonstrate the lack of a credible managerial commitment. In 1984, General Motors' assembly plant in Pontiac was assigned to build the Fiero sports car, in return for workplace reforms that included job enlargement. After initial successes and productivity improvements, engineering flaws resulted in a rapid decline in sales. The General Motors management responded by closing the plant and firing 1,100 employees. This, as the dissidents correctly pointed out, demonstrated that the management commitment did not include a guarantee of employment, contrary to the ideal "high-involvement" managerial style. Nor has the commitment to share profits been fully realized. In 1989, when General Motors profits were at record levels, each worker got a bonus of $250 – less than one-third that of Chrysler.

219

Cooperation and leadership

In defense of jointness, UAW president Owen Bieber has pointed out that the union made it through the difficult decade of the eighties without pay cuts and with managerial concessions on work pensions and cost-of-living adjustments. Overall, the employees of the UAW have seemed satisfied with the results of jointness to this point, voting overwhelmingly in favor of the current leadership and its policy.

Still, the issue of a credible commitment by management has not been resolved. To the extent that management at General Motors is perceived as not being credibly committed to job safety and fair compensation for higher levels of worker cooperation, the employees themselves can be expected to hedge their investments in the new system. This brings up the question, What can management do to make a credible commitment to jointness?

Commitment and political economy

While the potential for cooperative play is very real, the realization of this potential leaves us with the same conclusion that we reached at the end of Chapter 7: There is a tension between the self-interest of profit-oriented executives and the overall long-run efficiency of the firm. The solution must rest with the credible commitment of the executive to long-run, cooperative, efficient behavior. The solutions to the commitment problem take us out of the mechanical world of incentive systems and hierarchy and into the organic world of leadership and political power.

The problem is isomorphic with the political problem addressed by North and Weingast (1989) in their seminal paper, "Constitutions and Commitment." There, they address the hierarchy of the seventeenth-century state and show that the absolute ruler and citizen are involved in the kind of "trust-honor" game described in Table 10.1. If the citizen (merchant-banker) can trust the ruler not to confiscate the wealth he accumulates, both could be better off; however, if the merchant-banker believes the ruler will give in to the temptation to tax or borrow that wealth out of existence, he has no incentive to take productive actions that will increase his wealth.

North and Weingast (1989) point out that the primary political problem in this setting is for the ruler to find a way to make a credible commitment to abjure the temptation of violating the citizen's trust, thus making it possible for the citizen to accumulate the wealth that makes them both better off:

There are two ways in which a rule can establish such commitment. One is by setting a precedent of "responsible behavior," appearing to be committed to a set of rules that he or she will consistently live up to and enforce. The second is by being constrained to obey a set of rules that do not permit a degree of leeway for violating commitments. (1)

The political economy of hierarchy

The first method is basically reputational – creating confidence that the ruler will not forsake cooperation for short-term self-interest. The second consists in binding the manager's hands – depriving the manager of the opportunity to pursue self-interest. North and Weingast argue that the first is rarely used in the world of national politics. Be that as it may, in the most successful cases of organizational cooperation, both methods seem to be used simultaneously. The rest of this chapter will examine each of these in turn.

LEADERSHIP: CREATING EXPECTATIONS

Each individual's perception is always affected by a variety of signals and communication by the players. A player's reputation is based on a psychological perception by other players about how the given player prefers to play a game. Thus, the employers of a firm may create a reputation for being cooperative. They could create a reputation for being willing to pay more than the market-clearing wage for labor in exchange for more than effort-minimizing behavior on the part of laborers. Such a reputation could be created by past play, by public pronouncements, or by the imaginative use of symbols and manipulation of myths. Cultures are affected by the individual choices of members of the organization, especially those in a leadership position who make conscious and sophisticated use of the technology of mass communication.

Role of the leader: communication

One of the things that an effective manager does well is enhance communication. Communication, as we have emphasized before, is not sufficient to solve social dilemmas, but it does seem to be a necessary part of the culture building that solves social dilemmas. This is illustrated by the story of the Dana Corporation.

Dana is in the business of making propeller blades and gearboxes for autos and trucks. As such, it is in the least dynamic, most unionized, and most bureaucratic part of the economy. Yet in 1973 a man named Rene McPherson came to Dana with a new philosophy that produced outstanding results. In the early seventies sales per employee were the same as the all-industry average, but within a decade (and without any massive capital spending) they had tripled. At the same time, Dana's grievance rate fell dramatically.

For 22.5 inches of policy manuals McPherson substituted a one-page statement of philosophy:

– Nothing more effectively involves people, sustains creditability or generates enthusiasm than face to face communication. It is critical to provide and discuss all organization performance figures with all of our people.

221

Cooperation and leadership

– We have an obligation to provide training and the opportunity for development to our productive people who want to improve their skills, expand their career opportunities or simply further their general education.
– It is essential to provide job security for our people.
– Create incentive programs that rely on ideas and suggestions, as well as on hard work, to establish a reward pool. (Peters and Waterman 1982:248–49)

Notice the key role that communication plays in this philosophy. By communication, McPherson does not primarily mean communication with employees. Rather, he means learning from employees:

Until we believe that the expert in any particular job is most often the person performing it, we shall forever limit the potential of that person, in terms of both his own contributions to the organization and his own personal development. Consider a manufacturing setting: within their 25-square-foot area, nobody knows more about how to operate a machine, maximize its output, improve its quality, optimize the material and keep it operating efficiently than do the machine operators, material handlers, and maintenance people responsible for it. . . . We had better start admitting that the most important people in an organization are those who actually provide a service or make and add value to products, not those who administer the activity. . . . That is, when I am in your 25 square feet of space, I'd better listen to you! (Peters and Waterman 1982: 250)

McPherson emphasized personal communication in all ways possible. He required face-to-face meetings every month between every member of the organization and the division manager. The substance of these discussions was not the performance of the individual employees, but the performance of the corporation. He also ran ads in the firm newspaper saying, "Talk Back to the Boss" and "Ask Dumb Questions."

Clearly, McPherson believed that this high degree of interpersonal communication was necessary to support the shared beliefs necessary for mutual cooperativeness. An example of the importance of communication is the case of two hospitals in the St. Louis area. In one of them, communication between the nutritionists and the subordinate food preparers was limited to the formal dispensation of written menus. The chief nutritionists sat in their offices and planned menus, and then sent them out to the relatively untrained cooks. The cooks had not been given any measuring utensils, for fear that they might be stolen. Consequently, they had to estimate amounts of ingredients using a medium-sized soft-drink cup. It is not surprising that the food on the patients' trays bore little resemblance to what the nutritionists envisioned.

The other hospital was run by an administrator we will call Sister Patty. Sister Patty was a firm advocate of what Peters and Waterman call MBWA, or "management by walking around." She was frequently seen on all floors, eating in the employee cafeteria, observing the tray line, asking how things were done, reaffirming the hospital's commitment to quality care. Employees in this hospital frequently discussed how to pursue their ap-

222

pointed tasks, with the conversation ending, "We will have to do it this way, because Sister Patty wouldn't have it any other way." MBWA allowed Sister Patty to communicate the values of the organization graphically and clearly to the organization: to communicate the importance of those values and to impart a sense of team spirit and cooperation, not just in individual work groups, but among all groups in the hospital.

Communicating symbolically

Because a leader's job is to communicate organizational goals and build mutual trust, symbols are very important. Symbols can be defined as signals that communicate some aspect of an organization's self-definition clearly and with emotional impact. Renn Zaphiropoulos, head of Versatec, a Xerox subsidiary, is concerned with the symbols that encourage what he calls "symbiosis," a word I regard as a wonderful communicator of the mutual interdependence that characterizes cooperative efforts in repeated Prisoners' Dilemma games:

There is basically one killer of successful and productive symbiosis, and it is contempt. Contempt tarnishes someone's self-image. The most commonly practiced crime in industry today is a fundamental insensitivity toward personal dignity. . . . Private parking places are contemptuous toward those who do not have them. (Peters and Austin 1985: 207)

Another administrator in the automobile industry said:

I've never seen people working in a factory angry because they were making nineteen thousand dollars while the manager was making seventy thousand dollars. What makes them furious, what demotivates and demoralizes, is that slushy, January 26th morning, when they arrive for their shift at five-forty-five a.m. They park their car one hundred yards away, amidst the muck and dirt and slush. And then they wander in, finally entering cold and wet through the door that's right next to the plant manager's empty parking spot. That's what certifies them as nonfull-scale-adult human beings. (207)

While the role of symbols may be interpreted from a psychological or a sociological standpoint, there is an obvious game-theoretic interpretation: Symbols are an efficient way to establish common knowledge about a group's conventions. For example, a firm like Lincoln Electric is dependent on the creation of common knowledge about managerial commitment to abstain from the short-run profit-maximizing use of piece rates; employees must know that the firm will not cut piece rates when employees make a large salary, managers must know that employees know this, and employees must know that managers know that employees know it, and so on. At Lincoln Electric, the sharing of a common cafeteria and parking lots symbolizes that managers regard employees as equal partners in the firm and increases the credibility of the norms in place.

223

Building reputation

The communication process can greatly increase the ability of a leader to build a reputation of trustworthiness. This trust is essential if employees are to find it rational to share private information and costly effort. The management of Volvo has worked hard to create a reputation of trustworthiness; that reputation is now an asset that enables Volvo to make a high-quality automobile that could not be manufactured with unmotivated, shirking employees. The president of Volvo, Pehr Gyllenhammar, has a management selection strategy that is intended to facilitate this reputation building. Gyllenhammar (1977) writes:

> Until the manager can earn the respect of employees, there will be mutual suspicion, and too little information will flow between them. Leaders who have the strength and self-confidence to respect their employees and the strength to talk about their own mistakes will earn respect. Once the employees trust and respect a manager, real progress is possible. That kind of strength is the focus for selection, training, and development of Volvo managers. (112)

Thus, Gyllenhammar sees the leader's reputation for trustworthiness as the basis for norms of cooperation between employees and management.

James Lincoln, the founder of Lincoln Electric, emphatically supported the notion that a primary function of the leader is to earn the trust of his or her employees. Lincoln (1951) claims that a primary reason that an incentive plan like that at Lincoln Electric might not work in another setting is

> lack of honesty on the part of management. . . . The cutting of piecework prices when a man earns more than a certain amount is done on the theory that the price is a mistake and was set too high. Cutting such a price does not disturb the boss, as he thinks it is honest to correct a mistake. The production worker knows differently, however. He has been cheated of his honest earnings and he knows it. . . . if there is to be successful incentive management, the wage earner absolutely must regard the boss as a trusted, reliable co-worker on and for the team. The boss can win this acceptance in only one way. He must deserve it. He must hold himself under sterner discipline. (151–2)

Lincoln anticipated the necessity of making a credible commitment and implemented a formula that made it possible for his employees to make a long-term investment in the firm's growth that made both owner and employees better off.

An effective leadership strategy

The four-point strategy for leaders provided by organization behaviorists Warren Bennis and Burt Nanus in *Leaders* (1985) may be taken as a formula for coordinating a cooperative equilibrium in a repeated social dilemma, although of course they had no such game-theoretic formalism in mind when they constructed it. These were simply commonalities observed in the study of ninety successful leaders. The strategy includes (1) attention through vision, (2) meaning through communication, (3) trust through positioning, and (4) the deployment of self.

The first point can be interpreted from a game-theoretic perspective as an attempt to solve the coordination problem in any Battle of the Sexes game – focusing attention on one of infinitely many possible equilibrium solutions. Indeed, all students of leadership emphasize the responsibility of clarifying and consistently stating a commitment to a particular set of goals. The second point of the strategy can be seen as creating a communication network for the perpetration of shared perceptions that will support the leader-defined goal. The third point is necessary to the extent that the prescribed solution to a social dilemma is a cooperative one; in that case, a high degree of shared belief in reciprocated cooperativeness is essential. The fourth point is the use of personal dedication to reinforce the other three points through the leader's own example of commitment and personal growth. It is easy to see how such a strategy, and a personality capable of enforcing that strategy, would be useful in a repeated-game version of the social dilemma.

SIGNALING COMMITMENT: CONSTITUTIONAL CONSTRAINTS

Many of the aspects of leadership discussed so far involved what North and Weingast (1989) termed "setting a precedent of responsible behavior, appearing to be committed to a set of rules that he or she will consistently live up to and enforce" (1). This behavior implies communication, reputation building, and the creation of trust.

The ability to build this trust through face-to-face communication varies among individuals. In any person, it is inevitably limited in large-scale organizations where the leader cannot establish face-to-face relations with most employees. Consequently, the most credible managerial commitments supplement personal leadership with what we might term constitutional solutions: permanent restrictions on the ability of managers to pursue self-interested behavior at the expense of long-term cooperation. The most effective way to build a credible commitment to cooperation in organizations is by making a permanent change in the system of property rights, a change that gives employees the confidence to invest in the economic development of the firm.

Employee representation

The most permanent and credible form of commitment is the sharing of centralized decision-making power with employee representatives. Because other forms of commitment may be only temporary, union critics of employee participation have focused on employees' sharing of power. "To American unionists, real participation means not only problem solving on the shop floor but also gaining a voice in higher-level decisions" (*Business Week* 1989e). Indeed, the firms that have had the most success with inducing serious investments in company productivity have incorporated some degree of constitutional representation by employees.

At Lincoln Electric, a system of employee representation encourages employee confidence in management's piece-rate policies. Employees elect members of an advisory board and have a major say in personnel policy. They voted down a dental insurance plan for fear that it would eat into their bonus checks (Baldwin 1982: 51). Polaroid has an elected employees' committee with which managers consult on wage, motivation, and employee satisfaction issues. Volvo has the Corporate Works Council for the same purpose. Other high-performance plants have similar schemes. These representative bodies generally have no formal veto power, but politically it would be counterproductive to set them up and then ignore their advice.

Pehr Gyllenhammar went even beyond employee advisory boards in 1971 when he invited factory hands to select employee representatives to serve as directors for the Volvo board. Polaroid is one of the U.S. firms that has followed suit, letting employees nominate three candidates from which management selects one to serve on the board. Employee representation on the board is of course a more substantial level of participation than membership in advisory committees.

Expanded property rights as a credible constraint

According to Libecap (1989):

Property rights are the social institutions that define or delimit the range of privileges granted to specific assets, such as land or water. Private ownership of these assets may involve a variety of rights, including the right to exclude nonowners from access, the right to appropriate the stream of rents from use of and investments in the resource, and the right to sell or otherwise transfer the resource to others. Property rights institutions range from formal arrangements, including constitutional provisions, statutes, and judicial rulings, to informal conventions and customs regarding the allocations and use of property. (1)

Many firms that are most successful at encouraging higher levels of commitment and non-monitored effort from subordinates have effectively reallocated to employees some of the property rights to the assets owned by the firm, creating a sense of what is significantly called employee "ownership," or long-term control over those aspects of the workplace that are most important to employees (Peters and Austin 1985: 216–17).

The political economy of hierarchy

As Libecap (1989) demonstrates in his study of property rights, such a change can "critically affect decision making regarding resource use and, hence, affect economic behavior and performance" (1). Just as the strengthening of property rights in seventeenth-century England gave entrepreneurs the sense that they could invest without fearing unilateral confiscation by the king, the redefinition of employee rights in some firms gives employees the sense that they can "invest" their human capital in the firm without being subject to unilateral confiscation by management.

The sense of ownership can be "constitutionally" guaranteed in a variety of ways. For instance, the manager can visibly deprive herself of the means of unilateral intervention in the workplace.

Constraints on supervision. The time clock is one of the most pervasive symbols of a noncooperative, bureaucratic mode of hierarchical interaction, in which rules and hierarchy are used to impose and enforce closely defined behaviors on the part of subordinates. As Gouldner demonstrated at the Indiana gypsum plant, the strict enforcement of rules regarding time clocks deprived the employees of a sense of participation and ownership in their own work roles. The elimination of the time clock at organizations like Hewlett-Packard and Dana was a means by which the managers could, in effect, say, "The management is hereby depriving itself of a tool of checking your coming and going. We are interested in outcomes, not the details of your personal behavior. We hope to embark on a mutually beneficial era of cooperation toward our shared goals. We grant you a degree of constitutional autonomy in your own use of your own time and space."

When Rene McPherson eliminated the time clock at Dana Corporation, there was some concern among members of the accounting and control group:

"Everybody complained," McPherson says. "What do we do without time clocks?" I said, "How do you manage any ten people? If you see them come in late regularly, you talk to them. Why do you need time clocks to know if the people who work for you are coming in late?" My staff said, "You can't get rid of the time clocks. The government requires a record of every person's attendance and time worked." I said, "Fine. As of now, everyone comes to work on time and leaves on time. That's what the record will say. Where there are big individual exceptions, we will deal with them on a case-by-case basis." (Peters and Waterman 1982: 250)

The time clock is a minor example: other changes in the workplace can more substantially commit superiors to participative leadership and to the inviolability of worker property rights. One key example is the work redesign that accompanies the emergence of "autonomous work groups."

Ownership through work redesign. The success of "high-commitment" management seems to be based fundamentally on the delegation of man-

227

agement authority to work groups themselves. Work groups are trained to set their own productivity goals, decide on the means of reaching those goals, allocate tasks to work group members, and enforce norms that stipulate high levels of effort and high degrees of information sharing. This implies a certain "ownership" of the assets contained in the group's work area, in the sense that the group itself controls who has access to those assets.

This management strategy has been successful in a sufficient number of workplaces to generate a great deal of interest. Procter & Gamble has closed its new-design plants to researchers and others in the belief that its plants constitute a trade secret and give it a vital edge over the competition (Lawler 1986: 180).

But the strategy is not foolproof. A frequent reason for failure is that management cannot restrain itself from preempting the supposedly delegated authority of the work group, validating the rational suspicions of employees. When this happens, the work group members naturally feel that it is not rational to commit high levels of effort and energy to the success of the group and they become passive receptors of hierarchical authority. This process quickly leads to the reemergence of a very traditional, hierarchical equilibrium.

Thus, the key to success in high-commitment work groups is a credible commitment by plant managers to group autonomy. The redesign of the workplace that accompanies a commitment to the concept of work teams is normally quite expensive. Indeed, entirely new plants may have to be built to make small work teams the primary unit of production. Once built, these plants cannot be cheaply returned to a traditional supervisory style. The capital investment that accompanies a shift in managerial style thus stands as the organization's "bond" – forfeited if the management attempts to renege on the autonomy of the work groups.

Volvo's managers, for example, were quite aware of the commitment value of the company's work redesign and made the most of it politically. Gyllenhammar (1971) writes that Volvo's plant at Kalmar "is designed for a specific purpose car assembly in working groups of about 20 people. If it didn't work, it would be a costly and visible failure, in both financial and social terms. We would lose credibility with our own people" (106). Gyllenhammar's commitment of funds to such a plant was a conscious part of his plan to make his cooperative management style credible:

It was also clear that technical changes would be fruitless if they were not accompanied by organizational changes and evolution toward a climate of cooperation and partnership. So the second major change over the last five years has been Volvo's investment in tens of millions of dollars to improve the physical working environment for employees. That was simply part of the cost of achieving cleaner, more pleasant surroundings. . . . It demonstrates in concrete, visible ways that we value the people who work for Volvo. (106)

228

Volvo therefore built the Kalmar plant in order to "break up the inexorable assembly line" and instead installed individual car carriers on which groups of people, working cooperatively, built individual, identifiable parts of the car: "Each work group has its own buffer areas for incoming and outgoing carriers so it can pace itself as it wishes and organize the work inside its own area so that its members work individually or in sub groups to suit themselves" (107). The team gets a sense of "ownership" not only by pacing and organizing its own work, but also by inspecting its own product. Volvo is quite happy with the productivity results; indeed, a series of other plants have been created to duplicate the productivity gains observed at Kalmar.

The "ownership" rights that are granted individual work teams at Volvo would be worth very little to the employees if a great deal of uncertainty surrounded those rights. The major source of uncertainty, managerial authority, has been limited at Volvo both by consistent leadership styles and by the credible commitment that goes with the capital investment in the workplace.

Commitment and training. Like an investment in redesigned plants, an investment in human capital can serve as a credible commitment device. The expenditure of resources on training and education for employees is not rational if management regards employees as expendable. A highly visible training and education program, then, increases employee confidence that managerial assurances regarding long-term cooperation are not simply propaganda.

The successful operation of the cooperative work team concept requires a great deal of employee training. Training is offered because each job is likely to be "enlarged" so as to reduce boredom and increase motivation. More important, every member of a work team should be able to help any other member of the work team – exactly the kind of behavior that is discouraged in traditionally designed factories such as the Hawthorne plant. Mutual reciprocity requires that every person be trained for every other team member's job.

In a high-involvement firm that emphasizes training, pay is based mostly on skills acquired. Contracts based on pay for training once again signal the employee that the firm is willing to reciprocate the kind of individual effort and commitment to the firm that acquiring new skills requires. It contrasts starkly with the normal hierarchical pay system, which rewards employees primarily by means of promotion – with the message that the only worthwhile people in the organization are at the top.

Incentives and ownership. While there are logical limits on the degree to which an incentive system can realign individual and organizational self-interest shirking, incentive plans can also secure managerial commitment.

An incentive system can represent a contractual constraint on the firm that signals a willingness to invest employees with "property rights" in the surplus that their cooperative effort generates.

Once again, Lincoln Electric serves as an outstanding example of success. Along with high piece rates, the company has a profit-based bonus plan. Twice a year, every person in the company is evaluated on the basis of output, quality, dependability, innovation, and cooperation. The average score is set at 100, with highs up to 140 and lows down to 60. A large share of the firm's profits are then allocated to employees in proportion to their scores. Over the decade from 1978 to 1988, which included a major recession, more than 12 percent of revenues was handed out in bonuses. In 1987, the average bonus was $18,773, about 70 percent of the average worker's piece-rate earnings (Posner 1988: 96).

Profit-sharing and gain-sharing plans are favorite incentive systems for firms trying to induce high degrees of employee involvement. The gain-sharing plan attempts to provide a baseline or equilibrium level of organizational performance. It then fixes a formula for rewarding employees based on improvements in that performance (Lawler 1986: 144). The most famous gain-sharing plan is the Scanlon Plan, developed in the thirties by union leader Joe Scanlon.

Incentive systems such as profit sharing and gain sharing can be easily criticized on economic grounds. Each individual's share in the extra profits generated by his or her own marginal effort is so tiny as to have no effect whatsoever on that individual's self-interested behavior. However, these criticisms miss the point. The notion of plans such as the Scanlon Plan is not to harness individual self-interest in the interest of the firm; it is rather to serve as a symbolic commitment of managers to a shared ownership in the firm.

Furthermore, the Scanlon Plan, most notably, vests employees with a property right to the productivity gains generated by individual sacrifice and cooperation. By vesting this property right in employees, the gain-sharing system legitimizes the informal work norm in which workers urge one another on to higher levels of productivity, rather than the informal work norm in which workers discourage one another from making a greater effort. Further, a profit-based bonus plan serves as an effective constitutional constraint on the opportunistic behavior of managers. When Lincoln Electric hands out 12 percent of revenues in bonuses, it has a sizable impact on employee perceptions of managerial intentions: It creates a common knowledge of a shared fate.

The record of success with gain-sharing plans is mixed. Some companies report astounding increases in earnings, while others report that the plans have little effect (Lawler 1986: 159). This conflicting evidence is to be expected. Because gain sharing is valuable only as a signal of intended cooperative play, it is neither a necessary nor a sufficient condition for an efficient, cooperative outcome in a repeated social dilemma. The effectiveness of this signal can certainly be undercut by managerial behavior in other ways. Or managers can successfully create appropriate mutually reinforcing expectations of cooperation by other means. But there is no doubt that gain sharing has been used effectively not to change incentives so much as to alter organizational culture.

Employee stock ownership plans. Among the fastest-growing forms of employee power sharing are employee stock ownership plans (ESOPs). Procter & Gamble – one of the pioneers in participative management – has one of the two or three largest ESOPs, with close to $2 billion in stock. Avis has a stock ownership plan of equal size, and Penney, Anheuser-Busch, and Texaco all have plans involving more than $500 million in stock ownership. Partly in response to the tax advantages provided under the new tax law, two hundred publicly owned companies set up plans between May 1987 and May 1989 (*Business Week* 1989b: 116–17).

The motivation for this boom has in part been tax avoidance and protection against takeovers. However, it has also been the communication of an irreversible commitment to worker participation. The hope is that this will "seal the bargain" and motivate high levels of employee effort and involvement in the future of the organization.

Once again, however, there is nothing mechanical about the connection between an ESOP and employee productivity gains. The fact that each employee owns a tiny fraction of the stock does not create a sufficient economic interest to make employees feel it is economically worthwhile to increase efforts. ESOPs do not constitute a perfect incentive plan, aligning individual and organizational interest.

On the contrary, ESOPs are only of potential value as a means of enhancing cooperation in both horizontal and vertical dilemmas. Horizontally, ESOPs can provide an incentive for employees themselves to be concerned about the group norms of productivity. With an ESOP in place, more employees may take the time and effort to monitor other employee effort levels and to support and sanction social norms of high productivity. Thus, ESOPs can serve as a symbol or "coordinating device" that encourages commitment to a cooperative style of play among employees. If ESOPs encourage productivity, it is because they enforce social norms that encourage productivity, not because of their direct effect on productivity.

Similarly, ESOPs can help solve the vertical dilemma between employees and management by serving as a symbol of managers' commitment. An ESOP does not by itself make up for years of mutually reinforced negative interaction between employees and superiors. In such a setting, it will still be rational for employees to shirk and misrepresent information in the expectation that this will be reciprocated by an exploitative management. If

231

managers establish an ESOP simply for tax avoidance or protection from takeover, there will be no automatic implications for employee productivity. But if the same ESOP is established as part of a conscious strategy of employee participation and involvement, as at Procter & Gamble, then it can serve as a cornerstone of credible commitment by managers.

SUMMARY

The ideal incentive system would be one in which subordinates found it in their interest to share private information and to make costly efforts to achieve the organization's goals. It would also be one in which superiors found that the residual generated after inducing subordinates to take efficient actions could not be increased by providing a set of less efficient incentives.

If the ideal incentive system were available, no doubt it would never be abandoned. It would be a self-perpetuating machine that, once inaugurated, would harness the engine of individual self-interest to the end of social efficiency and, as a perfect machine, would glide smoothly into the future. There would be no reason for subordinates to worry about the trustworthiness of their co-workers and superiors, because each employee would know that every other's efficient behavior was constrained by self-interest; no reason for midlevel managers to concern themselves with the appropriateness of work group norms, because there would be no need for norms to constrain individually self-interested behavior; no reason for executives to worry about the accuracy of information supplied to them or to engage in strategic misrepresentation of their own, because every individual would find truth a dominant strategy.

But in the presence of marked information asymmetries and team interdependence, there is no such ideal incentive system. Individuals in hierarchies inevitably find themselves in situations in which their own self-interest is clearly in conflict with organizational efficiency. These situations seem to be increasingly the norm in contemporary society. Vertical dilemmas in hierarchy create an environment for politics and political leadership. Rather than relying only on a mechanical incentive system to align individual interest and group efficiency, hierarchical leaders must create appropriate psychological expectations, pay the "startup costs" for appropriate cooperation norms, kick-start the secondary norms that will be the primary enforcers of cooperation norms, and create institutions that will credibly commit the leader to the nonexploitation of employee "ownership rights" in the organization.

The analysis of repeated game theory has demonstrated that sustainable cooperation among rational individuals is one among many logical possibilities. The plethora of sustainable equilibria in repeated games puts the study of organizations back in the realm of the "organic" rather than "mechanical." The solution to the coordination problem – achieving more efficient rather than less efficient solutions to repeated social dilemma games – involves the personal characteristics and shared perceptions of the actors involved, the political skills of organizational leaders, and the constitutional resolution of the ultimate political problems of power sharing in organizations.

Epilogue
Politics, rationality, and efficiency

Institutions may arise as inefficient equilibria of repeated coordination
games and persist because, though all would benefit from a change in
joint strategies, no one individual can benefit from a unilateral change.
Binger and Hoffman (1989: 68)

Part II of this book documented the existence of a central managerial dilemma: Managers face short-term incentives to choose inefficient incentive
regimes for subordinates. Employees, knowing this, have no reason to trust
employers with the information that would make it possible for employers
to make efficient decisions. Hierarchy is thus a setting for a commitment
problem. The problem can be resolved, but only through a set of strategies
that are essentially political. To the extent that information asymmetries
and team production externalities exist in firms, efficiency requires a political leadership style projecting trustworthiness and/or a constitutional
constraint on the political authority of hierarchical superiors.

The picture of hierarchy that emerged in Part III is a long way from that
provided by most organizational economics analyses. Managers spend
scarce resources on communication and symbolic politics. Employees in
small work groups monitor one another and sanction violations of work
group norms. Managers and employees meet (formally or informally) to
define constitutional rules that reallocate property rights and decision-
making authority. This is a striking contrast to the normal pictures of managers writing "forcing contracts" and employees acting as self-interested
expected utility maximizers subject to the incentive systems imposed by
contracts. But because the analysis is different from normal organizational
economics, is it inconsistent with economics? Is the organizational actor described in Part III necessarily irrational?

I would argue that the way people behave in hierarchical organizations is
often quite different from the way they behave in competitive markets, but

that the difference is due to the institution, and not to irrationality (North 1990). Rational people necessarily behave differently in markets and hierarchies. Take, for example, Ms. Smith who works as a futures trader for a large investment company. In the futures market, Ms. Smith finds herself a price taker in an information-rich environment. There is little that she can do to affect prices by boycotting the market. But she has available through the market all the information she needs to make profit-maximizing adjustments in trading patterns; she can hear a large number of buyers and sellers making bids and offers, can project trends, and can easily figure how many units to buy or sell with trading partners in order to maximize profits. If she contracts with one trader or another, then no one's feelings are hurt, since contracts are normally short term, and at any rate there are few norms limiting social acceptance beyond minimal honesty. Other actors in the market assume that Ms. Smith and everyone else are primarily and legitimately motivated by pecuniary wealth. In the market, the scope of conflict is limited, since property rights are (ideally) clearly defined and everyone is operating on similar margins of price and quantity. Nor is there reason to attempt political organization of any sort since, in the absence of externalities, competitive forces drive the market to efficient outcomes anyhow. The formation of a coalition among a group of traders could potentially result in a profitable cartel, but it would be subject to instabilities and would at any rate be illegal.

These characteristics of Ms. Smith's market interactions stand in sharp contrast to her interactions as an employee of a large investment firm. In the firm she is not a price taker; she has specialized skills for which she was hired in the first place, and these have been supplemented by unique human capital that goes with her experience on the job and with her co-workers. She can be replaced only at great expense to the company. At the same time, however, the company pays her well as an inducement to accept company authority over matters of policy and disputes with other groups in the firm. She knows that she could not quit without losing a great deal of her labor market value and waiting in a queue for some time for another job. Thus, she and her employer are in a long-term bilateral monopoly position in which each side has to fear exploitation by the other. The problem is compounded by information asymmetries on both sides; Ms. Smith's boss may not really be able to second-guess her judgment in her area of expertise, and she may have only a vague notion of what the organization's long-term goals and strategies are. The opportunity and motivation for strategic misrepresentation are present; she quickly find out that, in an information-poor office environment, good information is a valuable commodity not to be shared openly with anyone. Office politics is therefore at a premium, and coalition formation seems to be the quickest route to success.

Hence, the rational behavior that Ms. Smith follows in her transactions in the market is likely to be very different from that which she follows in the firm. In the one case, she has the information, motivation, and authority to engage in simple expected utility maximization subject to price information that is common knowledge among the traders; in the other, rational behavior may involve strategic misrepresentation, complex coalition formation, conflict over property rights and decision-making authority, and attempts at coordination through norm building. As an employee of a hierarchy Ms. Smith may sense a fundamental threat of inefficiency that is not present in the futures market: Both she and other members of the firm could realize shared benefits by a form of cooperation that would make everyone in the firm better off. She then has an inducement to support the formation of conventions (e.g., mutual sharing of valuable market information among firm members) and to sanction noncooperators (e.g., by shunning). Since the internal interactions are long term and intense, nonpecuniary motivations such as shunning are more powerful than they are in the marketplace and are a basic medium of exchange. Furthermore, Ms. Smith may establish a long-term personal loyalty to a superior or to the firm as a whole, which makes her willing to take nonmonitored, nonrewarded costly efforts as long as she has faith that in some medium of exchange they are being reciprocated. Finally, she may take an intense interest in the institutional rules that determine property rights and the sharing of power in the organization. In short, in all her dealings within the firm, Ms. Smith will be a rational political animal.

Does all of this political activity imply that an efficient resolution to hierarchical dilemmas is inevitable? To the extent that a particular hierarchy is subject to competitive pressures from the marketplace, firms that find effective political leaders and achieve effective political institutions will certainly have an efficiency advantage. However, to the extent that an organization is partially protected from competitive pressures by entry barriers and government regulation, or protected from financial market pressures by corporate governance features such as poison pills, there may well be a range of more or less efficient resolutions to hierarchical dilemmas.

This is especially the case since efficiency is achieved through coordinated efforts to reach one outcome in a repeated game rather than another. As economic historians Binger and Hoffman (1989) so aptly describe it:

> In games with many possible strategies there are likely to be many possible inefficient equilibria, some of which are more or less efficient than others. Thus, just because we observe that an institution endures and seems to "do better" than some other institutions does not mean that it is necessarily efficient. Arguments to the effect that individuals will exhaust any gains from exchange and that institutions must be efficient do not apply when there are externalities and public goods. (71)

For this reason, it is to be expected that hierarchies only rarely and briefly achieve anything that may be regarded as a full resolution of the problems of information asymmetry, team production externalities, and market power. Rather, hierarchies are political settings in which people continually struggle to achieve the potential made possible by specialization and cooperation. They do so as purposive, rational actors who are aware that it is their own conflicting self-interest that is the primary obstacle to the achievement of their shared goals. The tools for dealing with this dilemma are the classic political tools: the enforcement of social norms, political leadership, and the credible constraint of hierarchical authority.

References

Akerlof, George. 1970. The market for "lemons": Qualitative uncertainty and the market mechanism. *Quarterly Journal of Economics* 84:488–500.

——. 1982. Labor contracts as partial gift exchange. *Quarterly Journal of Economics* 97:543–69.

Akerlof, George A., and Janet L. Yellen. 1986. *Efficiency wage models of the labor market.* Cambridge University Press.

Alchian, Armen, and Harold Demsetz. 1972. Production, information costs, and economic organization. *American Economic Review* 62: 777–95.

Aldrich, John. 1977. The dilemma of a Paretian liberal: Some consequences of Sen's theorem. *Public Choice* 30:1–21.

Arrow, Kenneth J. 1963. *Social choice and individual values.* New York: Wiley.

Auletta, Ken. 1986. *Greed and glory on Wall Street: The fall of the House of Lehman.* New York: Random House.

Aumann, Robert J. 1981. Survey of repeated games. In *Essays in game theory and mathematical economics in honor of Oskar Morgenstern,* edited by Robert Aumann et al. Mannheim: Bibliographisches Institute, 1–29.

Axelrod, Robert. 1984. *The evolution of cooperation.* New York: Basic Books.

Baker, George B., Michael C. Jensen, and Kevin J. Murphy. 1988. Compensation and incentives: Practice vs. theory. *Journal of Finance* 43:593–616.

Baldwin, William. 1982. This is the answer. *Forbes,* 5 July, 50–52.

Banks, Jeffrey S., and Randall L. Calvert. 1988. Communication and efficiency in coordination games with incomplete information. University of Rochester, Department of Political Science.

Barnard, Chester I. 1938. *The functions of the executive.* Cambridge, Mass.: Harvard University Press.

Barney, Jay, and William Ouchi. 1986. Agency theory. In *Organizational Economics,* edited by J. Barney and W. Ouchi. San Francisco: Jossey-Bass.

Barzel, Yoram. 1989. *Economic analysis of property rights.* Cambridge University Press.

Bavelas, Alex, and George Straus. 1955. *Money and motivation.* New York: Harper & Bros.

Bendor, Jonathan. 1985. *Parallel systems: Redundancy in government.* Berkeley and Los Angeles: University of California Press.

References

Bennis, Warren, and Burt Nanus. 1985. *Leaders: The strategies for taking charge.* New York: Harper & Row.

Berle, Adolph A., and Gardiner C. Means. 1932. *The modern corporation and private property.* New York: Macmillan.

Bhagat, Sanjai, and James A. Brickley. 1984. Cumulative voting: The value of minority shareholder voting rights. *Journal of Law and Economics* 27:339–65.

Binger, Brian R., and Elizabeth Hoffman. 1989. Institutional persistence and change: The question of efficiency. *Journal of Institutional and Theoretical Economics* 145: 67–84.

Brudney, Victor. 1985. Corporate governance, agency costs, and the rhetoric of contract. *Columbia Law Review* 85:1403–44.

Bull, Clive, Andrew Schotter, and Keith Weigelt. 1987. Tournaments and piece rates: An experimental study. *Journal of Political Economy* 95: 1–33.

Burrough, Bryan, and John Helyar. 1990. *Barbarians at the gate: The fall of RJR Nabisco.* New York: Harper & Row.

Business Week. 1986. And now, the post-industrial corporation. 6 March, 63–6.
1989a. Is the boss getting paid too much? 1 May, 46–50.
1989b. ESOPs: Are they good for you? 15 May, 116–23.
1989c. The cultural revolution at A. O. Smith. 29 May, 66–8.
1989d. The payoff from teamwork. 10 July, 56–62.

Buttrick, John. 1952. The inside contract system. *Journal of Economic History* 12:205–21.

Calvert, Randall L. 1987. Coordination and power: The foundation of leadership among rational legislators. Paper presented at the APSA annual meeting, Chicago.

Case, John. 1990. The open-book managers. *Inc.* 12 (September):104–13.

Chandler, Alfred. 1962. *Strategy and structure: Chapters in the history of the industrial enterprise.* Cambridge, Mass.: MIT Press.
1977. *The visible hand: The managerial revolution in American business.* Cambridge, Mass.: Harvard University Press.

Cheung, Steven N. 1983. The contractual nature of the firm. *Journal of Law and Economics* 26:1–21.

Coase, R. H. 1937. The nature of the firm. *Economica* 4:386–405.
1960. The problem of social cost. *Journal of Law and Economics* 3:1–44.

Collier, Peter, and David Horowitz. 1987. *The Fords: An American epic.* New York: Summit Books.

Crenson, Matthew A. 1975. *The Federal Machine: Beginnings of bureaucracy in Jacksonian America.* Baltimore: Johns Hopkins University Press.

Dann, Larry Y., and Harry DeAngelo. 1983. Standstill agreements, privately negotiated stock repurchases, and the market for corporate control. *Journal of Financial Economics* 11:275–300.

Darman, Richard G. 1986. Business, government, and education: The end of the rope-a-dope. *United States Treasury News,* 24 November.

Davis, Gerald, and Suzanne Stout. 1989. *The rise and fall of the market for corporate control: A dynamic analysis of the characteristics of large takeover targets.* Photocopy.

Eccles, Robert G. 1985. *The transfer pricing problem: A theory for practice.* Lexington, Mass.: Heath.

Edney, Julian. 1979. Freeriders en route to disaster. *Psychology Today* 13 (December):80–102.

Edwards, Richard. 1979. *Contested terrain: The transformation of the workplace in the twentieth century.* New York: Basic Books.

References

Eswaran, Mukesh, and Ashok Kotwal. 1984. The moral hazard of budget breaking. *Rand Journal of Economics* 15:578–81.

Fama, Eugene F. 1980. Agency problems and the theory of the firm. *Journal of Political Economy* 88:288–307.

Farrell, Joseph. 1987a. Cheap talk, coordination, and entry. *Rand Journal of Economics* 18:34–9.

1987b. Information and the Coase theorem. *Economic Perspectives* 1:113–29.

Fast, Norman. 1975. *The Lincoln Electric Company*. Boston: Harvard Business School.

Follett, Mary Parker. 1940. The giving of orders. In *Dynamic administration: The collected papers of Mary Parker Follett*, edited by Henry C. Metcalf and L. Urwick. New York: Harper & Row, 50–70.

Gibbard, Alan. 1973. Manipulation of voting schemes: A general result. *Econometrica* 41:628–37.

Gouldner, Alvin. 1954. *Patterns of industrial bureaucracy*. New York: Free Press.

Green, Jerry, and Jean-Jacques Laffont. 1977. Characterization of satisfactory mechanisms for the revelation of preferences for public goods. *Econometrica* 45:427–38.

Grofman, Bernard, and Scott L. Feld. 1988. Rousseau's general will: A Condorcetian perspective. *American Political Science Review* 82:567–87.

Grossman, Sanford J., and Oliver D. Hart. 1980. Takeover bids, the free-rider problem, and the theory of the corporation. *Bell Journal of Economics* 11:42–64.

Groves, Theodore, 1973. Incentives in teams. *Econometrica* 41:617–31.

1985. The impossibility of incentive-compatible and efficient full cost allocation schemes. In *Cost allocation: Methods, principles, applications*, edited by Peyton Young. Amsterdam: Elsevier, 95–100.

Groves, Theodore, and John O. Ledyard. 1977. Optimal allocation of public goods: A solution to the "free rider" problem. *Econometrica* 45:783–809.

Groves, Theodore, and Martin Loeb. 1975. Incentives and public inputs. *Journal of Public Economics* 4:211–26.

1979. Incentives in a divisionalized firm. *Management Science* 25:221–30.

Gyllenhammar, Pehr G. 1977. How Volvo adapts work to people. *Harvard Business Review* 55:102–13.

Halberstam, David. 1986. *The reckoning*. New York: Avon Books.

Halperin, Maurice. 1974. *Bureaucratic politics and foreign policy*. Washington D.C.: Brookings Institution.

Hammond, Thomas H., and Gary J. Miller. 1985. A social choice perspective on expertise and authority in bureaucracy. *American Journal of Political Science* 29:1–28.

Hammond, Thomas H., and Paul A. Thomas. 1989. The impossibility of a neutral hierarchy. *Journal of Law, Economics, and Organizations* 5:155–83.

Hardin, Russell. 1982. *Collective action*. Baltimore: Johns Hopkins University Press.

Harris, Marvin. 1974. *Cows, pigs, wars and witches: The riddles of cultures*. New York: Random House.

Harsanyi, J., and Richard Selten, 1988. *A general theory of equilibrium selection in games*. Cambridge; MIT Press.

Hayek, Friedrich A. 1948. *Individualism and economic order*. Chicago: University of Chicago Press.

Hechter, Michael. 1987. *Principles of group solidarity*. Berkeley and Los Angeles: University of California Press.

Heckathorn, Douglas D. 1989. Collective action and the second order free rider problem. *Rationality and society* 1:78–100.

References

Hobbes, Thomas. 1952. *Leviathan, or, matter, form, and power of a commonwealth ecclesiastical and civil* (1651). Chicago: Benton.

Hogarth, Robin, and Melvin Reder, editors. 1986. *The behavioral foundations of economic theory.* Chicago: University of Chicago Press.

Holmstrom, Bengt. 1982. Moral hazard in teams. *Bell Journal of Economics* 13:324–40.

Homans, George. 1950. *The human group.* San Diego, Calif.: Harcourt Brace Jovanovich.

———. 1954. The cash posters. *American Sociological Review* 19:724–33.

Hurwicz, Leonid. 1973. The design of mechanisms for resource allocation. *American Economic Association* 63:1–30.

Jacoby, Sanford. 1985. *Employing bureaucracy: Managers, unions and the transformation of work in American industry, 1940–1945.* New York: Columbia University Press.

Jarrell, Gregg A., and Annette B. Poulsen. 1987. Shark repellants and stock prices: The effects of antitakeover amendments since 1980. *Journal of Financial Economics* 19:127–68.

Jensen, Michael C. 1984. Takeovers: Folklore and science. *Harvard Business Review* 62:109–21.

Jensen, Michael C. 1986. Agency costs of free cash flow, corporate finance, and takeovers. *AEA Papers and Proceedings* 76:323–9.

Jensen, Michael C., and W. H. Meckling. 1976. Theory of the firm: Managerial behavior, agency costs, and ownership structure. *Journal of Financial Economics* 3:304–60.

Jensen, Michael C., and Richard S. Ruback. 1983. The market for corporate control: The scientific evidence. *Journal of Financial Economics* 11:5–50.

Josephson, Matthew. 1962. *The robber barons: The American capitalists, 1861–1901* (1934). New York: Harcourt Brace Jovanovich.

Katz, Daniel, and Robert L. Kahn. 1978. *The social psychology of organizations.* New York: Wiley.

Katz, Donald R. 1987. *The big store: Inside the crisis and revolution at Sears.* New York: Penguin Books.

Kilbridge, Maurice D. 1960. The effort bargain in industrial society. *Journal of Business* 33:10–20.

Klein, Benjamin, Robert Crawford, and Armen Alchian. 1978. Vertical integration, appropriable rents, and the competitive contracting process. *Journal of Law and Economics* 21:297–326.

Knott, Jack, and Gary Miller. 1987. *Reforming bureaucracy: The politics of institutional choice.* Englewood Cliffs, N.J.: Prentice-Hall.

Koford, Kenneth. 1988. *Testimony before the Delaware House and Senate Judiciary Committees.* Dover, Del.: Michael E. Harkins, Secretary of State, 20 January.

Kreps, David M. 1990. Corporate culture and economic theory. In *Perspectives on positive political economy,* edited by James Alt and Kenneth Shepsle. Cambridge University Press.

Latane, Bibb, Kipling Williams, and Stephen Harkins. 1979. Social loafing. *Psychology Today* 13 (December):104–110.

Lawler, Edward E. 1971. *Pay and organizational effectiveness.* New York: McGraw-Hill.

———. 1986. *High-involvement management.* San Francisco: Jossey-Bass.

———. 1987. Pay for performance: A motivational analysis. In *Incentives, cooperation, and risk sharing: Economic and psychological perspectives on employment contracts,* edited by Haig R. Nalbantian. Totowa, N.J., Rowman & Littlefield, 69–86.

242

References

Leibenstein, Harvey. 1982. The prisoners' dilemma in the invisible hand: An analysis of intrafirm productivity. *American Economic Review* 72:92–7.

———. 1987. *Inside the firm: The inefficiencies of hierarchy*. Cambridge, Mass.: Harvard University Press.

Lewis, David. 1969. *Convention: A philosophical study*. Cambridge, Mass.: Harvard University Press.

Libecap, Gary D. 1989. *Contracting for property rights*. Cambridge University Press.

Lincoln, James. 1951. *Incentive management: A new approach to human relations in industry and business*. Cleveland: Lincoln Electric Co.

———. 1961. *A new approach to industrial economics*. New York: Devin-Adair.

Luce, R. Duncan, and Howard Raiffa. 1957. *Games and decisions: Introduction and critical survey*. New York: Wiley.

Machiavelli, Nicolo. 1952. *The prince* (1513). Chicago: Benton.

Marwell, Gerald, and Ruth Ames. 1979. Experiments on the provision of public goods. *American Journal of Sociology* 84:1335–60.

Masten, Scott E. 1984. The organization of production: Evidence from the aerospace industry. *Journal of Law and Economics* 27:402–17.

McClelland, David C. 1961. *The achieving society*. New York: Van Nostrand.

McCraw, Thomas K. 1984. *Prophets of regulation*. Cambridge, Mass.: Belknap Press.

Meyer, Stephen, III. 1981. *The five dollar day: Labor management and social control in the Ford Motor Company, 1908–1921*. Albany: State University of New York Press.

Miller, Gary. 1977. Bureaucratic compliance as a game on the unit square. *Public Choice* 30:39–52.

Miller, Jeffrey, and Peter Murrell. 1981. Limitations on the use of information-revealing incentive schemes in economic organizations. *Journal of Comparative Economics* 5:251–71.

Myerson, Roger B., and Mark A. Satterthwaite. 1983. Efficient mechanisms for bilateral trading. *Journal of Economic Theory* 29:265–81.

Nelson, Daniel. 1975. *Managers and workers: Origins of the new factory system in the United States, 1880–1920*. Madison: University of Wisconsin Press.

Neuhauser, Peg, C. 1988. *Tribal warfare in organizations: Turning tribal conflict into negotiated peace*. New York: Harper & Row.

New York Times. 1986. America's imperial chief executive. 12 October.

———. 1989. More companies raise dividends. 13 February.

North, Douglass C. 1981. *Structure and change in economic history*. New York: Norton.

———. 1988. *Institutions and a transaction cost theory of exchange*. St. Louis: Washington University Political Economy Working Paper No. 130.

———. 1990a. *A transaction cost theory of politics*. St. Louis: Washington University Political Economy Working Paper No. 144.

———. 1990b. *Institutions, institutional change, and economic performance*. Cambridge University Press.

North, Douglass C., and Barry Weingast. 1989. *Constitutions and commitment: The evolution of institutions governing public choice in 17th century England*. St. Louis: Washington University Political Economy Working Paper No. 129.

Oliver, Pamela. 1980. Rewards and punishments as selective incentives for collective action: Theoretical investigations. *American Journal of Sociology*, 85:1356–75.

Perrow, Charles. 1987. *Complex organizations: A critical essay*, 2d ed. Glenview, Ill.: Scott, Foresman.

References

Perry, Nancy. 1988. Here come richer, riskier pay plans. *Fortune* 120:50–8.

Peters, Roger. 1988. Working smarter: The business of practical intelligence. *National Forum* 68;15–16.

Peters, Thomas J., and Robert H. Waterman, Jr. 1982. *In search of excellence: Lessons from America's best-run companies.* New York: Warner Communication.

Peters, Tom, and Nancy Austin. 1985. *A passion for excellence; The leadership difference.* New York: Random House.

Plott, Charles R. 1986. Rational choice in experimental markets. *Journal of Business* 59: S301–28.

Posner, Bruce G. 1988. Right from the start. *Inc.* 10:95–6.

Radner, Roy. 1987. Decentralization and incentives. In *Information, incentives, and economic mechanisms: Essays in honor of Leonid Hurwicz,* edited by Theodore Groves, Roy Radner, and Stanley Reiter. Minneapolis: University of Minnesota Press, 3–47.

Raff, Daniel M. 1988. Wage determination theory and the five-dollar day at Ford. *Journal of Economic History* 48:387–99.

Roethlisberger, F. J., and W. J. Dickson. 1939. *Management and the worker.* Cambridge, Mass.: Harvard University Press.

Roto, Hilton L. 1989. Tying the king's hands: Royal fiscal policy during the Old Regime. *Rationality and Society* 1:240–59.

Roth, Alvin, and J. Murnighan. 1982. The role of information in bargaining: An experimental study. *Econometrica* 50:1123–42.

Rubinstein, Ariel. 1982. Perfect equilibrium in a bargaining model. *Econometrica* 50:97–109.

Rutten, Andrew. 1990. The Coase theorem and the unfinished revolution in law and economics. Photocopy.

Ryngaert, Michael. 1989. The effect of poison pill securities on shareholder wealth. *Journal of Financial Economics* 20: 377–417.

Sahlins, Marshall. 1972. *Stone age economics.* New York: De Gruyter.

St. Louis Post Dispatch. 1987. Pickens says he's shareholders' friend. 17 May.
    1988. Dallas at 10: Ewings are older, hardly wiser. 27 March.

Samuelson, William. 1985. Comments on the Coase theorem. In *Game theoretic models of bargaining,* edited by Alvin Roth. Cambridge University Press, 321–40.

Satterthwaite, Mark A. 1975. Strategy-proofness and Arrow's conditions. *Journal of Economic Theory* 10:187–217.

Schofield, Norman. 1985. Anarchy, altruism and cooperation: A review. *Social Choice and Welfare* 2:207–19.

Sen, Amartya K. 1970. *Collective choice and social welfare.* San Francisco: Holden-Day.
    1976. Liberty, unanimity, and rights. *Economica* 43:217–45.
    1983. Liberty and social choice. *Journal of Philosophy* 80:5–28.
    1986. Rationality in psychology and economics. In *Rational choice: The contrast between economics and psychology,* edited by Robin Hogarth and Melvin Reder. Chicago: University of Chicago Press, 25–40.

Smith, Adam. 1952. *An inquiry into the nature and causes of the wealth of nations* (1776). Chicago: Benton.

Spence, A. Michael. 1974. *Market signalling: Informational transfer in hiring and related screening processes.* Cambridge, Mass.: Harvard University Press.

Stiglitz, Joseph E. 1987. The design of labor contracts: The economics of incentives and risk sharing. In *Incentives, cooperation, and risk sharing: Economic and psychological perspectives on employment contracts,* edited by Haig R. Nalbantian. Totowa, N.J.: Rowman & Littlefield, 47–68.

References

Sutton, John. 1986. Noncooperative bargaining theory: An introduction. *Review of Economic Studies* 53:709–24.

Taylor, Frederick W. 1895. A piece rate system. *American Society of Mechanical Engineers Transactions* 16:856–93.

——— 1911. *Principles of scientific management.* New York: Norton.

——— 1947. *Scientific management.* New York: Harper Bros.

Taylor, Michael. 1982. *Community, anarchy, and liberty.* Cambridge University Press.

Tideman, T. Nicolaus. 1985. Efficient local public goods without compulsory taxes. *Perspectives on Local Public Finance and Public Policy* 2:181–202.

Tideman, T. Nicolaus, and Gordon Tullock. 1976. A new and superior process for making social choices. *Journal of Economic Theory* 84:1145–59.

Tirole, Jean. 1988. *The theory of industrial organization.* Cambridge, Mass.: MIT Press.

Trist, E. L., and K. W. Bamforth. 1951. Some social-psychological consequences of the longwall method of coal-getting. *Human Relations* 4:3–38.

Tversky, Amos, and Daniel Kahneman. 1986. Rational choice and the framing of decisions. *Journal of Business* 59:S251–78.

Wall Street Journal. 1988a. All eyes on Du Pont's incentive pay plan. 5 December.

——— 1988b. How underdog KKR won RJR Nabisco without highest bid. 2 December.

——— 1989a. GM woos employees by listening to them, talking of its "team." 12 January.

——— 1989b. Pity the poor shareholder in wake of Time decision, advocates say. 1 August.

——— 1989c. At an Arizona mine workers were wooed away from the union. 8 August.

Walton, Richard E. 1985. From control to commitment in the workplace. *Harvard Business Review* 63:77–84.

Ward, B. 1961. Majority rule and allocation. *Journal of Conflict Resolution* 4:380–9.

Weber, Max. 1946. *The theory of social and economic organization,* edited by Talcott Parsons. New York: Oxford University Press.

Whyte, William Foote. 1955. *Money and motivation: An analysis of incentives in industry.* Westport, Conn.: Greenwood Press.

Williamson, Oliver E. 1975. *Markets and hierarchies.* New York: Free Press.

Williamson, Oliver E., and W. G. Ouchi. 1981. The markets and hierarchies perspective: Origins, implications, prospects. In *Assessing organization design and performance,* edited by A. Vade Ven and W. F. Joyce. New York: Wiley.

Yamagishi, Toshio. 1986. The provision of a sanctioning system as a public good. *Journal of Personality and Social Psychology* 51: 110–16.

Name index

247

Name index

Name index

Subject index

accountants, 84–5
adverse selection, 95–6
agency costs, 2, 160–4, 183, 214
Arrow impossibility theorem, 59–64
authority, political, 6–8, 11–13, 18
  and bargaining failure, 37–57
  created by efficiency wage, 67–75
  at Ford, 75–6, 98–100
  and market failure, 27–35
  misuse of, 24
  as replacement for price mechanism, 4
  at Sears, 92–3
  undermining of, by market competition,
    65–7

bargaining, 10, 11, 36–57
  advantages of, compared with hierarchy,
    38–9
  disadvantages of, compared with hierar-
    chy, 39–43
  and distribution, 42–3
  and incomplete information, 47–9
Battle of the Sexes game, 43–9, 52
  as a model for bargaining, 47–9
  as a model for coordination prob-
    lems, 202
behavior, organizational, 3–6, 12–13
binging, 189, 193, 205
Borda count, 62–4
budget balancing
  as an axiom in Holmstrom theorem, 129
  inconsistent with incentive compatibility,
    147–55
  inconsistent with Pareto optimality,
    134–5
  and separation of ownership and con-
    trol, 165

commitment, xi, 3, 11
  through constitutional constraints, 220,
    225–32
  and cooperation, 218–21
  failure of, 115–16
  to implement incentive-compatible mech-
    anisms, 154–5
  to implement joint forcing contract, 135
  at Lincoln Electric, 116–19
  through reputation, 220–5
  as solution to piece-rate dilemma, 113–19
  as a strategy in bargaining, 45–7
  and training, 229
competition, 6, 12–13
  in capital markets, 2, 170–7
  and efficiency, 26–7, 160–4
  among firms, 3, 5–7
  in labor markets, 65–7
  in market for managers, 2, 170–7
  undermining of hierarchical authority by,
    65–7
Condorcet jury theorem, 80–2
constitutions, 10, 217, 220–1, 225–6,
    230–1
contracts, 4, 11–13, 16, 36–43; see also
    forcing contract; inside contracting
  hierarchical, 4, 5, 11, 49–50, 69–74,
    176–7
  incomplete, 40–1, 55–6
  labor, 7, 67–75
  nonhierarchical, 36–8, 65–7
  at Volvo, 180
convention, 201–4
  defined, 201
cooperation, xi, 2, 3
  evolution of, 184–6
  among firms, 37

250